Zákyrilrios

'the jewel of Greece'
Third edition

Gail Schofield

SUNFLOWER BOOKS

Third edition © 2011
Sunflower Books™
PO Box 36160
London SW7 3WS, UK
www.sunflowerbooks.co.uk

ISBN 978-1-85691-401-7

Important note to the reader

We have tried to ensure that the descriptions and maps in this book are error-free at press date. The book will be updated, where necessary, whenever future printings permit. It will be very helpful for us to receive your comments (sent in care of Sunflower Books, please) for the updating of future printings.

We also rely on those who use this book — especially walkers — to take along a good supply of common sense when they explore. Conditions can change very rapidly on Zákynthos, and *earth tremors, storm damage or building works may make a route unsafe at any time*. If the route is not as we outline it here, and your way ahead is not secure, return to the point of departure. *Never attempt to complete a trip by car or on foot under hazardous conditions!*

Photograph credits
© i-stockphoto: cover and pages 5, 20, 32, 36, 40 (both), 47, 73, 76, 79, 103 (hedgehog), 111 (grass snake), 115 (common tree frog), 147 (hare), 167 (monk seal), and all birds (bottom right-hand photographs on pages 91, 95, 99, 103, 107, 111, 115, 119, 123, 127, 131, 135, 139, 143, 147, 151, 155, 159, 163, 167, 171, 175)
© Esa Eskelinen: pages 107 (Balkan whip snake), 123 (four-line snake), 127 (Montpellier snake), 135 (Greek *Algyroides*)
© Anna Proctor: pages 7, 14, 91 (pear tree) and 99 (charcoal burning)
© Giorgos Skoufas: page 95 (red-star starfish)
© Laurent Sourbes: page 109 (Panagía Skopiótissa)
© National Marine Park of Zákynthos: page 13
© Gail Schofield: all other photographs
Maps: 3D walking maps © Gail Schofield; fold-out maps by Sunflower Books, based on the author's originals (© Gail Schofield)
Sunflower Books is a Registered Trademark.
A CIP catalogue record for this book is available from the British Library.
Printed and bound in China by WKT Company Ltd.

Contents

❀ Preface

The successful mass tourism island of 'Zante' is a quick hop across Europe, and if you are seeking something more than sun, sea and nightlife in the company of crowds of drunk and sweaty tourists, I doubt it is on your list of places to visit.

So instead let me introduce you to 'Zákynthos'...

... an island described by writers and poets through the centuries as 'the jewel of the east', 'the emerald isle' and 'the island of dreams';

... an island of just 406 square kilometres, characterized by Cretaceous limestone mountain formations, Pleistocene sea clays, flood plains and many more geological formations and rocks rich in fossils;

... an island shaped by a succession of cultures since neolithic man — including Grecian states, Byzantine dynasties, Franks and Russians, Turkish pirates, Venetian monk-warriors and British bureaucrats until just over 100 years ago;

... an island rich in layers of forgotten archaeology — from ancient tombs, churches, monasteries and mansions to simple dwellings where relics of once-traditional ways of life now lie abandoned and reclaimed by nature;

Limestone rock formations on the northwest coast

... an island with an agricultural tradition so old that gnarled and twisted 400-year-old olive trees support their own ecosystems of plants, invertebrates, lizards, owls and bats;

... an island with more than 800 species of flowering plants, including fritillaries, 50 types of orchid and several other unique specimens;

... an island rich in rare and interesting invertebrates, amphibians, reptiles and mammals — and an essential migratory route for over 200 species of birds;

... an island surrounded by marine life — not only fish, but visiting dolphins, critically endangered Mediterranean monk seals, and the largest loggerhead sea turtle breeding population in the Mediterranean;

... an island where I still have not seen everything despite 17 years of exploring.

Zante is the more easily pronounced Italian name for the Greek island of Zákynthos. The car tours and walks in this book are designed to provide all visitors with a fascinating perspective on the island's cultural and natural heritage. You can visit Zákynthos at any time of year:
— May to October, when you can fly direct to the island, is the perfect time to see the endangered loggerhead sea turtles and the grape harvest for wine and raisins;
— March to May and September to November are the best times of the year for flowering plants and bird-watching;
— November to March are characterized by the slow winter rhythm, when the locals focus on the olive harvest and crop-planting; you may well bask in the warmth of a

winter sun, but be prepared for some wild storms too!

My own favourite time is from March to June; there are heavy showers interspersed with glorious sunshine, meadows full of orchid species, fritillaries, snakes, lizards and invertebrates. The birds migrate north and sea turtles migrate into Laganas Bay to mate, and if you are brave enough to swim in the cool sea, you will likely encounter a turtle or two!

There is something here for everyone, and you don't have to travel far to find it. I hope that this book will encourage you to visit and explore the island, and that you will agree that Zákynthos truly is the 'Jewel of Greece'.

About the author

I first visited Zákynthos during my holidays as a zoology student at the University of Bristol, on a volunteer project to help protect the sea turtles. I had planned to stay a month, but these 'ancient mariners' — with ancestors older than the dinosaurs — became my passion, and I now live here permanently.

My idea for this book developed partly as an excuse to explore every nook and cranny of this island, partly as a way to show my 90-year-old Nan (who could not travel) the place where I live, partly because there is no in-depth guide like this about Zákynthos and, finally, to correct the impression that the island is devoted solely to mass tourism and the clubbing scene.   — GAIL SCHOFIELD

Acknowledgements

I could not have written this book without the generous gift of time and companionship given by Amanda Banks, Sandra Beavis, Christina Davy, Frances Engle-hardt, Sabrina Fossette, Ilias Gounaris, Anastasía Kolokotsás, Martin Lilley, Roz Mills, Anna Proctor, Spíros Vertzágias, Katie Visvardi, TyAnn Lee and Ines Palomares, who bravely explored most of the back roads, footpaths and more than occasional thorny bushes with me!

Thanks also to Esa Eskelinen, Anna Proctor and Giórgos Scoúfas for donating some photographs, and to Dimítri Vardakastánis for GPS assistance. Special thanks to my parents who, as well as being walking companions, proof-read the book and improved its content as a direct result of their years of experience as dedicated walkers and users of walking guides. And a final thank you to Kóstas Katselídis who gave me critical advice, essential computer assistance and inspirational island bike rides.

Introduction

Zákynthos, with 300,000 visitors from Britain every year, is the third largest of the Ionian Islands off the western coast of Greece. The Ionian Sea constitutes the southern part of the Adriatic, separating Greece and Italy. It has seven main islands, often called the 'Eptánissa' (literally 'Seven Islands') — Kérkyra (Corfu), Paxoí (Paxos), Lefkáda (Levkas), Itháki (Ithaca), Kefaloniá (or Kefalloniá/ Cephaloniá), Zákynthos (also called Zante), and Kýthira — far to the south, off the coast of the Peloponnese.

Geography

Zákynthos (longitude 20° 52' E; latitude 37° 43' N; 406 sq km) is the second most southerly Ionian Island and the eleventh largest island in Greece. It is 9.5 nautical miles west of the Peloponnese, 8.5 nautical miles south of Kefaloniá and approximately 300 kilometres west of the Greek capital, Athens.

The island is approximately 40km long and 17km wide, with about 154 kilometres of coastline. Forty percent of the land is mountainous, primarily covered with Aleppo pine forests, while the rest is alluvial flood plains. The highest peak is Mount Vrachíonas at 756m. There are numerous beaches along the south and east coasts, while the

There are also many smaller islands, many of them inhabited seasonally or not at all. The islands are mostly hilly (up to 500m/1650ft) or, in the case of Kefaloniá, Ithaca and Levkas, mountainous (over 1000m/ 3300ft). The land is covered with pine forests, *maquis* (dry shrubs) and fir forests, surrounded by cultivated olive, vine and cypress groves. Their coastlines are very indented and largely rocky, with small sandy/shingly coves tucked in amongst the cliffs.

The six municipalities of Zákynthos

north and west coasts are characterized by precipitous cliffs.
The population numbers approximately 45,000 inhabitants. The Prefecture of Zákynthos covers the whole island, and includes six municipalities (see opposite) comprising some 50 villages and settlements. The prefecture is responsible for economic development, tourism, administration, public health, labour and citizenship.

Climate and weather

This is one of the sunniest places in Greece, and its geographical location is responsible for its typical Mediterranean climate of mild winters and warm summers cooled by seasonal breezes called the *meltémia*. Due to the high level of rainfall in winter, Zákynthos is considerably greener than many other Greek islands and has a climate favourable for the cultivation of olives, citrus fruits and vines. The island's temperature varies from an average of 11° C to 26° C — with extremes of 1° C in

January to 38° C in July. There are, on average, 105 dry days, with from about 810-970mm rainfall annually.
The tourist resorts are generally 'open for business' from May until mid-October, when the charter flights operate. Expect visitor facilities to be closed outside these months (and at minimal operation in May and October). April, May, September and October are the best months to visit; July and August can be very hot … and crowded.
There's more detailed information for walkers (and independent travellers) and on page 83.

Geology

Zákynthos lies between the Hellenic Trench, the deepest marine valley in the Mediterranean, and the Hellenides mountain range, covering most of mainland Greece. Both were created as a result of the sideways and downward movement of the African tectonic plate under that of the Eurasian. The Ionian Islands were formed as a result of the convergence and underthrusting of two geotectonic zones from the Hellenides — the pre-Apulian Zone and the Ionian Zone. The pre-Apulian Zone consists of pelagic and detrital limestones formed from marine sediment deposition

Monthly averages			
tempera-tures		days of sun	rain-fall (mm)
air	sea*		
Jan.	11°C	13°C	18	158
Feb.	12°C	13°C	20	104
Mar.	13°C	14°C	25	90
Apr.	15°C	16°C	29	49
May	19°C	19°C	30	21
Jun.	23°C	23°C	31	7
Jul.	25°C	25°C	31	6
Aug.	26°C	26°C	30	10
Sep.	24°C	24°C	28	35
Oct.	20°C	22°C	23	136
Nov.	16°C	19°C	20	159
Dec.	13°C	15°C	18	195

near the shore

Pre-Apulian Zone

Cretaceous Plio-Pleistocene IONIAN THRUST

Miocene Eocene Quaternery Ionian Zone

Oligocene Triassic

during the Cretaceous and Eocene, while the Ionian Zone is made up of Miocene evaporates and gypsum, Pliocene sea clays and Pleistocene sandstone conglomerates. The Quaternary alluvial landscapes and sedimentary substrates formed as a result of intense salt and compressional tectonics and uplift of evaporates and carbonates.

The island is still seismically active, as indicated by the presence of sulphur and bitumen springs, with many epicentres along the Hellenic Trench to the west of the island and the sea canyon system to the east.

Economy

On Zákynthos 40% of the land is farmed, 35% is grazed and 18% is forested. Of the cultivated land, 42% is covered in olive groves and 18% in vineyards.

Agriculturally, Zákynthos is a productive island and is famous for its olives and wine — in particular the semi-dry *masteládo* wine. Other produce includes grapes, raisins, citrus fruits, almonds, wheat, maize, fodder, pulses, melon, potatoes, cabbages, cauliflowers, onions, and tomatoes. Keep an eye out for the 'Zákynthos melon', the 'Zákynthos water onion', round courgettes, local olives and the red *Avgoustiátis* grapes.

Livestock is kept on the island primarily for domestic needs rather than for commercial exploitation— sheep, goats, pigs, cattle, rabbits and chickens. Dairy products include milk, meat and hard cheeses; honey is collected from the local beehives.

There is also a domestic **fishing industry**. The boats are generally small, and their owners are careful about their fishing methods, hence the fish stock is not subject to intensive exploitation.

The island also has a major **limestone quarrying** industry, as you will see from the scars on many of the mountains.

However, the successful **tourism industry** is the main source of income on the island. Between 1994 and 2001 the number of tourists doubled (from 232,520 to 435,833) due to an increase in international and charter flights, but has stabilized since (476,097 visitors in 2006). Tourism was introduced by the Greek government in the 1970s as a way of stemming emigration from island and rural communities (in particular to Germany, Canada and Australia) due to increasing economic difficulties. The government did not anticipate the potential success of this industry, which has given rise to increasing environmental conflicts and damage (hence the establishment of the National Marine Park; see pages 13-15).

Ecology

Since the end of the last century the European Union has made a dedicated effort to protect the wild flora and fauna throughout the member states, hence the formation of the **Natura 2000 habitats network**.

Greece has some of the most varied and unique ecosystems in Europe, making it essential to conserve its habitat and species biodiversity.

Zákynthos has three Natura 2000 Specially Protected Areas:

GR2210001: extending along the west coast to the northern tip of the island;

View over Sekánia Beach, an area only open to researchers with a park permit

GR2210002: within Laganás Bay in the National Marine Park of Zákynthos;

GR2210003: at the Strophádes Islands, 22 nautical miles south of Zákynthos (but within the boundaries of the National Marine Park).

Zákynthos is covered in a combination of settlements, farmland and typically Mediterranean semi-natural habitats.

The vegetation is xerophytic, meaning that it has developed a tolerance to water shortages in the hot, dry summer months. Mediterranean vegetation is divided into five altitude-based 'life zones', of which Zákynthos encompasses two — the 'thermo-Mediterranean' and 'meso-Mediterranean', with Mount Vrachíonas as the highest peak at 756m/2480ft and Mount Skopós in the National Marine Park at 491m/1610ft.

The terrestrial habitats of Zákynthos include

- sandy and stony beaches
- coastal sand dune systems with interesting plant species (particularly those at Laganás, Banána Beach, Alikés)
- a natural wetland with reeds and rushes (Lake Kerí)
- a man-made salt flat (Alikés)
- a drained lake (near Laganás)
- vast flood plain (extending up to Alikés)
- permanent and seasonal flowing rivers
- cliffs and caves with rare and endemic chasmophytic plants (especially on the west coast)
- broadleaved evergreen oak and coniferous pine and cypress forests
- *mattoral* (*maquis* of wild olive and carob, *garrigues* of rosemary, rock roses, heather and broom and *phryganas* of thorny burnet and thyme)
- human settlements
- viticulture and agricultural land (orchards, olive groves, hay meadows, vegetables and wheat fields) which, when managed organically, encourage an incredible wealth of annual flowering species.

island is the conservation of the most important loggerhead sea turtle *(Caretta caretta)* nesting beaches in the Mediterranean (concentrated in Laganás Bay) , a population of resident Mediterranean monk seals *(Monachus monachus)* and over 200 species of resident and migratory birds. Furthermore, by protecting the National Park ecosystems, other threatened wildlife and plants also receive protection.

Threats

As with many other protected areas, the NMPZ and wider area of Zákynthos is subject to a number of economic pressures and human conflicts. The most obvious of these is mass tourism. In addition to the conflicts encountered when protecting sea turtles in the marine area and on the nesting beaches, other pressures include:

- uncontrolled development
- illegal dumping of rubbish and sewage
- arson
- agricultural encroachment into important habitats
- off-road vehicle use on beach, dune and scrub habitats
- contamination of water by chemicals from agriculture and olive processing
- illegal bird-hunting during the migratory seasons.

European Law, under the Habitats Directive 92/43/EEC, protects Natura 2000 habitats, and any threat to these habitats must therefore be taken very seriously.

Wildlife and plant life

Within the National Marine Park of Zákynthos, a total of 1228 species (approximately 800 flora and 400 fauna) have been recorded. Of these species, 124 currently receive international protection status (89 species of reptiles, amphibians, mammals and birds; 35 plants).

Across the entire island landmass, there are at least 500 more species of flora and maybe a few unidentified mammals, reptiles and amphibians.

The number of terrestrial, marine and flying invertebrates and marine vertebrates found on and around the island is at present unknown.

Of prime importance to the

12

THE NATIONAL MARINE PARK OF ZÁKYNTHOS

The National Marine Park of Zákynthos (NMPZ) is the first National Park in Greece to function under a management body and has been in operation since 1999.

The fundamental aim of the National Park is to monitor various aspects of the natural environment (species, habitats and impacts), to facilitate the growth of environmentally compatible activities (such as sustainable tourism and recreation), while simultaneously safeguarding the natural and cultural landscape through environmental education, provision of information and various public awareness programmes.

The NMPZ is situated in the southern part of the island. It covers 11% of the island's landmass. In total, the Park comprises 89.2 sq km marine area and 14.2 sq km core land area,

with an additional buffer land area of 31.2 sq km. It includes the marine area of Laganás Bay, the islets of Peloúso, Marathoníssi and Ágios Sóstis, and the Strophades Islands.

The terrestrial region of the Park lies within the municipalities of Zakynthíon (comprised of the old Municipality of Zákynthos and the communities of Vassilikós and Argássi) and Laganás (a grouping of the former communities of Kalamáki, Pantokrátora, Lithakiá and Kerí).

For information read the National Marine Park of Zákynthos Visitors' Guide or visit the National Park's website (www.nmp-zak.org).

The National Marine Park of Zákynthos Terrestrial and Maritime Protection Zones (Source: National Marine Park of Zákynthos)

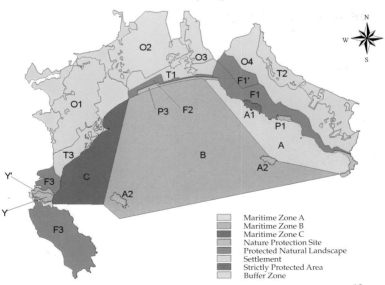

Maritime Zone A
Maritime Zone B
Maritime Zone C
Nature Protection Site
Protected Natural Landscape
Settlement
Strictly Protected Area
Buffer Zone

Visitor rules in the National Marine Park of Zákynthos

Below is a summary of the National Park guidelines, extracted from the park's 'Visitors' Guide'.

In the **'Marine Region'**, all sea craft are prohibited in **Zone A**. In **Zone B**, sea craft are permitted at a speed limit of 6 knots, but may not anchor. In **Zone C**, sea craft are permitted at a speed limit of 6 knots and may anchor.

In the **'Area of Absolute Protection'** (Sekánia region), only researchers with special permits are permitted on the beach.

In the **'Nature Protection Areas'** the following is prohibited:
• public access to the nesting beaches from 19.00 to 07.00;
• the use of beach umbrellas, except in the strip of sand 3-5 metres from the waterline;
• digging sand, especially where turtle nests are located;
• disturbing cages protecting nests;
• all wheeled vehicles;
• horses, and dogs without leads;
• using any light source at night.

When visiting the beaches in the Park...
• Leave no rubbish. Place it in bins provided or, if there are no bins, take it away with you. When you leave the beach, collect all the rubbish you find around, even if left behind by someone else.
• Don't throw rubbish or plastic in the sea — sea turtles may mistake plastic for jellyfish, eat it and die from suffocation.
• Don't discard fishing nets or lines in the sea or on the shore, lest birds become entangled.
• Do not use torches, oil lamps or light fires on the beach.
• Do not remove sea urchins or starfish to use for decoration, etc.
• Please report recreational boats or ships that break NMPZ regulations or pollute the sea (including leaving oil slicks) to the Park or Port Police Authority.

When visiting a forested region of the Park...
• Do not pick flowers.
• Smoking is prohibited.
• Never light fires.
• Do not leave behind glass or other litter. Take a bag with you to take away your own rubbish — and that left by others.
• Do not play loud music or make noise.
• If you find a **fire**, immediately telephone the **emergency fire service on 199** and describe the exact location, size and direction of the fire, how to find the fire, your name and contact telephone number.

When visiting the islands and islets of the Park...
• Don't light fires, and turn off all light sources at night.
• Don't let domestic animals (e.g. dogs) run free without a lead, even if you are watching them. It is

advisable not to stay overnight on the islets/islands, as there is the risk of disturbing existing species or of introducing species (e.g. mice/rats) which could eat the eggs or nestlings of other animals.

• Do not remove or introduce any animal or plant organisms to the islands/islets.

• If, on approaching an islet/island, you see a bird rising into the air, you should not disembark: the bird is probably nesting and your presence is disturbing it. Be especially aware of this during the period from April to October.

On finding marine mammals in the sea, such as dolphins or seals...

• Decrease your boat speed and do not change direction abruptly. Do not approach the animal(s) at a distance closer than 100 metres. Do not chase or circle the animal(s), and do not rev your boat engine.

• Allow the animal(s) to approach or swim away from the boat in its own time. Do not try to touch, swim with or feed the animal(s) — this is to prevent the animal(s) from becoming dependant on humans, as well as the transmission of diseases/parasites.

• Depart immediately if you observe the animal(s) striking the head or fins on the surface of the sea: these actions indicate that the animal has been disturbed.

Loggerhead sea turtle (Caretta caretta) observation procedure from boats...

• Maintain a minimal distance from the animal of 15 metres when it is near the surface and 5 metres when it is resting on the seabed.

• The observation duration of the same turtle should not exceed 10 minutes per hour per boat when it is near the surface and 15 minutes per hour when it is resting on the seabed.

• There should be no physical contact with the animal.

• The boat should not approach the turtle from the front (i.e. blocking its direction of swim).

• More than two boats should not follow the same turtle at any one time.

• Swimming with the turtle from the boat is not permitted.

• The boat speed should not exceed 2 knots during the observation.

• Professional tour boats for sea turtle observation should operate only between the hours of 11.00 and 17.00.

• Boats waiting to observe the turtle should maintain a distance of 45 metres.

When a sea turtle is disturbed by your presence it will...

• Suddenly change direction or swimming speed.

• Sea turtles resting on the surface are likely to suddenly dive.

• The turtle will frequently ascend to the sea surface to breathe, or will show signs of exhaustion.

• Because of this, it is essential to be careful when in the presence of a turtle and to be prepared to take actions that cause minimum disturbance.

On finding an injured or sick animal (sea turtle, seal, dolphin or bird)...

• Contact the National Marine Park or the Port Police immediately. A list of useful telephone numbers can be found in the 'A-Z', on page 41.

Getting to Zákynthos
By air

The island's international airport, 'Dionýsios Solomós', is located 4km from Zákynthos town and about 2km from Laganás and Kalamáki. The airport only operates during the day, to avoid disturbance to sea turtles. There is a public transport service between the airport and the town, and a taxi rank in front of the airport.

Between May and October there are direct **charter and non-charter flights** from many UK airports — at time of writing: Birmingham, Bristol, Cardiff, Doncaster Sheffield, East Midlands, Edinburgh, Glasgow, Leeds/Bradford, London Gatwick, London Luton, London Stansted, Manchester, and Newcastle. There are also flights from Dublin (and many other European countries). Anyone travelling from outside Europe will have to fly in via Athens, as described below (or fly into London and take a package tour from there).

Prices are highest between June and early September, when there are also more flights. During the 'shoulder' seasons (May, late September and October) prices are considerably lower. **Package holiday** deals (including flight, accommodation and perhaps car hire) can sometimes be less expensive than paying for all the items separately.

Between November and April, when there are no charter flights, it's necessary to **fly via Athens**, and either take a connecting Olympic Airways flight to Zákynthos or travel by bus and ferry.

There are daily domestic flights from Athens International Airport ('Elefthérios Venizélos') to Zákynthos throughout the year. Flight time is approximately 45 minutes. There are also direct Olympic Airways flights from Zákynthos to Thessaloníki, Corfu and Kefaloniá. Contact the airline directly or search the web (www.olympicairlines.com) for flight times and frequency.

By car and ferry

Driving to Zákynthos is *possible* for those with plenty of time (allow 4-5 days; about 20 hours' driving after crossing the Channel, and 20 hours or so on ferries). You will need an international driving licence, the

---

Ferries to neighbouring islands

Between May and October there is a twice-daily car ferry service from Ágios Nikólaos in the north of Zákynthos (09.45, 19.15) and Pessáda on the island of Kefaloniá (returns from there at 07.45 and 17.30). Tickets can be reserved at Ágios Nikólaos port or at ticket offices in Zákynthos town. The journey takes about one hour. You must take your hire car, as there is no connecting bus or taxi service from Pessáda Port.

From Kefaloniá there are connecting ferry services from Fiskárdo to the island of Levkas and from both Fiskárdo and Sámi to Ithaca Island.

To travel between Zákynthos and Kefaloniá from November to April, you must go via Kilíni in the Peloponnese (one hour from Zákynthos), then take another ferry from Kilíni to Póros or Argostóli on Kefaloniá (one hour).

vehicle's registration documents and valid Third Party insurance. From France you would make for Venice, Ancona, Bari or Brindizi, from where there are ferries to Patras, Greece. Patras is some 80km/50mi north of Kilíni on the northwestern coast of the Peloponnese, from where there are at least four departures per day to Zákynthos.

Be aware that ferry services can be disrupted by strong winds, especially in winter. In fair weather the crossing from Kilíni takes about one hour. Note that the ferry timetable is changed frequently during the summer and around festivals. You can check **timetables and prices** for both the crossing from Italy and onward travel from Kilíni in advance at www.ferries.gr.

> **Tip:** for air, bus and ferry travel (including ferries to Kefaloniá) see zanteweb.gr/transportation.html

By coach/bus

A minimum of four bus services connect Zákynthos with Patras and Athens daily, and twice-weekly with Thessaloníki. The journey from Athens to Kilíni is 286km and takes about five hours. From there you have a direct link by car ferry to Zákynthos. Note that bus timetables are regularly changed, especially during the summer months. KTEL (www.ktel.org) is the company providing bus services in Greece, so check their website for **timetables** before you travel.

There is a bus service (line E93) connecting Athens International Airport and the KTEL 'Kiffisós' bus station in Athens.

Getting around Zákynthos

By car

Having your own **car** is the best, and safest, way of getting around the island (and to the walks described in this book). At any time of year you can hire a car locally when you arrive. But to save money, hire through your travel agent when booking your holiday or book in advance on the internet — even the day before you travel.

If you would like to explore the island's back roads or cover some of the walking routes by car, I advise hiring a **four-wheel drive** vehicle. (But 4WD vehicles are *not* necessary for reaching the *starting points* of the walks).

Prices of car hire vary with the tourist season, and of course are at their highest in summer. Be sure to check the **insurance coverage** of the car and alert the owners to existing damage before you take it on the roads — you might even take photos of any existing damage.

Drive defensively, and always *expect the unexpected* — buses, coaches, water trucks, cement trucks, speeding taxis, cars on the wrong side of the road, etc. The tarmac roads on the island are generally in poor condition, with potholes, water and oil spills, slippery, smooth surfaces and gravelly hairpin bends. It is usual to sound your horn when approaching a bend, to alert oncoming traffic.

Should you be unfortunate enough to be involved in an **accident**, you must *not* move the vehicle. Place a warning triangle 100 metres behind the car, then summon the police (a police

Mediterranean traffic jam: a loggerhead being cleaned by fish

report is mandatory for any insurance claim). *Do not sign any report which you cannot read* — or make a note on the report that you could not read it.

Keep the following **regulations** in mind: the **maximum speed** in built-up areas is 30-40km/h; on main roads 50-60km/h. The **blood-alcohol limit** for drivers is 0.5mg/l (generally equivalent to two glasses of wine). **Seat belts** must be worn; **mobile phones** may not be used while driving. Beware: short distances can often take much longer than expected. When touring always carry plenty of water and, if you plan to stay out until after sunset, remember to take a jumper. There are plenty of **petrol stations** (see fold-out map) on the main roads, but fewer in the mountains. Lead-free petrol (*amólivthi venzíni*) is readily available.

By *bus*

The road network covers the entire island, with a public bus service to almost all destinations. It is relatively easy to travel to the main towns by bus, with regular services between villages like Alikés, Tsiliví, Argássi and Laganás.

However, while smaller villages may have services once or twice a day, they are likely to be at irregular or inconvenient hours for your needs. Moreover, many services do not run at weekends. Sometimes the buses pass intermediate places on their route much earlier or later than expected, so it's a good idea to keep a radio taxi service telephone number to hand in case you get stranded!

The **bus schedules** are updated monthly during the summer and can be obtained from the bus station in Zákynthos town (west of the hospital; 11 on the town plan on pages 42-43).

There are buses from Zákynthos town to Agalás, Ágios Léon, Ágios Nikólaos, Alikanás, Alikés, Anafonítria, Argássi, Éxo Chóra, Galáro, Girí, Kampí, Katastári,

18

Kerí, Ksirocástello, Kypséli,
Laganás, Lithakiá, Macherádo,
Orthoniés, Plános, Pórto Róma,
Tragáki, Tsiliví, Vassilikós and
Volímes.
The local bus company also offers
organised tours around the
island, with stops in the main
villages and resorts en route.

By taxi
Taxis are easily available all over
the island, and there is a taxi rank
in most resorts. By law, all taxis
should turn on their meters at
your request (make sure it is set
to the day-time rather than night-
time rate). However, for tourists
there is a fixed rate for the
popular destinations.
Generally the taxis are good
value and relatively cheaper than
in the UK. But before getting into
a taxi, check the routes and
journey length on a map and
check the cost (your local hotelier
or a shopkeeper will be able to
advise you on the approximate
cost of a proposed taxi ride). If
the price sounds too high, then
perhaps you are being ripped off
— so just return ten minutes later
and ask a different taxi.
Be positive about where you
want to go and don't let the taxi
driver persuade you that you
want to go elsewhere. Most taxi
drivers have a relative who runs
a taverna, apartment or car rental
business, and some will try their
best to get you there, even if it's
well off the itinerary you have
chosen.

By boat
It's worth taking at least one boat
trip around Zákynthos to truly
appreciate the island's beautiful
and varied coastlines. **Large tour
boats** depart daily from

Touring and picnicking
*On pages 42-79 I have outlined
one city tour and four car tours,
integrating cultural and environmental themes with all the
practical information you should
need. The maps at the start of
each tour are only intended to
show the route; **for full details
see the fold-out map**. Using the
fold-out map, it is also possible to
explore the unpaved back roads
— or even integrate parts of the
walks in your tour, but to do this a
4WD vehicle is essential.
If possible, allow a full day for
each tour, to ensure plenty of time
to explore. On the fold-out map I
have highlighted several potentially pleasant picnic spots, all
within about a 10 minute walk
from a road. Some of these picnic
spots feature in the walks, and a
glance at the sketch map for the
relevant walk may inspire you to
go a bit further!
When picnicking, do remember
that bonfires and barbecues are
prohibited within the National
Park, and it is unwise to light fires
anywhere on the island.*

Picnic overlooking a Blue Cave

Zákynthos town to many places around the island that can only be reached by sea — Marathoníssi Islet, the Shipwreck, the Kerí Caves and Blue Caves, and many isolated beaches.

Additionally, **smaller tour boats** depart from most local ports (Ágios Sóstis, Makrís Gialós, Ágios Nikólaos, Skinári, etc) to visit specific nearby sites. Alternatively, **boats can be hired privately** for the day at most major resorts (but there are restrictions on how far you can take them).

On the nearby islands of Kefaloniá, Levkas and Ithaca, **flotilla sailing holidays** are a popular way of exploring the coastlines and islets of the central Ionian, and you could plan your holiday to take in a week's sailing and a week's walking.

Yachting by the Keri caves and arches

By *moped, motorbike or quad-bike*

While it is certainly possible to hire mopeds, motorbikes and quad-bikes (it is mandatory to wear a **helmet**), I advise against it. This is partly because there is no quality control on bike condition, partly because of the road surfaces and partly due to traffic conditions — including fast local drivers, uncertain tourist drivers, water trucks, buses and coaches. There are many bends on which mopeds and motorbikes may easily skid, and unstable quad-bikes tend to turn over.

By *bicycle*

The Municipality of Elatíon have created a 2km/1.3mi linear tarmac **bicycle path in the valleys between Volímes and Anafonítria**. It begins by a church on the main road leading into Volímes and is clearly sign-posted. It is also shown on the fold-out map at the back of this book. (Of course this bicycle path may also be walked — it leads through meadows and pine forest with fine mountain views, and can be made into a loop by returning along the main road or by following one of the many tracks in this area, also shown on the fold-out map.)

Another popular place for cycling is the flat terrain by the **Alikés salt pans**, and bicycles can be hired nearby.

Naturally, since they mostly follow dirt tracks, **the walks may also be used for cycling**. But these tracks are usually fairly rough and best suited to sturdy mountain bikes. The walking sketch maps differentiate between surfaced (orange) and unmade (white) roads — so you can try out a couple of routes and select those that reflect your ability.

Alternatively you can **use the fold-out map** at the back of the book (which shows five grades of road surface) to design your own cycle routes along back roads. However I do recommend that, wherever possible, you avoid all main roads leading from Zákynthos town to Kerí, Katastári and Vassilikós.

Please also remember that *cycling along the protected nesting beaches in the National Marine Park is prohibited by law* — this includes the stretch of beach between Ágios Sóstis, Laganás and Kalamáki.

By hitchhiking

When buses have not turned up, or when they have passed earlier than expected, it is not unusual for the locals to hitchhike — I have frequently been hailed down by old women, and even the occasional priest. But I would advise you against hitchhiking — not only is it unreliable, but potentially dangerous.

Accommodation

There are many holiday resorts on Zákynthos, all of which are coastal and in close proximity to sandy beaches. The walks in this book are spread across the entire island, so wherever you are based, some of them will be easily accessible.

There are **hotels, apartments, apart-hotels, campsites** and **rooms to rent** to suit all budgets. If you have not pre-booked a package holiday, the web is an excellent way to find somewhere in advance. For example, the web site www.zanteweb.gr lists all different types of accommodation, with facilities and sometimes photographs. If you wait

Some of the walking routes are suitable for cycling, such as the Korakoníssi trail shown above (Walk 16)

until you get to the island, you can ask in village bars or restaurants.

In the touring section on pages 42-79, I have highlighted (under the relevant village) about 25 of the best places to stay on the island, with approximate prices, and indicated with asterisks *my own personal 'star ratings'*. Accommodation is cheapest at the start and end of the holiday season (**May** and **October**) and most expensive in August, the peak season, with a rising scale in the months in between. If you visit the island in **July or August** it is *essential to pre-book* rooms. During the other months it is relatively easy to find accommodation on arrival.

From **November** to **April**, all

There are many vineyards on the island, and in a taverna you are likely to find very good carafe wine made from the owner's own grapes. — rosé (rozé), red (kókkino) or white (áspero).

tourist villages and associated amenities shut down. Contact the owners in advance to check if they are willing to open for you (the winter is the only time of year when they can travel). Check, too, if they have heating (otherwise the accommodation will be damp and cold). Alternatively, you can stay at one of the hotels in Zákynthos town, which are equipped with both air conditioning and heating systems, and you will be close to all the town amenities which function year-round. (Remember, most restaurants are open for just three or four days a week in winter, so it's worth checking in advance which are open and when!)

Food and drink

The food on Zákynthos is similar to that on other Ionian Islands, with local variations and specialities. Some **Zakynthian specialities** are
• stuffed chicken *(yemistó kotópoulo)* or rabbit *(kounéli)*;
• *melitzánes skordostoúmbi:* aubergines in garlic sauce
• beef ragout *(stifádo);*
• *mageirítza* or *sgantzéto* (the Zakynthian equivalent of *mageirítza*): an Easter Saturday dish made from pressure-cooked intestines and offal of a baby goat or lamb, in an egg-lemon sauce;
• *kokorétzi*, barbecued intestines;
• *pantséta* (cured bacon)
Zákynthos produces **cheeses** (including *ladotíri* (meaning 'oily cheese'), **cold salted meats** called *chiroméri* and **special sweets**, including *mandoláto* (nougat with almonds) and *pastéli* (caramelized sesame seeds with honey). Naturally, in common with all the Greek islands, Zákynthos has a wide range of **seafoods** — from mussels, scallops and fish to octopus, squid, cuttlefish and lobster.

Eating Greek-style

Eating is one of my greatest pleasures in life, and the Greek style of eating is a perfected technique.

I cannot recount the number of times I have been in a restaurant and despaired as I overheard tourists order a meal as they would in northern Europe, and their subsequent dismay at the meagre starter and vegetable-lacking main course which arrived later.

To save you disappointment, below are the fundamental rules of eating out in Greece:

Rule 1: Greeks eat to be social and hence share their food;

Rule 2: Greeks eat to enjoy the combination of tastes.

So because Greeks eat together as part of being social (Rule 1) it means that several people usually share a meal and hence a variety of small dishes, known as 'mezés', will inevitably be selected (Rule 2).

Greek food is prepared and served to fulfil the above rules.

So forget about trying to order a set dish per person or selecting one starter each and one main course each and be prepared to share your food.

If there are two of you I suggest you order one main dish and, depending on how hungry you are, a selection of three to five starters — including a Greek salad. If you are four, order two main dishes and again a selection of three to five starters. You can always order more if there isn't enough — or if something is particularly tasty. Most of all, enjoy the Greek experience of sharing and tasting.

Typical Zakynthian mezé with mixed salad, bread with tomato and garlic sauce and cheese pies

In the touring section on pages 42-79, I have highlighted (under the relevant village) about 35 of the best places to eat on the island and indicated with asterisks *my own personal 'star ratings'*. A price guide is given as well (€ very inexpensive; €€ moderate; €€€ fairly pricey).

More about Greek food

To learn more about Greek food, just do an internet search … or buy a copy of 'Walk & Eat Kefaloniá'. This guide can not only be used for excursions to Zákynthos's near neighbour, but contains a wealth of illustrated articles (and recipes!) for dishes common to both islands.

HISTORY

The early history of the island has been gleaned from poets and storytellers such as Homer in the *Iliad* and the *Odyssey*, in which he describes Zákynthos as 'Iliéssa' (wooded). Mythology includes a tale about Zeus, the father of the Olympian gods: he frequently bathed in the channel between Zákynthos and Kefaloniá. After a swim he would stand on Zákynthos and take up handfuls of water to wash his face. He would then gather up rocks and throw them over to Kefaloniá. This is why Kefaloniá is more mountainous than Zákynthos!

The oldest records of human existence on Zákynthos are bone fossils of neolithic man during the palaeolithic period. Due to the island's fertile soil and strategic location on the sea route to the Middle East, Zákynthos (in common with the other Ionian Islands) has had a turbulent past. Initially it was fought over by various Greek states and was then occupied by the Romans, Byzantines, Normans, Italians, Turks, Venetians, French, Russians and British — while the rest of Greece was primarily under Byzantine or Turkish rule. Then, after almost a century of union with Greece, the island was subject to a final, brief period of occupation, under German and Italian rule during the Second World War.

Beginning opposite is a more detailed chronology of the island's history.

The timeless Gérakas sunset

Dates (approx.)	Occupier	Details
3000 BC	Neolithic man	Indigenous inhabitants (remains of neolithic man found).
1600-1500 BC	Trojans	According to Homer, Prince Zákynthos, the son of King Dárdanos of Troy and grandson of Zeus and Electra, brought the first settlers to the island from the Arcadian city of Psophís in the Peloponnese. At that time the modern town of Zákynthos was still under water; they built their acropolis, Psofída (or Psophís), on what is now Bóchali Hill (the remnants are under the Venetian castle). The inhabitants worshipped the Goddess Artemis.
1500 BC	Arcadians	The Arcadians settled on the island to take advantage of the fertile soil.
from 1200 BC	Kingdom of Ithaca	Zákynthos was part of the kingdom ruled from Ithaca by Odysseus (Ulysses), and sent him ships for the Trojan War.
	Kefalonians	Under the rule of King Arkísos, Kefaloniá invaded the island.
	Kingdom of Ithaca; then independence	Odysseus recaptured the island, then returned to Ithaca — having both ignored the Zakynthian contribution to the Trojan War effort and slain all Zakynthian suitors for his wife Penelope's hand during his long absence. The island rebelled, demanding independence. A treaty was finally mediated by a Zakynthian, Neoptolémos, granting the island autonomy and democracy — the first example in Greece.
6th century BC		The island was flourishing and one of the first places in Greece to circulate silver currency (depicting Apollo … with three legs).
479 BC		Neutral for most of the Persian Wars, Zákynthos finally sided with Sparta against the Persians at the Battle of Plataéa.

Dates (approx.)	Occupier	Details
from 455 BC		Having previously been allied with Sparta, Zákynthos now joined Corfu and Athens during the Peloponnesian Wars.
404-371 BC	Sparta	Sparta prevailed in 404 BC and imposed an oligarchic regime on Zákynthos. The inhabitants rebelled and re-established democracy in 371 BC.
217-214 BC	Macedonians	Conquered the island, under the rule of Philip V, during the Macedonian Wars.
214-191 BC	Romans	Zákynthos fell under Roman occupation. From 210 BC Zákynthos was given as a gift to different Roman rulers.
191-150 BC	Macedonians vs. Romans	The islanders were under siege, while the two powers fought for supremacy.
from 150 BC	Romans	The Romans won and granted the islanders the right to have their own parliament and laws and mint their own currency. Zákynthos became a part of the Kingdom of Achaea, a province of the Roman Empire.
34 AD		Christianity was brought to the island by Mary Magdalene and Maria Klopa (St. Beatrice); the village of Mariés is named for them.
from 395	Byzantine Empire	The Roman Empire split in two on the death of Emperor Theodosius I, with Zákynthos (and all of Greece) falling into the Eastern Roman Empire (the Byzantine Empire). Christianity boomed under Byzantine rule, during which time Constantine the Great included Zákynthos in the province of Illyria. But it was far from Constantinople and difficult to protect: the island suffered successive raids by Goths, Vandals, Saracens and, later, even the Crusaders.

Dates (approx.)	Occupier	Details
1185-1479	Normans, Italians	Normans, having previously attacked the Ionian Islands, finally prevailed in 1185. At the start of the 13th century the Palatine County of Kefaloniá and Zante was founded, which survived for three centuries under the Orsini family (who imposed Roman Catholicism and forbade Greek Orthodox worship), then the de Tocchi dynasty.
1479-1485	Turks	Unable to stop Turkish attacks, the last de Tocchi rulers sold up to the Venetians and fled to Italy, while the islanders fled to the Peloponnese. Turkish forces searching for escaped refugees invaded the island, having already sacked Kefaloniá.
1485-1797	Venetians	The Venetians negotiated a treaty with the Turks whereby they could occupy the island at a 'rent' of 500 gold ducats a year. The inhabitants returned to their homes, with the population quickly swelling to 25,000. The island (called 'Fior di Levante' or 'Flower of the East') flourished, and the capital was rebuilt — becoming known as the 'Florence of Greece'. But the strict class structure, whereby the lowest classes were treated as surfs, gave rise to 'the People's Rebellion' (1628-1632), against the Venetian nobility; this was quickly suppressed.
1797-1798	French	Venice was defeated by Napoleon, and the Ionian Islands became French possessions. The class structure was removed and local mayors had authority to rule under French supervision.
Oct. 1798	Turks and Russians	Re-invasion of the island by a Russian and Turkish fleet. The conquerors quickly reinstated the hated oligarchy.

Dates (approx.)	Occupier	Details
1800-1807	Turks and Russians	Russia and Turkey established a new 'State of the Seven Ionian Islands', under Russian protection. Although it only lasted seven years, and the islanders had to pay tax to the Turks, this was the first time they had not been directly governed by foreigners since antiquity.
1807-1809	French	With Napoleon's defeat of the Russians, the islands returned to France under the Treaty of Tilsit.
1809	British	The British Navy defeated the French fleet and took Zákynthos. Under British rule, the island became the capital of the Ionian State, while the rest of Greece remained under Turkish Ottoman Rule. The British modernised the island and built many bridges, as well as the water pipeline near Argássi.
1814		With the defeat of Napoleonic France, Britain received control of the Ionian State at the Congress of Vienna.
1830		At the end of the War of Independence, Greece won freedom from Turkish rule (Zákynthos had been a centre for British supporters of independence, most famously Lord Byron). Now the Ionian Islands asked to be reunited with Greece.
21 May 1864	Greece	Following years of negotiation, all seven of the Ionian Islands were united with Greece. Campaigning had begun in 1851 when a member of Parliament, Ioánnis Typaldós Kapelátos, suggested the union, but met with British opposition. Eventually Britain, France and Russia signed a treaty in June 1863, in which Britain gave up its role as the power protecting the Ionian Islands.

Dates (approx.)	Occupier	Details
1941-1943	Germans and Italians	Zákynthos was subjected to Axis occupation by the Italians and Germans during World War II, until its liberation on September 12, 1944. Many islanders participated in the resistance against the occupying army, resulting in much conflict and sacrifice. Zákynthos town has the only synagogue on the island in which there is a special plaque thanking the Zakynthians for their courageous efforts during the war. While the island shares similar experiences with many places worldwide during the war, Zákynthos was the only place in Greece where all the Jewish inhabitants (275 people) survived the atrocities of the Holocaust. This was due to the bravery of the inhabitants, the mayor and the Orthodox church, who all cooperated in hiding the Jewish population from capture (see page 47). Zákynthos has been included in the 'Righteous Among Nations ' for the efforts and actions of its inhabitants.
September 12th, 1944	Greece	The island was liberated and re-united with the rest of Greece.
August 1953		Earthquakes (see page 30) caused extensive damage on the island (the neighbouring island of Kefaloniá was virtually destroyed). Although rebuilding began, there was a great exodus to find work overseas.
from the 1980s		Emigration was stemmed by the burgeoning tourist industry, a key element of the Zakynthian economy.

CULTURAL HERITAGE

Zákynthos has inspired writers such as Homer and has been the home of great Greek poets — Fóskolos, Kálvos, Xenópoulos and Dionýsios Solomós (writer of the Greek National Anthem, the *Hymn to Liberty*). The island remains a cultural blend of Venetian and Greek traditions and is renowned for its music, especially the *kantádes* — polyphonic songs accompanied by guitar or mandolin.

Tragically, most of the historical buildings, monuments and artefacts mirroring the island's cultural development have been destroyed by earthquakes. The last major quakes occurred on 11-12 August 1953, measuring 6.8 and 7.3 respectively on the Richter Scale. Some 70% of the island's buildings were destroyed; only four in Zákynthos town survived the tremors and subsequent fire storms — the churches of Ágios Dionýsios and Ágios Nikólaos tou Mólou, Ámmos Primary School and the National Bank of Greece. Today there are stringent building regulations regarding earthquake protection. Information about churches, monasteries and other historical sites and museums can be found in the touring section on pages 42-79. Below is a summary of the island's celebration days.

Date	Name	Location	Details
1 Jan.	New Year's Day	**public holiday** throughout Greece	This is the name day of St. Basil and is associated with an old Byzantine custom of slicing the *Vassilópita* (Basil cake or New Year's cake), a sweet bread with a coin inside which brings good luck to the finder for the coming year. This is also the day when children receive their gifts.
6 Jan.	Epiphany	**public holiday** throughout Greece	This is the feast day of Agía Theofánia, or 'Fóta' (in reference to the day being a Feast of 'Light'). Priests lead processions to the waterside (lakes, rivers or the sea), then throw a cross into the water to bless it. With this rite, the malicious *kalikántzari* (hobgoblins) who have been active above ground during the 12 days of Christmas, are banished back to the bowels of the earth. Young locals compete to retrieve the cross, which will bring them good luck for the whole year.

Date	Name	Location	Details
31 Jan.–22 Feb.	Greek Carnival season	throughout Greece	The Carnival is called *Apókries* and is celebrated by three weeks of feasting and dancing before the start of Lent *(Katharí Deftéra).* The festivities are particularly enjoyable on Zákynthos and are a major event in Patras (the ferry and bus trip takes two hours from Zákynthos).
Feb.	Funeral of the Fagade	**public holiday** throughout Greece	'Halloween'-like festival celebrated in Zákynthos town, with a parade on the last day (which is a public holiday)
varies year to year	Katharí Deftéra (Shrove Monday)	**public holiday** throughout Greece	Celebrated 40 days before Easter, 'clean' or Shrove Monday marks the first day of Lent. It is customary to visit the countryside, fly paper kites and picnic on seafood (not meat).
25 Mar.	Greek Independence Day and Feast of the Annunciation	**public holiday** throughout Greece	This day celebrates Greece's victory in the War of Independence against the Turks who had occupied the country for 400 years. March 25th, 1821 was the day Archbishop Germanós of Patras raised the flag of national rebellion at the monastery of Agía Lávra in the northern Peloponnese and war was declared. It is also a major religious holiday, a feast celebrating the Angel Gabriel's announcement of the birth of Christ to Mary. It is customary to bake special loaves of bread and cover them in fragrant spring flowers.
varies year to year	Greek Orthodox Easter	**public holiday** throughout Greece	**Good Friday:** A sombre day of fasting and remembering the dead. In the evening, villagers from each church take part in a candlelit procession, following the *Epitáphios* (the funeral bier of Christ) from their church to the local square, where more candle-carrying villagers from other churches will be gathered.

Date	Name	Location	Details
varies year to year	Greek Orthodox Easter (cont'd.)	**public holiday** throughout Greece	**Holy Saturday:** The ceremony of the Resurrection takes place: on Zákynthos the crucifix is carried through the streets from the church of Ágios Nikólaos Mólou to Solomós Square. Everyone follows the icons as they are carried around the town; then, at midnight, a first candle is lit and the flame is quickly passed from candle to candle. Fireworks and church bells sound. Afterwards people go home for the traditional feast of red-dyed Easter eggs and *mageirítza* (a soup made from lamb innards).
varies year to year	Greek Orthodox Easter (cont'd.)	**public holiday** throughout Greece	**Easter Sunday:** This is the biggest church holiday in Greece. All over the country, lambs are roasted on spits and wine flows abundantly. Red Easter eggs are cracked against each other, and the person with the last egg remaining uncracked will have good luck all year.

Greek Easter eggs

Date	Name	Location	Details
1 May	Labour Day and May Day (Feast of Flowers)	**public holiday** throughout Greece	This is celebrated by hanging flowers and home-made multi-coloured wreaths outside houses, and decorating car windscreens with flowers. This ancient custom of celebrating spring is world-wide. On Kefaloniá the tradition is to place some garlic with the flowers, to protect the house from bad luck and to ward off the evil eye and ill fortune.
21 May	Ionian Day	**public holiday** on the Ionian Islands	On this day in 1864, the Ionian Islands gained independence from British occupation and were united with Greece. It is also the name day of saints Konstantínos and Eléni.

Date	Name	Location	Details
varies year to year	Whit Monday	**public holiday** throughout Greece	This religious holiday marks the descent of the Holy Spirit (*Ágio Pnévma*) to the assembled disciples, 50 days after Easter. Church services are held, as well as picnics or barbecues, with dancing after evening services. Families visit graveyards or pray in remembrance of deceased family and friends.
late June/ early July	Navy Week	throughout Greece	Coastal towns, fishing villages, and ports celebrate the nation's long relationship with the sea and honour the Greek Navy with festivities and entertainments lasting the whole week.
early August	Interna-national Meeting	Zákynthos	The International Meeting of Medieval and Popular Theatre is held in Zákynthos town.
15 Aug.	Assump-tion Day	**public holiday** throughout Greece	This religious festival celebrates the ascent of the Virgin Mary (*Panagía*) to Heaven. All churches named after the Virgin Mary have celebrations. On Zákynthos, locals travel up the mountain to celebrate at the Church of Panagía Skopiótissa (see pages 104-105), the only day on which this church is opened. In the afternoon Lithakiá's priest gives a celebration service on the beach of Marathoníssi islet, where there was once a monastery dedicated to the Virgin.
24 Aug.	Saint Dionýsios (Patron Saint of the island)	**public holiday** on Zákynthos only (but shops stay open)	Mass is held in memory of the transfer of the saint's body from its original burial place at the monastery in the Strophades Islands, where he spent most of his life, to the church of Ágios Dionýsios in Zákynthos town. The patron saint is on display for 24 hours and paraded throughout town. The celebrations last three days, with various religious cere-monies followed by traditional

Date	Name	Location	Details
			dances and music, accompanied by local food and wine. Pilgrims by the thousands visit the island to crawl on their knees up the steps to the church that holds the holy icon. There are fireworks and hundreds of street stalls. After Easter, this is the island's most important celebration.
late Aug./ early Sep.	Wine Festival	wine-growing regions throughout Greece	On Zákynthos this festival is held in Zákynthos town, where the tasting of local wines and raisins is organised. There is also dancing and theatre.
14 Sep.	Holy Cross	**public holiday** throughout Greece	On this day all churches around the island decorate the cross with basil. *Vassilikó* (basil) means 'belonging to the king'. After the services all the parishioners are given a bunch of basil to take home. This plant is grown in and around most gardens and verandas. The celebration of the Holy Cross originated with Helena, mother of Constantine the Great (the first Christian emperor). She allegedly found the true Cross of Christ in Palestine and in turn became a saint herself.
28 Oct.	'Óchi' Day	**public holiday** throughout Greece	This day commemorates General Metaxá's famous 'Óchi!' ('No'!), refusing Mussolini's demand to occupy the country under Fascist rule during World War II. The Italians invaded, but were driven back into Albania and nearly back to Italy. The day also marks Greece's entry into the war on the side of the Allies and is celebrated by military parades and folk dancing.
17 Nov.	Students' Uprising	near universities throughout Greece	This is the anniversary of the student uprising at the Polytechnic University in Athens in 1973. The demonstrations against

Date	Name	Location	Details
			the national military dictatorship (the 'Regime of the Colonels') gained momentum and were crushed when tanks crashed the gates of the university, killing many students. The annual commemoration ceremonies end with a march (not always peaceful) that begins on the Polytechnic campus and ends at the American Embassy.
17 Dec.	Saint Dionýsios (Patron Saint of the island)	**public holiday** Zákynthos (businsses close only on the 17th, but most shops stay open)	This is the date of the death of the island's patron saint and the 'name day' of all people named Dionýsios (Dennis). The event lasts three days and includes various religious ceremonies, followed by traditional dances and music accompanied by local food and wine.
24 Dec.	Christmas Eve	throughout Greece	Young children walk around singing carols (*kálanda*) on trains, buses and in neighbourhoods.
25 Dec.	Christmas Day	**public holiday** throughout Greece	The traditional Greek decoration for this important festival celebrating the birth of Christ was a wooden boat, but today Christmas trees and lights are used. Greeks traditionally give presents on the 1st of January — the name day of St. Basil (who, rather than St. Nicholas, is 'Father Christmas' in Greece).

PRACTICALITIES A-Z

Beaches

Every beach on the island is described in this book — and there are beaches to suit all tastes. If a beach is described as having 'facilities', this will usually include sunshade and sunlounger rental, freshwater showers, and usually a café/bar and/or nearby taverna. '*Ample facilities*' means a lot more will be on offer — from multiple refreshment opportunities to some water sports and boat rentals. '*All facilities*' indicates the whole range — banana boating, jet skiing, paragliding, and perhaps diving tuition. Remember, however, that

facilities may be more limited at the start and end of the 'season'. **Naturism** is not acceptable on public beaches, but on some secluded beaches they will turn a blind eye. Beaches where you can expect to find naturists are mentioned in the text.

Camping

There are currently five camping sites on the island; all are very well equipped: Ágios Sóstis, Alikés, Mésa Gerakári, Lithakiá and Tragáki. For locations, see the fold-out map. Otherwise you may only camp with the land-owner's permission. *Camping and bivouacking are prohibited in the National Park.*

Churches, visiting

Go quietly and wear appropriate dress (no bare shoulders, long trousers for men, knee-length skirts for women). At the more important churches and monasteries clothing is often available at the door. Please remember to leave a small donation.

Consulates

The **British Honorary Vice Consulate** is at 5 Fóskolos Street, 291 00 Zákynthos town. It is open to the public from 08.00-13.00 Mon.-Fri; tel. 26950-22906/48030/45386; fax 26950-23769; zakynthos@british-consulate.gr.

Crime

Sensible precautions should ensure you are not a victim of crime — or end up in jail! Keep valuables locked in your hotel safe or car boot; keep your wits about you late at night (especially women on their own); *never* try to bring drugs into Greece — the penalties are far more stringent than in the UK.

Electricity

The power supply is 220 volts, and two round-pin plugs are the norm, so take your continental or international adaptor.

Holidays

Public holidays are shown on pages 30-35. In tourist centres, shops and tavernas will remain open, but bus services will be less frequent and many petrol stations are closed.

Information

There is still no official tourist office on the island, but there *is* information galore about the island on the web; to maximise your search results try using the following spelling variations: Zante, Zákinthos and Zákynthos.

Some general web addresses

www.zakynthos.gr *(official site of the Prefecture of Zákynthos, with links to the web sites of the island's six municipalities)*
www.zanteweb.gr *(general site)*
www.olympicairlines.com
www.ionianferries.gr *(ferries)*
www.ktel.org *(the bus company)*
www.panhellenic-camping-union.gr *(campsites and facilities)*

Hatchlings making their way to sea

Conservation web sites

Greek Ministry of the Environment: www.minenv.gr
National Marine Park of Zákynthos: www.nmp-zak.org
WWF Greece: www.wwf.gr
Friends of the Ionian: www.foi.org.uk
Archelon (The Sea Turtle Protection Society of Greece): www.archelon.gr

MEDASSET (Mediterranean Association to Save the Sea Turtle): www.medasset.gr
Earth Sea & Sky (Ionian Nature Conservation): www.earthseasky.org
Ionian Dolphin Project: www.tethys.org
MOm (Hellenic Society for the Study and Protection of the Monk Seal): www.mom.gr
Hellenic Ornithological Society: www.ornithologiki.gr
Natura 2000: www.eu.int

Language

The majority of Greeks working in and around tourist resorts speak English, if not perfectly then at a level that can be understood. However, this is not necessarily the case in the hilly regions and mountain villages, so a simple Greek phrase book or pocket dictionary can often prove invaluable — you can at least point to words. It is a good idea to learn the Greek alphabet, too, as many signposts are only in Greek.

The list of words and phrases below, with approximate pronunciation, is a small selection of what you might need.

Some common words and phrases

Good morning	Ka-lee-**me**-ra
Good afternoon	Ka-lo-ap-**o**-yev-ma
Good evening	Ka-lee-**spe**-ra
Good night	Ka-lee-**neeh**-ta
Hello/goodbye (formal)	*Yeea*-sas
Hello/goodbye (informal)	*Yeea*-soo
Cheers	*Yeea*-mas
Yes	*Ne*
No	*O*-hee
OK	En-**daks**-ee

Please	*Pa-ra-ka-lo*
Thank you	*Ef-ha-ree-sto*
I'm lost	*E-ha-sa to dro-mo moo*
I don't understand	*Den ka-ta-la-ve-no*
Do you know English? French? German?	*Kse-re-te an-glee-ka? gha-lee-ka? yer-ma-nee-ka?*
Open	*A-neek-to*
Closed	*Klee-sto*
How much does it cost?	*Po-so ka-nee?*
What?	*Tee?*
When?	*Po-te?*
Why?	*Yeea-tee?*
Where is …?	*Poo ee-ne …?*
It is beautiful	*Ee-ne po-lee o-re-a*
Could you help me?	*Bo-ree-te na me vo-ee-thee-se-te?*
Now	*To-ra*
Where is the toilet?	*Poo ee-ne ee toua-le-ta?*
I don't know	*Dhen kse-ro*
Private	*A-pa-go-re-ve-te*
It is allowed to be here	*E-pee-tre-pe-te*
Stop! (doing …)	*Sta-ma-ta!*
Don't	*Me*

Mini-vocabulary

Bank	*Tra-pe-za*
Beach	*Pa-ra-lee-a*
Bus stop	*Sta-see*
Church	*E-klee-see-a*
Doctor	*Yat-ros*
Food	*Tro-fee-ma* or *Fa-gee-to*
Appetizers	*Me-ze-dhes*
Footpath	*Mo-no-pa-tee*
Hill	*Lo-fos*
Hotel	*Kse-no-dho-hee-o*
Hospital	*No-so-ko-mee-o*
House	*Spee-tee*
Market	*A-go-ra*
Medical centre	*Ken-tro ee-yee-as*
Mill	*Mee-lo-nas*
Mountain	*Voo-no*

Petrol	*Ven-zee-nee*
Pharmacy	*Far-ma-kee-o*
Police	*As-tee-no-mee-a*
Post office	*Ta-hee-dhro-mee-o*
Quay	*Lee-ma-nee*
Restaurant	*Ta-ver-n*
Road (main)	*Dhro-mos*
Rock	*Vra-hos*
Sea	*Tha-la-sa*
Spring	*Pee-ghee*
Square	*Pla-tee-a*
Street	*O-dhos*
Town hall	*Dhee-mar-hee-o*

Maps

I think the fold-out map at the back of the book is the most accurate available (see page 85).

Medical care

For minor ailments, visit the nearest pharmacy; they are used to dealing with problems and usually speak English. They should also be able to direct you to an English-speaking doctor or dentist if need arises.

By all means take your European Health Insurance Card, but using it is complicated. It must first be verified by the Social Insurance Office (IKA, 12 on the plan on pages 42-43). This office is on the second floor; they will then direct you to a doctor on one of the floors below. If you are not based in Zákynthos town, seek medical assistance directly, pay for it yourself, then get a receipt (*apódixi*) stating what the ailment is and cost of treatment. You can then present this to the IKA and hope to have some of the cost refunded. **In an emergency**, go to Zákynthos Hospital emergency room immediately. If you are admitted, be aware that if you require nursing you will have to hire a nurse or rely on friends to carry out basic nursing.

Holiday insurance with health cover is strongly recommended. Look for a policy with a 24-hour help line, to make arrangements should you need to be transferred to Athens or repatriated. Look also at the coverage for any sports — even riding mopeds: so many people in swimwear come off bikes on the gravelly bends that 'Honda rash' is a well-documented injury…

Money

The currency is the **euro**. Cash (not travellers' cheques) can often be changed at post offices and banks, but the best rates are at the tourist supermarkets. There are **ATMs** in all significant towns and resorts. Greeks have a huge mistrust of **credit cards**, and they are often not accepted, so *always be sure to have enough cash!*

Name days

In Greece, 'name days' are more celebrated than birthdays. Since it is common to name children after saints, a person's 'name day' is the feast day of the saint after whom they were named. If you visit a village on the name day of the saint to whom the church is dedicated, you can watch the festivities!

Newspapers, etc

Available at 'Períptera' (see below), hotels and some tourist shops and supermarkets. The local weekly newspaper can be read online in English at www. imerazante.gr/imera/news/en.

Opening times

Most businesses close in the afternoon because of the heat, reopening late-afternoon and staying open late in the evening. **Banks:** Mon.-Fri., 08.00-14.00 (Fri. 13.30).

Churches and monasteries: as a rule of thumb open from 08.00 until 12.00, then again from 16.00/17.00 until 20.00. But many are *not open at all,* and you will have to track down the keyholder (best to ask at a bar or café). **Museums:** irregular hours/days; opening times (at time of writing) are shown for each museum. **Post offices:** Mon.-Fri. from 07.30-14.00 (but in high summer the post office in Zákynthos town may be open until early evening). **Shops:** usually open from 08.00/ 09.00 until 13.00/14.00, then from 17.00 until 21.00/22.00 or even later. Tourist shops may stay open all day. **Travel agencies:** officially they keep shop hours, but at the height of the tourist season are likely to be open all day.

Períptera

A *períptero* is a kiosk. *Períptera* can be found on street corners and in squares and are often open day and night. They sell practically everything — books, magazines, newspapers, sweets, cigarettes, toiletries, cough sweets, pain killers, snack foods, dairy products, water, soft drinks, alcohol, ice cream, etc. They also have pay telephones.

Pharmacies

These keep normal shop hours; if the pharmacy is closed, there should be a notice on the door about the nearest emergency pharmacy. Medicines are usually cheaper than in the UK, and often drugs like antibiotics can be obtained without a prescription.

Post offices

There are post offices in Zákynthos town and in most decent-sized villages. There are also **collection boxes** in most villages, easily recognised by their yellow colour. Tourist supermarkets sell **stamps**.

Souvenirs

Along with the usual tourist tat, there are some lovely gifts on offer — ceramics from Vassilikós or Macherádo, lacework and woven goods from Volímes, superb honey, good wines and cordials, island cheeses and cold meats. Of course you *must* buy something depicting a sea turtle — from a carpet or mug to a stuffed toy. CDs of *kantádes* are popular too.

Sports

Naturally, with so many beaches, **watersports** dominate. At beaches with 'all facilities' you can usually rent anything from paddle boats to jet skis. You can also rent surfboards, but the

Walk 21 starts not far from this windmill above the Blue Caves.

wind isn't really strong enough for good surfing. **Sailing** is extremely popular, too (see page 20), with yachts for hire, for instance at www.bestour.gr/zakynthos-sailing.htm.

Horse riding is quite popular; there are stables in Ksirocástello, Vassilikós, Laganás, Kalamáki, Alikés and Alikanás.

Snorkelling is permitted everywhere, but **scuba diving** is only possible in limited areas, due to zoning and to minimize damage to the environment. The best beaches for snorkelling are all mentioned in this book.

Tennis: the larger hotels have courts, where you can often pay to play even if you are not staying there.

Walking is the most pleasurable and environmentally-friendly activity you can indulge in. You will learn so much about the island, and often you can combine a walk with a swim. See the special section devoted to walking on pages 80-87. But even if you are not a walker, *do* dip into the notes following each walk — where island geology, habitats, agriculture, culture, flora and fauna are described and illustrated.

Telephones/internet

There are many **card telephones** round the island. Cards, in 100-unit increments, are available from nearby shops and kiosks (*períptera*). You can also buy 'pay as you go' dongles at the Vodaphone or Cosmote **mobile phone** shops in Zakynthos town. *Beware of telephoning from your hotel room;* calls are often charged at extortionate rates — make a quick call and ask to be called back, directly to your room.

Most built-up areas have **internet access**. A few hotels offer free access in their lobbies, but you will have to pay for connection to your room.
To telephone anywhere on the island, just dial the number, *including* the Zákynthos area code (26950). To call mainland Greece, omit the country area code (0030). To call overseas, first dial 0044 (UK), 00353 (Republic of Ireland), 001 (USA and Canada), 0030 (Greece), 0061 (Australia), 0064 (New Zealand).

Some useful telephone numbers
Airport 26590 28322
Bus (KTEL)
  Zákynthos town 26590 42656
  KTEL, Athens 210 5129432
  KTEL, Patras 2610 274938
Coast Guard (*see under* Police, Port)
Customs offices 26590 26119
Emergencies, general . . . 26590 **112**
  Ambulance 26590 166
  Tourist Police 26950 171
Fire Brigade 26590 22161
Environment Dept. . . . 26590 22518
Ferries (Ionian Ferries)
  Zákynthos . . . 26590 41500/22083
  Kilíni 26230 92422/92100,
  Athens 210 3249997
First Aid (EKAB) 26590 23166
Forestry office 26590 41125
Health centres
  Volímes 26590 31201
  Kallipádo 26590 61301
  Katastári 26590 83208
  Macherádo 26590 92217
  Pantokrátora 26590 51210
Hospital 26590 25902/42514/42515
Information, tourist . . 26590 22518
Motorists' aid 26590 26064
National Marine Park
  . . . . 26590 29870-72
Olympic Airways
  Airport counter 26590 28322
  Reservations 26590 28611
Police
  Airport 26590 28668
  Alikanás 26590 83217

Ágios Nikólaos, Skinári
  . . . . 26590 92249
Katastári 26590 83217
Laganás 26590 51251
Port (Coast Guard)   26590 28117/8
Port Authority, Kilíni
  . . . . 26230 92211/92000
Volímes 26590 83259
Tourist 26590 27367
Zákynthos town 26590 22100
Post office (ELTA) 26590 44875
Taxis . . . 26590 22280/48104/48261
  Radio taxis 26590 48400
Telephone company (OTE)
  . . . . 26590 59300/42499

Time
Greece is on Eastern European Time, two hours ahead of GMT, in both summer and winter (clocks go forward and back on the same days). At noon on Zákynthos, it's 10am in the UK, 5am in New York.

Tipping
Restaurants already include a substantial service charge by law (even if it is not itemised separately), so it is customary just to round up the bill; the same is true of taxis. Chambermaids (per day) and porters (per bag) will expect about 0.70 €. Tip hairdressers 10%.

Toilets
Men (*ándron*); ladies (*ginaíkon*); *never* put paper or sanitary materials down the loos; the narrow piping can't cope — especially in older establishments.

Water
Always drink **bottled water**. The tap water on the island is stored in large rooftop tanks, where it gets hot, promoting the growth of micro-organisms. Only use tap water for washing.

ZÁKYNTHOS TOWN

Even though Zákynthos town was shaken to ruins by the 1953 earthquake, it was rebuilt in keeping with its Venetian past. The capital has many churches, museums, monuments and squares in remembrance of the island's long and turbulent history. A walking tour is suggested opposite, taking in some of the highlights, which are described below *(in the order followed on the tour)*.

Bóchali

This upper district of the town, set round a tiny square below the Venetian Fortress, has been inhabited since ancient times. From the square there is a fantastic view to Zákynthos town and the Peloponnese. Besides the church of Panagía Chrisopigí (see page 44), there are several cafés, bars and ice-cream parlours. Bóchali can be reached by road or via the ancient cobbled trail suggested for the descent; unfortunately, it is partly concreted over now.

Places of interest

Amphitheatre: A modern concrete theatre built in traditional Greek style, over the site of an old English graveyard.

Ágios Geórgios Filikón: This little church is famous for its icon (now in the Museum of Post-

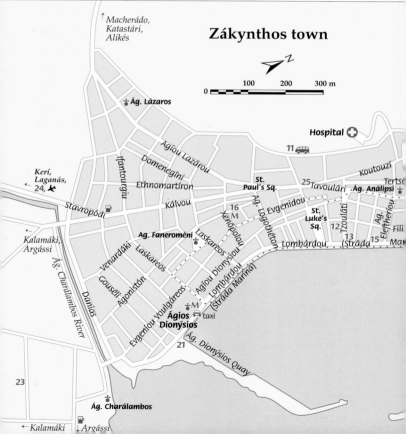

Zákynthos town

↑ Macherádo, Katastári, Alikés

↑ Ág. Lázaros

Hospital

Kerí, Laganás, 24, ✈

Agíou Lazárou

Ifantourgíu

Domenegíni

Ethnomartíron

Stavropódi

Kálvou

St. Paul's Sq.

Evgenidou

St. Luke's Sq.

Tavoulári

Koutouzí

Ág. Análipsi

Tertsé

Ág.

Kalamáki, Argássi

Venardáki

Laskaréos

Gouséli

Agonistón

Laskaréos

Xenopóulou

Ag. Faneroméni

Agíou Dionýsiou

Lombárdou

Tzoulátou

Eleftheríou

Fili

Lombárdou

(Stráda)

Mar

Evgeníou Voulgáreos

Danías

Ág. Charálambos River

Ágios Dionýsios

taxi

(Stráda Marína)

21

Ág. Dionýsios Quay

23

Ág. Charálambos

← Kalamáki   ↓ Argássi

Suggested walking tour of Zákynthos town

Start the tour at **Solomós Square** by taking a short taxi ride up to hillside Bóchali (via the **Amphitheatre**, **Ágios Geórgios Filikón**, the **Maritime Museum** and **Stráni Hill**). Once at **Bóchali**, follow the cobbled road to the **Venetian Fortress** for 360° views of the island.

From the castle take the old cobbled trail down into town via the church of **Panagía Pikridiótissa**, an **old fountain** [17], and **Kálvos Square**. This will bring you to **St. Mark's Square** and the **Solomós Museum** [7]. From here, follow 21 Maíou into the main pedestrianised shopping street, **Alexándrou Róma**, and into a maze of alleyways — past the **Xenópoulos Museum** [16],

the **Faneroméni Church** and on to **Ágios Dionýsios Monastery**, with museum and church. Return along the waterfront promenade, the **Stráda Marína**, to **Solomós Square**. The square was once an islet off the main town, with just the sailors' church, **Ág. Nikólaos tou Mólou**. Visit the **public library** [2, with post-earthquake pictures], the **Museum of Post-Byzantine Art** [5, free entry on Sundays], and take in the **monuments** to the poet Hugo Fóskolos and the World War II mayor, Loukás Kárrer, who protected the Zakynthian Jews from capture. Of course there is also a statue of Dionýsios Solomós, after whom the square is named.

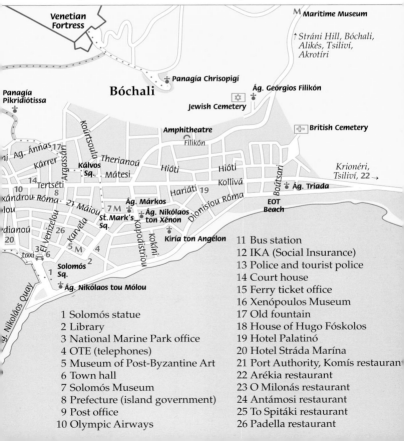

1 Solomós statue
2 Library
3 National Marine Park office
4 OTE (telephones)
5 Museum of Post-Byzantine Art
6 Town hall
7 Solomós Museum
8 Prefecture (island government)
9 Post office
10 Olympic Airways
11 Bus station
12 IKA (Social Insurance)
13 Police and tourist police
14 Court house
15 Ferry ticket office
16 Xenópoulos Museum
17 Old fountain
18 House of Hugo Fóskolos
19 Hotel Palatinó
20 Hotel Stráda Marína
21 Port Authority, Komís restaurant
22 Arékia restaurant
23 O Milonás restaurant
24 Antámosi restaurant
25 To Spitáki restaurant
26 Padella restaurant

Byzantine Art), in front of which the members of the Hetaeria fighters in the Greek Revolution took their vows in 1821.

Maritime Museum: Covers the naval history of Greece from 1700 to the present day, with displays of 140 paintings, models of Byzantine and Greek warships, naval uniforms, books, etc. Privately owned and *usually* open daily from 09.00-14.00 and from 18.00-21.00; admission fee.

Stráni Hill (Lófos Stráni): This park (not on the plan, but only about 100 metres above the Maritime Museum) is where Greece's national poet, Dionýsios Solomós, used to promenade; there's a statue of him in the square (see panel, right).

Panagía Chrisopigí: This church in Bóchali Square (also known as **Zoodóchos Pigí**) was built on the site of the ancient temple to Bacchus, God of Wine. It became a monastery, was rebuilt as a church in the 16th century, and rebuilt again after the 18th-century and 1953 earthquakes. It contains a gilded altar screen and some beautiful icons. The wood-carved icon of the Virgin Mary is

said to date from the middle of the 8th century and to have originated on Crete.

Dionýsios Solomós (1798-1857)

Born on Zákynthos but educated in Italy, he wrote his first works in Italian. Only when he returned to Zákynthos did he start writing in Greek — and not formal Greek, but the language of the people (inspired, it is said, by the simple songs of a blind singer). There had already been a Zakynthian poet, Doxarás, writing in the popular idiom, but only with the works of Solomós did the poetry become popular.

He lived in the family's estate on Stráni Hill. A statue marks the spot where he is reputed to have written the 'Hymn to Liberty' at the age of 26. The first stanzas of this poem were later set to music by the Corfiot composer Nikólaos Mántzaros and became the national anthem of Greece, and Solomós became the country's national poet.

Another famous poem is 'The Free Besieged', said to have been inspired by the sound of gunfire during the siege of Messolóngi during the Greek War of Independence — the gunfire could be heard on Stráni Hill. A third epic poem, 'On the Death of Lord Byron', was written when Byron died in the course of this same long siege. Solomós's work was much inspired by Byron and other Romanic poets.

Solomós moved to Corfu in 1828, where he formed the Ionian School of Poetry to further develop poetry in the modern Greek idiom. He died on Corfu in 1857, and his remains were taken back to Zákynthos in 1865.

Entrance to the Venetian Fortress

Venetian Fortress: The fort/castle is just above Bóchali Square. Completed in 1646, it was built over the ruins of the ancient citadel/acropolis of Psofída. Above the entrance gate the Venetian blazon of the Lions of St. Mark is carved in the stone. The original walled-in town was almost completely destroyed by earthquakes, but there are some remains of churches, gunpowder rooms, and the British prison. Recent archaeological findings from the small excavation site have also yielded prehistoric tools. The sprawling hilltop area has now been attractively planted with pines, and there are 360° views over the island from the highest point of the walls. Open Tue.-Sun., 08.00-19.30; admission fee.

Panagía Pikridiótissa: The campanile of this church, with its Alpine-looking onion dome, stands out in the landscape. A plaque recalls that it was here that Theódoros Kolokotrónis — looking to the mountains on the Greek mainland — decided to form the Hetaeria and fight the Turks (see also Ágios Geórgios Filikón above).

Food and drink

Gaídouri Taverna: On Bóchali Hill, overlooking the lowlands between Alikés and Kerí. (Take the main road from town towards Bóchali and, at the junction for Bóchali, continue straight on over the hill towards Plános/Tsiliví. This roadside taverna is about 500m further on, where the road bends left.) Seating inside or on an outside balcony. Starters are served on a tray, from which you make your selection; a range of traditional

fish and meat dishes, but some unusual mains too — rabbit, snails and emu. Plenty for vegetarians and vegans. Rating *****; open all summer and on certain days in the winter; €€€.

Lower town

The lower town, called 'Chora' stretches along the waterfront. What was once thought to be the most beautiful town in the Ionian Islands had to be completely rebuilt after the 1953 earthquake (when only four buildings remained; see page 30). Despite the sterile modern buildings put up in haste, some effort was made to recreate the past, with colonnaded streets reminiscent of the Venetian Era.

Places of interest

St. Mark's Square is at the heart of the town, an intimate but lively gathering place where restaurants and cafés line the triangular, paved piazza.

Ágios Márkos: The attractive Roman Catholic church of St. Mark's, with its detached campanile, adds to the Italianate feel of St. Mark's Square. It was built in 1518 by the Venetians and completely rebuilt in the 1960s. Very few of its treasures survived the 1953 earthquake.

Museum of Dionýsios Solomós and Eminent Zakynthians [7]: Next door to St. Mark's, this was built in 1966 over the ruins of the church of Pantokrátora, destroyed by the 1953 earthquake. It's chock-a-block with artefacts, coats of arms, statues, paintings and all sorts of amazing items collected from the island's aristocratic families. It also houses the mausoleums of the national poets Dionýsios

Saint Dionýsios (1547-1624)

The island's patron saint is revered throughout Greece. Born on Zákynthos to noble parents, at an early age he retreated to a monastery on one of the tiny Strophades Islands and when ordained as a priest took the name Daniel.

His charisma was soon recognised by the bishops, and he was sent back to his native island to preach, eventually becoming an abbot at Moní Anafonítria (see page 74). During a pilgrimage to the Holy Land he stopped over in Athens, where the archbishop persuaded him to become Bishop of Égina (1577), at which time he took the name Dionýsios.

Although he was much loved by the people during his 10-year stay on Égina, homesickness and a desire for tranquillity led him to return first to the Strophades and later to Moní Anafonítria (where he died), although he also served for a time at St. Nicholas on the Quay in Zákynthos town.

At his own request, he was buried in the Strophades Islands. The many miracles attributed to him led to his canonisation in 1703. A few years later the then abbot in the Strophades monastery had a dream: St. Dionýsios appeared to him, asking for his casket to be opened. His body was found to be completely preserved. (Later, when his remains were transferred to Zákynthos, they were still preserved.)

The saint is remembered on 17 December (the day of his death) and 24 August (the date when, in 1717, his remains were transferred to Zákynthos). On both days there are grand processions and festivities (see pages 33 and 35).

Solomós (1798-1857) and Andréas Kálvos (1792-1869). A good number of Solomós's manuscripts and belongings are stored here, as well as a rich collection of portraits of eminent Zakynthians. There are photographs and engravings of old Zákynthos, Venetian costumes and Byzantine icons. Open Mon.-Sat. 08.30-15.00; admission fee.

Museum of Grigórios Xenópoulos [16]: Situated on the eponymous street, this museum is devoted to the life and work of Grigórios Xenópoulos (1867-1951), a novelist, journalist and prolific writer of prose, plays and critiques. The museum houses his publications and manuscripts, personal belongings and furniture from the family house. Open Mon.-Fri. 09.00-14.00; admission fee.

Faneroméni Church: Built in the 15th century, it has a lovely bell tower and intricate stonework on the façade. It's hard to believe that it was badly damaged in 1953 — but there is hardly any decoration inside. Any treasures escaping the earthquake were taken to the Post-Byzantine Museum. This church was a focal point for commoners in times of Venetian rule, while the nobility gathered around St. Mark's.

Ágios Dionýsios: This church was built in 1708 over the site of an earlier church specifically to house the remains of the island's patron, St. Dionýsios (see panel left). Because of frequent pirate raids, his remains were removed from the monastery on the nearby Strophades Islands from 1764 onwards. They have since been kept in this church, in an ornate silver casket.

Rebuilt between 1925 and 1948 to resist earthquakes, the church survived the 1953 quake relatively unscathed. Many pilgrims from all over Greece visit the island to pay their respects to the saint. The tall bell tower resembles that of St. Mark's in Venice and dominates the waterfront. There is a **museum** (admission fee payable) in the monastery building behind the church, housing historical Greek Orthodox robes, documents, manuscripts, paintings, books and artefacts. The church is open daily from 07.00-13.00 and from 17.00-22.00. Suitable dress is required (long trousers and skirts are available for visitors).

Solomós Square: Named in honour of Zákynthos's most famous poet, **Dionýsios Solomós**, this large square is home to the church of **Ágios Nikólaos tou Mólou** (see page 48) and the **Statue of Liberty** commemorating Greek independence won in 1821 (inspiration for the statue's decoration came to Solomós in a dream). There is also a **statue of Loukás Kárrer**, the island's mayor during World War II. He was ordered by the Nazi occupiers to hand over a list of all Jews on the island: he prevaricated, then gave them a list of just two names — his own and that of the island's Greek Orthodox bishop. Zákynthos was the only place in Greece where a local population joined together to protect the Jewish population from certain death. There is **horse and carriage** hire opposite the square, which is also served by a **tourist train** from Argássi.

Museum of Post-Byzantine

The bell tower of Ágios Dionýsios dominates the waterfront.

Art [5]: On the north side of Solomós Square, this is one of the town's highlights. Of particular interest is the model of pre-1953 Zákynthos on the ground floor, from which its Venetian splendour can be appreciated. The museum's eight rooms have displays of art treasures — icons, altar screens and frescoes — collected from churches all over the island destroyed in the earthquake. There are also 17th- to 19th-century paintings from the Cretan and Ionian schools, clearly showing the influence of the Italian Renaissance and Flemish Schools. Open daily except Mon. from 08.00-14.30. Admission fee.

Ágios Nikólaos tou Mólou (St. Nicholas of the Quay): Built in the 16th century for sailors and fishermen, so that they could be blessed on their way in and out of port, this church on the seaward side of Solomós Square was once on an islet *(mólos)* off the town; the land has since been reclaimed over the centuries from earthquake rubble. In Venetian times, the campanile served as a lighthouse. St. Dionýsios, the island's patron, was ordained in this church (his robes are on display). The church was damaged in the 1953 earthquake, but each stone was labelled, so that it could be faithfully rebuilt.

Public Library and Cultural Centre [2]: The staircase to the library is lined with photographs of the town before and after the 1953 earthquake. There are also various artefacts, dolls in traditional costumes, rare photographs, manuscripts, historical documents and paintings on display. The library holds 55,000 books dating back 300 years, some very rare — there is, for instance, a two-volume book written in the 19th century by a German visitor to the island covering geology, geography, wildlife, etc; only one other copy is in existence. Open Mon.-Fri. from 08.30 until 13.30; free entry.

House of Hugo Fóskolos [18]: Hugo Fóskolos (Ugo Foscolo, 1778-1827), one of Italy's major poets and writers, was born on Zákynthos, and is considered Greek by the Greeks. The house holds various memorabilia. Admission fee.

Other places of interest

• **Agía Análipsi:** Located west of the post office, this 16th-century Church of the Ascension has a bell tower, three-aisled basilica and notable paintings;

• **Agía Triáda:** Behind the EOT beach, Holy Trinity Church has a square bell tower and tiled, vaulted roof; wonderfully decorated interior with wood-carved altar screen and icon of the Virgin;

• **Kiría ton Angélon:** Our Lady of the Angels, southeast of St. Mark's Square and dating from 1687, is set well below the road (its higher surroundings were built after 1953 on top of the earthquake rubble). The exterior is decorated with reliefs; inside is a wood-carved altar screen with icons by Zákynthos's most famous artist, Panatiótis Doxarás;

• **Ágios Charálambos:** On the west side of the river and dating from 1728, this church has a beautifully carved bell tower and interior, especially the intricate altar screen;

• **Ágios Lázaros:** On the north-western edge of town, it was founded in the 16th century. St. Gerásimos (patron saint of Kefaloniá) was a priest here;

• **Ágios Nikólaos ton Xenón:** Just east of St. Mark's, this church is the town's cathedral and is where foreigners *(xenón)* used to have their funerals. It is richly decorated, but only part of the altar screen remains.

• **British Cemetery:** On the east side of town, the tombs date from the British occupation; there are interesting old marble vaults, plaques and pillars surrounded by high trees.

Beaches

The town is not a place for beach-lovers, but there are some small pebbly beaches and outcrops at

Krionéri (good snorkelling; no facilities). There is a small **public town beach (EOT beach)**, which also has tennis courts (fee payable). Or you can swim off the rocks (facilities nearby). Locals swim off the rocky out-crops on the north side of the **port** (no facilities).

Accommodation

Hotel Palatinó [19]: newly-built four-star hotel in a quiet area north of Solomós Square and just 100m from the beach. Modern, comfortable rooms with private balconies overlooking the sea or the hill; 3-channel music system; air-conditioning. Rating *****; 90-200 € per night, depending on the time of year and number of people. Open all year. www. palatinohotel.gr.

Hotel Stráda Marína [20]: on the seafront by the port; the location is its greatest asset. Roof garden, air-conditioning. Rating ***; 80-200 € per night, depending on the time of year and number of people. Open all year. www. stradamarina.gr.

Food and drink

Komís [21]: On the seafront at the port, opposite Ág. Dionýsios. An atmospheric fish taverna decorated with fishing-related items. Delicious fish dishes prepared in an unusual way — at British prices. Rating *****; open all year for lunch and dinner; €€€.

Arékia [22]: On the main port road towards Krionéri and Akro-tíri, this is a small cosy taverna, with seating outside in summer. Fish, meat and vegetable dishes. Features live traditional music (*kantádes*; see page 30). In August reservations mandatory. Rating ***; open for dinner all year; €€.

O Milonás [23]: On the south side of town (take the Argássi road, turn right at the T-junction for Kalamáki, then take the first right: it's about 500m along, on the left). Old advertisements line the walls inside; outside there's a wooden veranda. Delicious traditional Greek fish and meat dishes; vegetarian meals are often available at lunchtime. Very popular at lunchtime (when all the food will be gone by 2pm!). Rating ****; open for lunch and dinner all year; €€.

Antámosi [24]: Take the main road towards Laganás and Kerí; it's 500m out of town (after the traffic lights). Inside an old building; grilled or oven-roasted fish and meat. Gets very full in the evenings. Rating ***; open Oct.-May for lunch and dinner; *closed in summer*; €€.

To Spitáki [25]: At the junction of **Tavoulári and Koutouzí**. Tradi-tional town taverna, small and friendly; grilled or oven-roasted fish and meat. Rating ***; open for lunch and dinner all year; €.

Padella [26]: On the second road to the right off El Venizelou, above the National Park office. Delicious mousakas, meat dishes and plenty of vegetarian starters. Rating ***; open for lunch and dinner all year; €.

Popoláros: near the village of Ampelókopoi, halfway along the main (Kerí) road between town and the turn-off for Laganás. Both indoor seating and an outdoor veranda. Grills and oven dishes, meat and fish. Plenty of salads and starters for vegeta-rians. Features traditional *kan-tádes*. Rating ***; open Oct.-May for dinner; *closed in summer*; €€.

Car tour 1: THE SOUTH

Zákynthos town • Argássi • Vassilikós • Cape Ágios Nikólaos to Pórto Róma • Cape Gérakas area • Kalamáki • Laganás • Ágios Sóstis • Lithakiá • Lake Kerí and Marathoníssi Islet

This tour takes in Laganás Bay and the area's golden sandy beaches and dunes covered with aromatic sea daffodils. You'll enjoy stunning sea views from both the hilly Vassilikós peninsula and, later, the precipitous limestone cliffs of the mountainous Kerí peninsula.

Argássi to the Ksirocástello area

This is *the* tourist centre on the Vassilikós peninsula, full of package-holiday hotels, bars and supermarkets, but lacking in character. Attracts the young set, with plenty of nightlife.

Buses: up to 8 a day to/from Zákynthos town.

Taxis: rank on the main road 200m east of the bridge.

Tourist train to Solomós Square in Zákynthos town.

Parking: free parking near the church of Ágios Státhis.

Places of interest

Panagía Skopiótissa: This church and monastery is located near the top of **Mount Skopós** (only accessible by 4WD or on foot; see Walk 5, pages 104-107). The original buildings rose in the 1400s over the ruins of an ancient temple dedicated to the goddess Artemis; the monastery, now in ruins, was fortified by the Venetians as a military outpost. The whole area has been renovated, with pleasant walkways and seating; one can really get a feel for the past.

The interior of the church holds frescoes, marble carvings, 17th-century murals and an unusual stone-carved altar screen. A twin-headed eagle, the symbol of the Byzantine Empire, is depicted on the floor. But what attracts

pilgrims is the famous silver icon of the Virgin Mary holding Jesus, brought to the island from Istanbul when the Byzantine Empire fell. The church is the only one on Zákynthos with a central Byzantine-style octagonal dome, more common to the Aegean.

Ágios Nikólaos Megalomáti: On the hillside below Panagía Skopiótissa, this post-Byzantine church was built over the remains of a sacrificial temple of justice. Sections of the mosaic flooring and some of the hanging arches of the southern and central walls still remain. Some of the 12th/13th-century décor is now on display in the Post-Byzantine Museum in Zákynthos town. Access as for Skopiótissa.

National Marine Park of Zákynthos Thematic Sea Turtle Exhibition: On the road to Dáphne, just past Ksirocástello village. Housed in a traditional stone building, with photographic displays of the region's flora and fauna, as well as 3D sculptures of turtles and videos of sea turtle behaviour taken in Laganás Bay. You can take one of the NMPZ guided beach tours at Dáphne Beach, to see the sea turtle tracks remaining from the previous night. Admission fee.

Panagía Evangelístria: This monastery-fort, built by the Venetians on **Peloúso Islet** (see

Suggested car touring route

60km/37mi
Walks en route: 1-12

First explore the **Vassilikós peninsula** between Argássi and Gérakas. After **Ksirocástello**, you might like to detour to the Sea Turtle Exhibition on the road to Dáphne. Make a first swim-stop to admire the fossil-filled rocks at the southern end of **Pórto Zórro Beach**, and be sure to take in the dune and forest system of **Banána Beach**. Visit the folk museum in **Vassilikós** and the chapel at **Cape Ágios Nikólaos**. Take a walk along the rocky coastline of **Pórto Róma** and visit the sea turtle nesting beach of **Gérakas** (16km), with its stunning Pliocene-Pleistocene rock formations and Wildlife Information Centre.

Then return to **Argássi** (28km) and, at the local church (Ágios Státhis), turn left and drive into the hills to see the British-built aqueduct of **Vrysákia**. Then continue along the road leading into the hills where you can take in views of Laganás Bay and

drive down to **Kalamáki** (36km). Stop for a swim along the 3km protected nesting beach and admire the dune system, covered in sea daffodils in summer.

At **Laganás**, follow signs up to the ruins of the **Sarakína Mansion**, then drive down to the natural harbour at **Ágios Sóstis** (43km). Continue to **Pórto Koúkla** and through the ancient olive groves.

Turn left when you return to the main road for Kerí (48km) and, after crossing the **Ávyssos Gorge** (created by the earthquake of 1633), visit **Lake Kerí** (54km), to see the natural bitumen springs. If you have time, take a boat trip to the Kerí sea caves and natural arches or over to **Marathoníssi Islet**. Visit **Marathiá Beach** (56km) for a swim — or a 30 minute walk along the peninsula. End the day at **Kerí** (60km), on the southernmost tip of the island — enjoying the sunset from the lighthouse, looking at the ancient tombs, the dancing 'Mizíthres' rocks and the limestone cliffs.

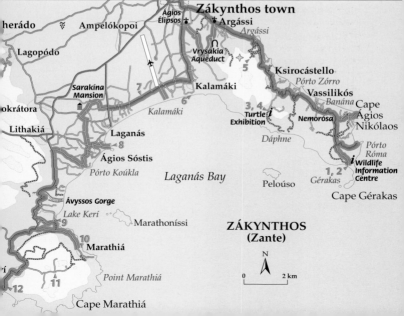

pages 94-95), was abandoned after the 1893 earthquake, after which it was looted and its irreplaceable library lost. Since the 1953 earthquake only a couple of walls remain standing. There is a good view to the ruins on Walk 2. It can only be seen up close by boat but, as it is in the Marine Area Protection Zone B, mooring is prohibited.

Venetian ruins: The remains of the churches of St. Constantine and St. Spirídon are literally sinking into the sea off Argássi Beach. In the sea near the old harbour in the town centre are the ruins of a watchtower.

'Venetian' bridge: There is also a well-preserved three-arched bridge by Argássi harbour. It once carried the old main road, but now stands in the sea, due to coastal erosion. Although it is dated 1885, it is usually referred to as the 'Venetian' bridge and is similar to the Venetian bridge at Alikés, thus the date may refer to its refurbishment.

Vrysákia Aqueduct: This 15m-high bridge on the road above Ágios Státhis was built during British rule to supply Zákynthos town with water. Legend has it that Theódoros Kolokotrónis, founder of the Hetaeria, used to ride his horse over the bridge.

Beaches

Argássi Beach: a narrow, dark strip of sand runs the length of

Loggerhead tracks

the resort; there's hardly room to put down a beach towel in summer. All facilities.

Kamínia Beach: a golden-sand beach backed by a lawn area, reached from Ksirocástello by a narrow winding road. Ample facilities, including snack bar. Good for children.

Dáphne Beach (also called Mélla Beach): a sand-and-pebble beach within the NMPZ, visited on Walk 2 and an option on Walk 3. The same rules apply as at Gérakas, and there is the same danger from rockfalls if you sit below the cliffs. This is a fine snorkelling beach, fronted by reefs rich in sea life. There is an an unofficial naturist section at the far eastern end of the beach. Facilities, but the restaurants/bars are only operational during daylight hours.

Sekánia Beach: guarded beach in the core area of the National Marine Park; access allowed only for park-permitted research. This is the most densely-nested sea turtle beach in the Mediterranean (about 700 nests per year). You would have a good view of the beach, shown on page 11, from Walk 3. No facilities.

Pórto Zórro/La Mare Beach: a small sandy cove with pictur-esque rocky outcrops — excellent for snorkelling. The shore slopes gently, so it's good for children. Ample facilities.

Peloúso Islet: There are two small, pebbly beaches on the islet, near the monastery ruins.

Accommodation

Sea Castle Luxury Villas: A sea-front complex of three indivi-dually styled stone buildings in the Ksirocástello area, just 150m off the coastal road. Studios, apartments or maisonette houses, all with easterly views towards the Peloponnese (fantastic sunrises). All accommodation has a balcony or veranda, fully equipped kitchen or kitchenette, air-conditioning, bathroom with robes/hair dryer, satellite TV, CD/DVD player, daily maid service. Outdoor jacuzzi, private pool, bar/snack bar open all day, mini-market. Internet access/PC available on request. Rating *****; 110-320 € per night, depending on the time of year and number of people. Open 1st May-31st Oct. www.seacastle-zante.com.

Fiore Studio Apartments: Just off the main road at Kamínia Beach. Studios and apartments, all with sea views. Restaurant; beach bar. Rating **; 40-120 € per night; can be open all year. www. zantefiorestudios.gr.

Food and drink

Portokáli: on the main road in Argássi village. This restaurant/bar has an interesting selection of nouvelle cuisine dishes; good décor both indoors and out on the veranda. Rating ****; open for dinner and drinks all year; €€.

Taverna Theodorítsis: signposted just off the main Argássi/Vassilikós road below Mount Skopós, near the road to Walk 5 (see map page 105). Good views across to Argássi and Zákynthos town. Grills and oven roasts, meat and fish. Particularly large choice of meats and salads. Rating **; open for lunch and dinner all year; €€.

Taverna Agnádi: on the main road from Argássi to Vassilikós. Clifftop setting with view to the Peloponnese. Grills and oven

roasts, meat and fish. Family-run. Unfortunately, service is sometimes slow. Rating **; open for lunch and dinner in summer; €€.

O Milonás: on the main road in Ksirocástello; specialises in spit-roasted pork. There are also locally produced cheeses. *No fish.* Fantastic views towards the Peloponnese. Rating ***; open for lunch and dinner in summer; €€.

Dáphne Fish Taverna: on the road to Dáphne, just past Ksirocástello village, next to the NMPZ Thematic exhibition — in the hills above Sekánia Beach, overlooking Laganás Bay. A wide range of local dishes, both fish and meat. Rating ***; open for dinner all year; €€.

Vassilikós village area

This strung-out village, set amid woods and olive groves, boasts some of the island's finest sandy beaches.

Buses: up to 4 a day to/from Zákynthos town (stop on the main road in the lower village).

Taxis: rank at the turn-off to Ágios Nikólaos.

Places of interest

National Marine Park of Zákynthos Thematic Sea Turtle Exhibition: This new exhibition centre is on the left just as you enter Vassilikós village. (See also the reference to the NMPZ centre on the road to Dáphne in the right-hand column on page 50.)

Nemorósa Folklore Museum: The museum (signposted from near the petrol station) contains artefacts from traditional Greek life — household utensils and furniture, farming and milling equipment, clothing worn by the different classes of society. There are also pictures and photographs of the island over the last five centuries and histories of famous people who were born on or visited Zákynthos. Privately owned and *usually* open daily from 10.00-14.00 and 16.00-18.00. Admission fee.

Bridges: The arched bridges of the Vassilikós area were built during British rule and still form an essential part of the island road network.

Beaches

Banána Beach: several kilometres long, this beach is one of the island favourites. The eastern part has deep white sand (where some turtles nest); the western part (called **Ionian Beach**) has more pebbly sections, with jetties to access the water. Facilities along most of the beach, with the greatest concentration behind the Ionian Beach section.

Accommodation

Armonia Villas: Drystone hillside villas in traditional style (including a windmill and tower), on a road inland from Vassilikós village church. Each is set in its own garden, with an east-facing veranda for the sea and the sunrise. Fresh vegetables and eggs, local honey and wines available from the owners' farm. Open all year. Rating ***; 25-160 € per night, depending on the time of year and number of people. www.zakynthos-armoniahouses.com

Food and drink

Kostas Brothers Taverna: Set in a stone building in Vassilikós village, in a beautifully landscaped garden. A wide range of local dishes, both fish and meat. Home-made wines — and super

bread (baked in the stone oven outside). Live music some evenings. Rating ****; open for dinner Fri.-Sun. in Jun./Sep., every evening in Jul./Aug.; €€.

Skartsofoli: a new restaurant near Kostas Brothers; Greek food with an international accent. Worth a visit. Rating ***; €€.

Taverna Pórto Iónio: a lovely, old-fashioned place set above a stretch of Banána Beach, with seating indoors and out (nice walled terrace under tamarisks). The chicken dishes are especially good. Rating ***; open for lunch and dinner in summer; €€.

Cape Ágios Nikólaos to Pórto Róma

Buses: up to 4 a day to/from Zákynthos town to Ágios Nikólaos and on to Pórto Róma. In high season there is also a **shuttle bus** from Ágios Nikólaos to Kalamáki, Laganás and Argássi (departs 10.00, returns 17.00).

Taxis: rank at the turn-off to Ágios Nikólaos from the main road.

Parking: large car park at the end of the narrow 1km-long road to Ágios Nikólaos Beach.

Places of interest

Ágios Nikólaos Chapel: Set on a rocky outcrop between Ágios Nikólaos Beach and Pláka Beach, this pretty tiled-roof chapel is an oasis in the busy resort.

Beaches

Ágios Nikólaos Beach: This sandy beach, on the south side of the eponymous cape, is the busiest on the eastern side of the peninsula. Plenty of facilities; excellent water sports; diving school. In high season it can get a bit boisterous, to say the least. Two beaches on the north side of the cape (Pláka and Golden Bay) are somewhat quieter.

Koúkis Beach: This is a small sandy section of Ágios Nikólaos Beach, also with ample facilities.

Pláka Beach: A small sandy cove backed by a lawn area, just north of the cape; facilities include a taverna.

Golden Bay Beach: A bit west of Pláka, also sandy, and set within a hotel complex. Ample facilities.

Mavrátsis Beach: another sandy beach just south of Ágios Nikólaos, surrounded by steep rocks. Mostly used by guests from the surrounding luxury hotel complex. Facilities include a taverna.

Pórto Róma Beach: An enchanting small sand-and-shingle cove with a tiny harbour, south of Ágios Nikólaos. Facilities include a taverna.

Accommodation

Dáphnes Villas and Apartments: Set in a large olive grove just above Pórto Róma Beach. Lovely garden, buildings designed in the traditional Zakynthian country style with exposed beams, large private verandas and tiled roofs. Accommodation ranges from small one-room apartments sleeping two people to two-bedroom villas for 6-7 people. Air-conditioning; shared barbecue. Rating ****; 65-171 € per night, depending on the time of year and number of people. Open from mid-May till mid-Oct. www.daphnes-zakynthos.com.

Lithies Houses: Situated off the road between Ano and Kato Vassilikos, the six houses (some in traditional stone) have sea views and are set in an organic farm run by the Gianoylis family. Their olive groves, vineyards and vegetables are freely available to guests. All houses with air-conditioning. Open all year. Rating ***; 60-135 € per night, depending on the time of year and number of people. www.lithieshouses.gr.

Food and drink

Lithies Taverna, adjacent to Lithies Houses and run by the same family. Outdoor patio. Grills and oven roasts, meat and fish. Produce from their organic farm. Rating **; open for lunch and dinner in summer; €.

Taverna Pérasma: on the main road not far north of the turn-off to Mavrátsis Beach. In an old building full of original paintings, some hundreds of years old. Seating inside. Various types of cuisine — try the 'Perasma chicken'. Rating ****; open for lunch and dinner from Easter to Oct.; €€.

Mikrí Plateía, above Pórto Róma near the junction with the road to Cape Gérakas. A small taverna run by the same family for four generations. Outdoor terrace dining, with panoramic view over Pórto Róma and Gérakas. Both grills and oven-roasted dishes, meat and fish. You can go into the kitchen to watch the food being prepared. Rating ***; open for dinner in summer; €.

Cape Gérakas area

Access: There are no buses or taxis; the nearest place to alight from a bus and find a taxi is the junction for Gérakas and Pórto Róma on the main road (although taxis can be ordered from the Gérakas bars and tavernas).

Parking: both free and paid parking on privately owned land.

Places of interest

Gérakas Wildlife Information Centre:
Just above Gérakas Beach (starting point for Walks 1 and 2), this centre was established by the Vardakastánis family to provide information about the island's various conservation and wildlife organisations through photo-graphic and written displays. Run by volunteers and usually open from late May to early Oct. from 10.00-18.00. Free admission.

Kanónia: This area contains the concrete remains of Nazi cannon bunkers (maybe even a few unexploded bombs…). Only accessible on foot (Walk 1).

Beach

Gérakas Beach: a beautiful arc of golden sandy beach with a pebbly section to the west. This is a protected loggerhead sea turtle nesting beach (about 80 nests), with 24-hour guards, thus there are no water sports. Facilities include sunshades and sun-loungers, but no taverna on the beach itself (bars and tavernas on the access road). You must keep within 3-5m/yards of the sea and, in July and August, you are requested to stay no longer than two hours (to relieve pressure on the nesting beach). The cliffs running the whole length of the beach are subject to rockfalls, so don't sit below them. Unofficial naturist section at the far western side of the beach.

Accommodation

Logothetis Farm: holiday houses for 2-7 people, on an organic farm on the road to Gérakas, 1km above the beach. Surrounded by olive groves and pine forests. Very well equipped, decorated with great care in the local style. Rating ***; 60-140 € per night, depending on the time of year and number of people. Open all year. www. logothetisfarm.gr.

Food and drink

Gérakas Fish Taverna: a family-run restaurant on the road to Gérakas Beach. They offer a range of traditional Greek dishes, both fish and meat — the mousaka is particularly recom-mended. Rating ***; open for lunch and dinner in summer; €€.

Nikos taverna: another family-run restaurant on the road to Gérakas Beach, specialising in grilled meat dishes such as *souvláki*. Rating ***; open for lunch and dinner in summer; €.

Taverna Galini: signposted just west of the junction of the Pórto Róma/Cape Gérakas roads. Seating indoors and out; several terraces with wide-ranging views over the cape and to the Pelopon-nese (now marred by new build-ings). Grills and oven roasts, fish and meat. Sometimes the service is a bit slow. Rating **; open for lunch and dinner in summer; €€.

Kalamáki

After Laganás itself, this resort straddling the main road is the main tourist centre in Laganás Bay, much quieter and more 'up-market' than Laganás.

Buses: up to 8 a day to/from Zákynthos town, up to 4 a day to/from Laganás; all buses stop at the central crossroads and at other stops on the main road (blue signs).

Taxis: rank at the main cross-roads near the bus stop.

Parking: easiest on the road to the beach.

Places of interest

Ágios Élipsos: Stop to visit this small church on your way to Kalamáki from Argássi (see the map). Set on a hill, the little church rises above olive trees; the blue and white bell tower has two small bells and a cross on top. There is a fine view from here over Zákynthos town and the sea. Part of the original church still remains.

Beaches

Vrondónero Beach: a dark sand/pebble beach covered in seagrass, with amazing cliff geology (photograph below). Visited on Walk 6 (see pages 108-111). A few turtle nests each summer. No facilities; (unofficially) naturist.

Kalamáki/Crystal Beach: a protected golden sand beach with about 50-100 loggerhead turtle nests annually (24-hour guards). Visited on Walk 6. Not commercialised, but some facilities and very busy. Bar and taverna at the adjacent Crystal Beach Hotel.

Laganás/Kalamáki Beach: a protected (24-hour guards) golden sand beach at the quieter, eastern end of Laganás Bay, which extends from Hipsolíthos Rock (with World War II cannon bunker) as far as the Zante Beach Hotel fence. There are about 150 nests annually — and an additional 10-15 nests in front of the Zante Beach Hotel itself. The sea here is very shallow and warms up during the day. Some facilities, but not along the entire 3km length. Walk 7 explores this area in depth (pages 112-115).

Laganás

The island's largest resort, attracting primarily the younger set. Hotels, bars and nightclubs cheek-by-jowl.

Buses: up to 15 a day to/from Zákynthos town, up to 4 a day to/from Kalamáki, and once a day to Vassilikós, Pórto Róma and Ágios Nikólaos. Bus stops on the main roads have blue signs.

Taxis: ranks opposite the Hotel Victoria and at the beach.

Parking: is a big problem, as all the places near the beach are full up from early morning, so you are likely to have to look for a place quite a way from the beach.

Vrondónero Beach (Walk 6)

Places of interest

Sarakína Mansion: Signposted from Laganás, this estate, which belonged to the Loúntzi family, once controlled all the land as far as the neighbouring hills. The baroque-style family residence and servants' quarters were ruined in the 1953 earthquake. (See also 'Culture', pages 118-119).

Beaches

Laganás Beach: a hard-packed, golden sand beach full of sun-burned tourists packed in like sardines. It's a good place to go on a turtle-spotting trip, other-wise there is nothing of interest. Ample facilities (plenty of bars and tavernas, but no motorised water sports). A coastal path runs from here to Ágios Sóstis Port and beach (see Walk 8).

Ágios Sóstis

A small resort not far from Laganás, with none of the hustle and bustle of the latter. Natural harbour with colourful fishing port atmosphere. For an over-view of the beaches, see the walk sketch on page 117 (Walk 8).

Beaches

Ágios Sóstis Port Beach: a hard-sand beach next to the harbour, with good snorkelling. Facilities available in nearby bars and restaurants.

Cameo Islet: small stony beach in a little cove, good for snorkelling. The islet broke away from the mainland in the 1633 earthquake; access is by a footbridge (only in summer). Facilities.

Ágios Sóstis Beach: a small, gently-shelving sandy beach near many submerged reefs, good for snorkelling. Facilities.

Pórto Koúkla Beach: small sandy beach set under the trees below a steep little cliff. Facilities.

Kamínia Beach: a narrow strip of sand and pebbles. No facilities.

Accommodation

Kaliméra Koúkla: Surrounded by olive groves, near the beaches of Koúkla, Ágios Sóstis and Laganás. A modern Zakynthian building with balconies. 21 large studio apartments over three floors, some with sea views, others facing inland. Open-plan kitchenettes; satellite TV; air-conditioning at extra charge. Rating ***; 30-100 € per night, depending on the time of year and number of people. Open all year. www.kalimera-koukla.gr.

Kostas Kladis Apartments: in Ágios Sóstis village, 30m from the beach. Family-run studios and apartments, decorated by the daughter, Adrianna (a ceramicist with a nearby workshop where you can enjoy coffee and home-made cakes in a relaxing setting, while viewing ceramic works by artists from all over Greece). Private parking, landscaped gardens, verandas. Rating *****; 26-76 € per night, depending on the time of year and number of people. Open all year. www.zantekladis.com.

Food and drink

Harbour House: on the front under a pagoda of grapevines. In early evening you'll see the heads of turtles popping up from the sea to breathe. A wide range of dishes from mousaka to spaghetti. Specialities of both meat and fish; also special vegetarian dishes. This place has the best pizza on the island, but you will have to wait for it to be cooked! Rating ****; open late May-Oct. for lunch and dinner; €€.

Lithakiá

This is a fairly large and pictur-
esque village in the hills 3km
inland from Ágios Sóstis and
Laganás, above Laganás Bay.
Many of its traditional stone
buildings have been retained or
rebuilt, and there are several
mansions and churches of note.
Buses: twice a day to/from
Zákynthos town (Kerí bus).
Taxis: none (you can call a taxi
from one of the bars).
Parking: along the roadside.

Places of interest
Panagía Faneroméni: This 17th-
century church has a beautiful
carved-wood gilded altar screen
and some important icons.

Ágios Ioánnis: a typical example
of Zakynthian ecclesiastical
architecture, with a lovely
detached campanile.

Maloúchou Mansion: a richly
decorated 19th-century mansion.

Messála Mansion: one of the few
examples of 'Seven Island' (Eptánissa) architecture, renovated
after the 1953 earthquake and
now housing the Environmental
Educational Centre.

Accommodation
The Olive Groves Luxury Villas:
on a hillside overlooking the
island's stunning southern coast
— just three villas, each sleeping
8 people (10 at a pinch). Each
villa has its own private heated
pool. Stylish interiors, including
designer bedding and bathroom
suites, plasma satellite TV, etc.
Rating *****; 140-350 € per night,
depending on the time of year
and number of people. Open all
year. www.theolivegroves.com

Leeda's Village: set in olive
groves overlooking Marathoníssi
Islet, about 1km from Lithakiá

village (take the main road from
Lithakiá towards Kerí and turn
left at the local school). Five
traditional stone houses catering
for 2-9 people. Beautiful interiors,
verandas, barbecues, gardens
with vegetables that you can help
yourself to for free. Pool.
Welcome pack of local wine and
olive oil. Range of activities
available, including hiking and
even diet programmes! Rating
*****; prices on request. Open all
year. www.leedas-village.com.

Tsivouli Park: Just 7 rooms make
up this lovely b&b built of
traditional stone in Peloponnese
style. The rooms, although
simple (no tv or aircon), are
beautifully laid out, with
stunning views across Laganás
Bay. Leafy courtyard. The park is
an organic farm with emus and
other animals. Anglo/Swiss
ownership. Rating *****; prices
on request. Open all year.
www.tsivouli.com. Daily visitors
welcome to visit the farm (small
fee charged); also a farm shop.

Food and drink
O Milonás: on the main road
leading into Lithakiá village,
opposite a currently operational
olive mill. In a beautifully converted olive mill, with a range of
milling equipment on display. A
wide selection of Zakynthian
dishes, both meat and fish, and
delicious local wine. Live music
some evenings. Rating *****; open
all year for dinner (and lunch on
some days); €€.

Taverna Dennis: On the main
road to Kerí, this taverna boasts
an amazing view from Lithakiá
to Kalamáki. Good range of
home-cooked Greek food — meat
and fish, grilled or from the oven.
Greek dancing some evenings;

free transport can be arranged. Rating ****; open for lunch and dinner all year; €€.

Lake Kerí area and Marathoníssi Islet

The Kerí peninsula forms the base of the mountain chain extending to the north of the island. **Kerí** (Walk 12) is a beautiful, traditional stone village set in the mountainside, where you can explore the narrow alleyways. **Lake Kerí** village (Walk 9), at the bottom of the hills, adjacent to the lake, has a natural harbour and small fishing community. While there is some tourism here, it has not spoiled the local atmosphere. Opposite Lake Kerí is the islet of Marathoníssi, once a thriving monastery, now one of the protected sea turtle nesting beaches.

Buses: twice a day to/from Zákynthos town.

Boat trips: run all day to Marathoníssi Islet and the Kerí Caves.

Places of interest

Panagía Keriótissa: Despite the earthquake, most of the original baroque church in Kerí village remains, as does the huge, squat bell tower. Inside are some fine wood carvings and icons. Legend has it that the *Panagía* saved the village: as pirates approached one fine summer's day, she caused a dense fog to descend, and they turned back.

Tholos tomb: This stone tomb lies on the cliffs below the Kerí Lighthouse (access on foot; see Walk 12 sketch map on page 133).

Panagía Odigítrias: This 15th-century monastery and church on Marathoníssi Islet is in ruins, although traces of its ancient frescoes can still be identified.

Bitumen spring: The natural bitumen (tar) upwellings at Lake Kerí were historically used for tarring ships — as cited by Herodotus back in the 5th century BC. During the 1880s, tar was commercially exported and traded as a shipbuilding product. By the 1900s, however, the cost of export exceeded the profit, and this resource became limited to local use. See Walk 9, page 120-123.

Beaches

Límni Kerioú (Lake Kerí) Beach: a long, narrow yellow sand-and-pebble beach backed by the lake/marsh and an additional small strip of yellow sandy beach by the harbour. Facilities. Walk 9.

Marathiá Beach: a white-pebble beach with beautiful deep (cold) blue waters — a great place for snorkelling. There are natural bitumen and sulphur sea springs along this peninsula. Facilities nearby. Walk 10, pages 124-127.

Point Marathiá: Only accessible in 4WD, by boat, or on foot (see Walk 10, pages 124-127). The 'beach' is actually a slab of rock from which you can swim, near one of the Marathiá arches and sea cave. There are sulphur springs here. No facilities.

Marathoníssi Islet: There are three beaches on the islet. The white sandy beach on the north side is a protected sea turtle nesting beach (Maritime Zone B), and it is illegal to beach or moor a boat here. The stony beaches on the west (with cave) and north coasts are in Maritime Zone C, and mooring/beaching of boats is allowed. No facilities.

Accommodation

Villas Cavo Marathiá: Located in

1.5 ha of land, right on the sea, overlooking Marathoníssi. Villas with studios and apartments for 2-5 people. Free use of gym, billiards, table tennis; satellite TV room, internet connections on request. Restaurant. Rating *****; 110-160 € per night (including breakfast buffet), depending on the time of year and number of people. Open all year. www.zantiotis.gr.

Argastares Villas: 100m up the road from Marathiá Beach, these newly built stone houses in traditional style have fine views of Laganás Bay, Marathoníssi Islet and the sunrise. Just two buildings at present, each with two bedrooms, large sitting room with open fireplace. Barbecue. Nearest facilities are at Lake Kerí, 1km away. Rating ***; 25-200 € per night, depending on the time of year and number of people. Open all year. www.argastaresvillas.com.

Athenea Luxury Villas: also on the road to Marathiá Beach. Eight traditional drystone villas with wonderful views of Marathoníssi and Laganás Bay. Each villa is suitable for 4-6 people; some villas with private pool. Large bathrooms with hairdryer; kitchen or kitchenette; large balconies; air-conditioning (at extra charge). Maid service three times a week. Shared barbecue/outdoor oven. Rating ***; 50-150 € per night, depending on the time of year and number of people. Open May to Oct. www.atheneavillas.com.

Dolphins Villas: in the heart of Lake Kerí village, 150m from the harbour and beach, overlooking the lake (an ideal location for watchers of migratory birds in Apr., May and Sep.). 7 studios and 5 apartments. Kitchenettes with fridge and oven. BBQ, TV lounge, parking available; small extra charge for air-conditioning. Rating ***; 25-75 € per night, depending on time of year and number of people. Open all year. iedolphins@gmail.com.

Food and drink

Taverna Botsalo: in Marathiá village, with covered outdoor veranda and spectacular view to Marathoníssi and Laganás Bay. The whole building is decorated with inset stones and shells. The meat and fish dishes are typical — but the setting *is fantastic*. Rating ***; open for lunch and dinner in summer; €€.

Lighthouse Taverna: overlooking sheer chalk cliffs and the deep blue sea by Kerí Lighthouse. You can walk up to the lighthouse — the most popular place to watch the sun set, but in July and August it's *very* crowded. Grills and oven roasts, meat and fish. Rating ***; open for lunch, dinner and coffees in summer; €€.

Anemómilos: in a replica windmill on the main road to Kerí (past Lithakiá and before Lake Kerí, just after the Ávyssos Gorge), with a veranda overlooking Laganás Bay and Lake Kerí. Grills and oven roasts, meat and fish. Rating **; open for lunch, dinner and coffee in summer; €.

La Bruschetta: on the main road to Kerí, just before the turning for Marathiá. Outdoor seating on a veranda overlooking the lake and bay. Pastas and pizzas, the latter especially good. Rating ***; open for lunch and dinner in summer; €€.

Car tour 2: THE CENTRE

Zákynthos town • Krionéri • Akrotíri • Tsiliví and Plános • Tragáki • Gerakári • Alikanás • Alikés • Katastári • Pigadákia • Kallithéa • Agía Marína • Macherádo • Kilioménos • Agalás

Here we tour the agricultural heart of the island. Vineyards carpet the landscape, framed by olive groves in the west and sea in the east. In winter you will see the beating of olive trees to collect olives for making oil, in summer the grape harvest for both wine and raisins.

Coast north of Zákynthos town

The coastal plains between Zákynthos town and the foothills of the island's mountain chain are speckled with many small villages, surrounded by vineyards and olive groves.
Buses: up to 10 a day to/from Zákynthos town (Tsiliví/Plános route).

Krionéri

Places of interest: There's a **Venetian fountain** here, where the spring water was used to clean Venetian merchant ships. The name *krionéri* derives from the spring's cold, clear water.

Beach: on the south side of the village — a series of small pebbly beaches and outcrops — good snorkelling, but no facilities.

Food and drink: Green Boat, set on a veranda by the sea, a fish taverna with delicious fish, crab and lobster. Rating ***; open for lunch and dinner all year; €€.

Akrotíri

Food and drink: Akrotíri Taverna, on an outside patio covered with grape vines. A meat taverna, *no fish*, but vegetarians and vegans will be easily satisfied. Starters *(mezés)* are served on a huge tray — an experience not to be missed! Rating ****; open for dinner only, and only during the summer; €€.

62

Tsiliví and Plános

This area is a very popular family resort, with gently sloping child-friendly beaches protected from strong winds by Cape Gaídaros. In hot weather northerly breezes make it cooler here than on the Vassilikós peninsula beaches.
Buses: up to 10 a day to/from Zákynthos town; stop is on the main road opposite the Bar Reportage, where there are usually a couple of **taxis**.
Parking: early birds can find a place on the road to the beach.

Beaches

Plános/Tsiliví Beach: a long, gently shelving sandy beach, backed by sand dunes in the east and with a small fishing harbour at the northern end. Ample facilities.

Boúka Beach: the western part of Plános/Tsiliví Beach, a short, wide sand-and-pebble beach with a small fishing harbour by Cape Gaídaros. Facilities nearby.

Ámboula Beach (long and sandy), **Katragáki Beach, Pachiá Ámmos Beach** and **Drosiá Beach** (all three small and pebbly) lie further west along the coast — all of them lined with apartments, with facilities nearby.

Accommodation

Zante View Studios: apartments set in the hills above Tsiliví, with panoramic views of the island.

Suggested car touring route

56km/35mi
Walks en route: 14, 22 (13 is nearby)

Leave Zákynthos town via **Krio-néri** and take in views of the Peloponnese from the Venetian fountain. Beyond **Akrotíri** and **Tsiliví/Plános**, continue over the hills through **Tragáki** and **Kypséli** and into **Áno Gerakári** (with panoramic views of the island from St. Nicholas). Go for a swim at the old fishing port of **Alikanás** (possibly ancient Arcadia, where Mycenaean ships have been found). Drive into **Alikés** via the Venetian Pento-kámaro Bridge and past the man-made salt flats, stopping to look out for unusual waterfowl. Continue on to **Katastári** (20km), and cross over the main road, to follow a country lane running south through a series of old agricultural villages along the foothills of the Vrachíonas Moun-tains. There are stunning views, freshwater springs and many churches of historical interest to explore here.

At **Pigadákia** visit the church with its sulphurous spring and the folk museum, at **Kallithéa** drive up to the Black Cave, and at **Agía Marína** call at the natural history museum.

The Agía Mávra church is a must at **Macherádo** (36km), where you can also visit a local winery. Then take a scenic panorama road into the mountain village of **Kilio-ménos** and admire the intricately carved bell tower at St. Nicholas. Continue through the valleys to **Agalás** (56km). First visit the Andronios Venetian wells, then explore the old village ruins, museum and church, before descending to the two-tiered Damianós Cave, from where you can watch the sunset.

Rooms either facing the sunrise or sunset; 1km to the beach; 0.5km to shops and other facilities. Air-conditioning, TV. Basic kitchenettes only. Rating ***; 35-80 € per night, depending on the time of year and number of people. Open May-Oct. www.zanteview.gr.

Food and drink

Níonidos Taverna: in Plános. (When approaching from Bóchali via the hill, turn left at the hairpin bend. Follow this road for about 3km, to a junction where the taverna is signposted to the right. Follow the road until you reach the taverna, on your left.) Meat and fish taverna set in vineyards; dining indoors or out on the veranda. A wide range of local dishes done with individual flair. Rating ****; open all year for dinner; €€.

Le Maschere: on the main road leading out of Tsiliví village, overlooking Tsiliví Beach. Italian chef; pizzas and pastas in a fun atmosphere; play area for children. Rating **; open in summer for lunch and dinner; €.

Tragáki

A lovely little hillside village, quite unspoilt, despite its proximity to the coast. Some ruins of Venetian houses remain, and there is a memorial to the unknown soldier in the square.

Accommodation

Paliokalíva Village: traditional Zakynthian stone villas for 2-6 people, set in olive groves 1km above Tsiliví on the road to Tragáki, 600m above Boúka Beach. Views to either the garden and pool or over the bay. Air-conditioning, satellite TV, CD/DVD, daily maid service; kitchenettes. Rating *****; 80-190 € per night, depending on the time of year and number of people. Open May-Oct. www.paliokaliva.gr.

Kypséli

Surrounded by olive groves and orchards, an attractive hillside village dominated by its church.

Places of interest

Agía Paraskeví, the village church, has an old wood-carved altar screen and some beautiful frescoes.

Gerakári

This village is in three parts: **Káto** (lower) **Gerakári**, just a petrol station and shop on the main road; **Mésa** (middle) **Gerakári** — hidden by trees, on a hillside off the main road, and **Áno** (upper) **Gerakári**.

Places of interest

Agía Triáda: in Mésa Gerakári, Holy Trinity Church has a wood-carved and gilded altar screen and icons.

Ágios Nikólaos: in Áno Gerakári, a 16th-century church with onion dome, built over a former temple. There is a stupendous view over the whole of Zákynthos from this hilltop vantage point.

Beaches

Psarós Beach: off the coast road, about 1km east of the road to Gerakári. It's small, sandy, and kept in pristine condition. The beach hardly shelves at all, so the water stays warm. Facilities.

Gerakári Beach and nearby **Amoúdi Beach** are small and sandy, with facilities nearby.

Olive groves grace the foothills of the west coast mountains.

Alikanás

A family-orientated package tour resort, especially popular with the Brits. Plenty of bars and tavernas, but still nowhere near as frenetic as Laganás and quieter than Plános/Tsiliví. The loveliest part of this resort is the lively little **fishing port** at **Cape Agía Kiriáki**, where there is also a chapel.

Buses: some Alikés buses run via Alikanás (others take the inland route; check in advance).

Tourist train; horse and carriage: run to nearby Alikés and the museum at Pigadákia.

Beaches

Alikanás, eastern beach: a small cove with a narrow sandy beach set below a steep cliff; facilities nearby.

Alikanás, western beach: a sandy beach which begins at the Skoúrtis River — with dunes extending to the fishing port at Cape Agía Kiriáki (see above); facilities nearby.

Alikés

Once the quiet fishing port for Katastári, Alikés is now a popular, busy resort in a wide, curving bay. Again, well suited to families, and considerably livelier than Alikanás.

Buses: up to 6 a day to/from Zákynthos town.

Tourist train; horse and carriage: run to nearby Alikanás and the museum at Pigadákia.

Places of interest

Pentokámaro Bridge: an arched Venetian bridge over the Skoúrtis River; the name derives from its five arches.

Salt pans: They make an attractive picture just by the coast, but have not been worked for decades, as not enough salt was produced. It's a popular area for cycling on the flat terrain.

Spíros Vertzágias (owner of the museum and restaurant in Pigadákia), in front of a panoramic view of eastern Zákynthos

Accommodation
See under Katastári below.

Beaches
Alikés Beach: a good sweep of bay divided by two jetties. Sandy beach, sloping gently (fine for children). All facilities, centred on the main part of the beach. The further north you go, the more pebbly the beach becomes — and the quieter the surroundings. Another **sandy beach** (unnamed)

Typical old building; this is on Walk 14, near the Andronios wells.

lies between Alikés and Ksígia: to reach it by road you have to follow an unmarked track. This beach, at the bottom of a steep cliff, is sandy and backed by dunes. A few facilities.

Katastári

Straddling the busy main road to Zákynthos town, this is the island's largest village.
Buses: up to 7 a day to/from Zákynthos town; some run on the main road, others via the Macherádo/Pigadákia road.

Places of interest
Moní Ágios Ioánnis Prodrómou is signposted off the Ágios Nikólaos road about 4km north of Katastári. The current, simple building dates from the 17th century, with two floors and a defence tower with circular base. It was once a resting place for pilgrims and contains several fine icons. St. John (Ágios Ioánnis) was the island's patron saint before that honour went to St. Dionýsios.

Accommodation
Archontiko Village: 13 traditional villas and apartments for

2-6 people, built on the side of a mountain, surrounded by olive trees. All accommodation with sea view; only 0.8km from Alikés. Pool with bar; garden; TV room (satellite); air-conditioning/ heating; kitchenettes. Rating **; 50-90 € per night, depending on the time of year and number of people. Open 1 Apr. to 31 Oct. www.archontikovillage.com

Pigadákia

A small village scattered along a mountainside, named for its freshwater springs. Walk 22 is based here; see pages 172-175.
Buses: see under Katastári.

Places of interest
Ágios Pantelémon: This church (originally 17th century, but rebuilt after the 1953 earthquake) is located above a sulphur spring. The 'bad waters' (hold your nose!) that reputedly pour forth from the spring each year on the saint's day are said to have healing powers; St. Pantelémon was a doctor during his lifetime.

Vertzágio Museum: a family-run museum in an old building, with displays from domestic and agricultural life — olive/grape press; reconstruction of a traditional house with dining room, kitchen and bedroom, all authentically decorated, furnished and equipped. Exhibits have information in English. Open daily from 09.00-21.00; admission fee.

Food and drink
Taverna Kakí Ráchi: opposite Ágios Pantelémon Church, with a range of local fish and meat dishes and delicious wine from the surrounding vineyards. Rating ****; open all year; €€. Be sure to visit the nearby farming museum created by same family who run this taverna. The owner, Spíros, knows the area like the back of his hand (see page 172).

Kallithéa

Another characteristic hill village with traditional stone architecture and surrounded by vineyards.
Buses: see under Katastári above.

Places of interest
Black Cave (Spiliá Chagióti): Just off the 4WD track up to Girí, and reached by a steep, skiddy path. To explore the stalactites and stalagmites, *be sure to take a torch and go carefully!* Free entry.

Agía Marína

A small village, tightly clustered around the main square with church and fountains.
Buses: see under Katastári above.

Places of interest
Agía Marína: built in the mid-1800s over a previous church; its red and sky-blue clock tower catches the eye. Inside are impressive altar screens and frescoes.

Helmi's Natural History Museum: a privately funded museum in a lovely traditional building, with collections of flora and fauna from Zákynthos and around the world — birds, shells, fossils, rocks and minerals. Open 09.00-18.00 in summer, 09.00-14.00 in winter; admission fee. www.museumhelmis.gr

Food and drink
Taverna Dennis' Place: at the top of the village (well signposted). In summer you can sit out on the terrace with fine views over Agía Marína and the agricultural

plain; in winter there's cosy seating indoors. Superb local cooking — it's best to just ask for the dish of the day. Rating ***; open all year; €€.

Macherádo

As you approach this village, the third largest on the island, the towers of the main church and the nearby monastery rise above the surrounding greenery.
Buses: up to 7 a day to/from Zákynthos town (Katastári bus); up to 2 a day (Kiloménos bus).

Places of interest
Agía Mávra: dating from 1631, this church (with a huge detached Venetian bell tower) is one of the most important on the island. It is dedicated to the Egyptian St. Mávra, martyred in the 3rd century. The single-aisled church was badly damaged by fire in 2005 and is currently being rebuilt. It remains to be seen how many of the treasures have survived: there were frescoes, 19th-century ceiling paintings, and an altar screen with richly worked framing donated by

Kiloménos bell tower

Queen Olga of Greece. This iconostasis was surrounded by offerings (including a valuable jewel also given by Queen Olga) testifying to miracles attributed to Saint Mávra.

Panagía Eleftherótria: on the road to Kiloménos. The striking white and red buildings of this abbey and church, founded in 1962, look like a fairy-tale castle on the approach. There are 17 nuns and, while the abbey cannot be visited, the church is open to the public and has some fine frescoes. There's a pretty garden and cloisters. Open daily from 07.00-12.00 and 16.00-20.00. Dress code for the church is very strict; clothing is on loan at the door.

Kiloménos

This mountain crossroads has grown from just a few houses clustered round a tiny square to a fairly sizeable village.
Buses: up to 4 a day to/from Zákynthos town; some terminate at Kiloménos, others go on to Anafonítria.

Places of interest
Ágios Nikólaos: dating from the 15th century, this rebuilt church has a separate, most impressive, four-storey stone-carved bell tower built in 1893.

'**Melissiotisses**', a women's collective in the village, where you can buy local products.

Moní Iperagáthou: Founded by two brothers in the 1600s and dedicated to the Holy Virgin, this monastery was once the base for monks from the St. Catherine's Order of Mount Sinai. It is now abandoned, save for a keeper. In the past it was not only used for religious purposes — in 1944 it

Three of the 11 Andronios Venetian wells near Agalás, visited on Walks 13 and 14; 'Andronios' is a place near Agalás named for a legendary giant.

was made the first station of the Allied Military Mission to liberate the Ionian Islands. To get there, drive about 1.5km from Kilioménos towards Ágios Léon, then turn right on the signposted track. Walk 15 (pages 144-147) visits this monastery, but from Loúcha (on Car tour 3).

Accommodation, food and drink

Ampelostrates: family-run place offering horse riding, hiking on forest trails, wine-tasting from organic vineyards, ouzerie with snacks and home-cooked food, participation in farm life (olive picking, harvesting grapes, wine-making, cheese-/bread-making). Rating*****; arguably the best food on the island, at reasonable prices; €€; www.ampelostrates. com (under construction).

Taverna Alitzeríni: in a traditional stone farm building with narrow doorways, tiny windows and somewhat wonky chairs, this authentic place exudes bygone days. A range of local mountain (*dópio*) dishes (*no fish*) and local 'black' wine. Live music some evenings. Essential to book in advance in summer. Rating *****; open all year for dinner; €€.

Agalás

An isolated mountain village surrounded by pine woods. In the past the people lived from wood-cutting and their olive groves, but today the few inhabitants left work down on the coast. Walks 13 and 14 explore this area (pages 136-143).
Buses: up to 2 a day to/from Zákynthos town (Kerí bus).

Places of interest

Damianós Caves: These unusual caves (signposted from the village and visited on Walk 14) put Agalás on the tourist map. There are two shallow caves or grottoes, one lying on top of the other; the upper tier is slightly higher, with stalactites and stalagmites. Unfortunately, the caves have been victim to modern-day graffiti.

Andronios Venetian Wells: Visited on Walks 13 and 14, they were built in the 15th century by the Venetians to supply water locally; there are 11 springs.

Museum of Agalas Art Gallery: in the centre of Agalás, an **art gallery** with paintings ranging from traditional to modern.

Car tour 3: THE NORTH

Zákynthos town • Katastári • Ksígia • Makrís Gialós and Míkro Nissí • Ágios Nikólaos • Cape Skinári • Volímes • Shipwreck • Anafonítria • Orthoniés • Mariés • Pórto Vrómi • Éxo Chóra • Kampí • Loúcha • (Girí) • Ágios Léon • Pórto Róxi • Limniónas

In the most remote areas of the island, away from both resorts and agricultural land, you will discover pockets of traditional stone villages and hidden fertile valleys below mountains covered in pine and *maquis*. There are stunning views and, despite the lack of beaches, fantastic swim spots in turquoise waters backed by steep cliffs.

Zákynthos town to Ágios Nikólaos

The main road leads through fields of vineyards backed by olive groves on the foothills. From Katastári you gain elevation and can enjoy views east towards Alikés and south over the island, as the road cuts along precipitous cliffs. At the base of these cliffs are sea caves carved by the turquoise-blue waters, and small traditional fishing villages like Makrís Gialós and Míkro Níssi.

Katastári
See page 66.

Ksígia
Beaches: Only 4WD vehicles can get down the road to the **south Ksígia beaches**; otherwise it is a 10 minute walk to a small white-sand beach and a climb around fallen rocks to a larger, isolated, pebbly beach with nearby caves, sulphur springs and wonderful snorkelling; no facilities. **North Ksígia beach** is a small white-pebble beach at the base of a steep cliff. It is fantastic for snorkelling. If you swim north, you will find a 'blue cave' round the corner. There is sulphur bubbling up through the water — you will smell it, and you will smell *of* it after a swim! A few facilities nearby, at the top of the hill.

Food and drink: **Ksígia Taverna**, on the road to Makrís Gialós; on a hill overlooking Alikés and Zákynthos town. Typical Greek food, both meat and fish. Rating ***; open for lunch and dinner in summer; €€.

Makrís Gialós and Míkro Nissí
Beaches: **Makrís Gialós Beach** is a short pebbly beach, partly shaded in the late afternoon. Facilities nearby. Heading further north, there are two pebbly beaches without facilities: **Ágriosykia** and **Klimáti**.
Places of interest: There is a small **Venetian tower** in the hamlet of **Míkro Nissí**.

Ágios Nikólaos

This picturesque port is an oasis in a mostly barren landscape; tamarisk trees line the road, where there are a few bars and tavernas. There are two quays. **Boats to Kefaloniá** tie up at the newer one (see panel on page 16 for details). The older quay, at the north side of the bay, is where you will find the fishermen and the **excursion boats to the Blue Caves and Shipwreck**. On a hill above is the 'Art Café', decorated with art works and a fine selection of drinks and snacks. **Buses:** up to 4 a *week* to/from Zákynthos town (Skinári bus).

Suggested car touring route

96km/60mi
Walks en route: 15-21

Take the main road to **Katastári**
(16km) and, on leaving, stop to
visit **Moní Ágios Ioánnis Prodrómou** (see page 66). Further
on, take the turning to **Ksígia**, a
good swim spot. Then continue
north, past **Makrís Gialós, Míkro
Nissí, Ágios Nikólaos** and
Koríthi to **Cape Skinári** (47km),
from where I recommend a boat
trip to the **Blue Caves**.
Then drive up to **Volímes** and
explore its churches and streets
laden with handicrafts. Continue

to the '**Navagio**' (62km) — a
viewpoint over the smugglers'
Shipwreck (take a 10-minute
walk along the peninsula for
stunning views). Visit the nearby
monasteries of **Ágios Geórgios
Krimnón** and **Anafonítria**
(where the island's patron saint
spent his final years).
From here, make a detour to
Moní Spiliótissa near **Orthoniés**,
before driving south through
Mariés and stopping for a swim
in the crystal-clear waters at
Pórto Vrómi. Move on to **Éxo
Chóra** (72km), with Venetian
wells worth visiting. In **Kampí**
visit the memorial cross dedicated to the Civil War resistance
fighters and the Mycenaean
cemetery.
Then drive inland past the old
flour-grinding windmill to
Loúcha (and perhaps **Girí** and
the Black Cave). Loop back down
to **Ágios Léon** (87km) and to the
rugged coastline at **Pórto Róxi**,
then finish the day with a sunset
swim in the turquoise waters of
the **Limniónas** inlet (97km).

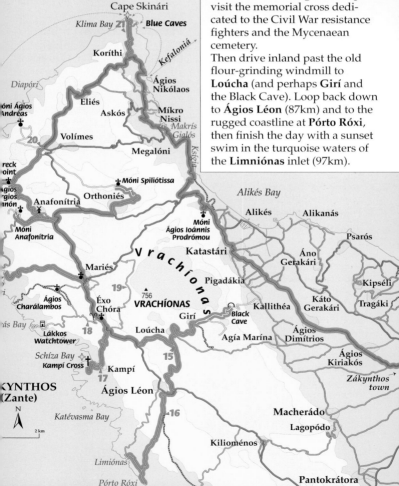

Beach

Ágios Nikólaos Beach is a small pebbly beach by the port, with facilities nearby.

Accommodation

Orfos Luxury Village: set near the port, four individually styled villas, each accommodating 4-8 people and each with private swimming pool overlooking the sea. Air-conditioning, satellite TV, CD/DVD players, fully equipped kitchens, hydro-massage, daily maid service. Rating *****; 140-320 € per villa per night, depending on the season. Open 1 May to 31 Oct. www.orfos-villas.gr.

Emerald Luxury Villas: on the hillside 300m above the port, 8 villas accommodating 4-8, each in an area of 1000sqm and each with private pool overlooking the sea. Fully equipped kitchen, jacuzzi, large veranda and balcony, air-conditioning, satellite TV, CD/DVD player, Internet access, washing machine, daily maid service. Rating *****; 140-360 € per villa per night, depending on the season. Open 1 May to 31 Oct. www.emerald-villas.gr.

Hotel Nobelos: just 300m from the picturesque port, this hotel (which has won several national awards) is built completely from stone in the old Zakynthian style and is reminiscent of the island's traditional mansions. It is divided into four spacious suites, each sleeping up to 4 people. Each room is decorated differently, with art objects, handmade Venetian-style furniture, traditional lace curtains, etc. Air-conditioning, TV, CD/DVD players, hydro-massage, twice-daily maid service (!), private balconies with sea view. Two of the suites have fully equipped kitchens. Rating *****; 240-420 € per suite per night, depending on the season. Open all year. www.nobelos.gr

Cape Skinári and the Blue Caves

From the crossroads at the hamlet of **Koríthi** the road descends to **Cape Skinári**, the northernmost cape on the island — and the famous 'Blue Caves'. Once there was only a **lighthouse** here (base for Walk 21; see pages 168-171), but the few new tourist developments have not spoilt the natural charm.

Places of interest

Blue Caves (Galázia Spiliá): a highlight on any island holiday. To see them at their best, *do* take a boat trip, either from Cape Skinári or Ágios Nikólaos. This series of caves and arches is famous for the brilliant play of light and shade — the brilliant turquoise sea reflected in the blinding white limestone rock.

Swimming

Blue Caves: You can swim through these arches, but beware of boat traffic. There is also a very strong current, making it easier to swim out than back. Facilities nearby.

Accommodation

Blue Caves Villas: just two traditional stone villas set directly above the caves, looking out to the island of Kefaloniá. The main villa accommodates 6-8 people; the 'studio' 2-3. Satellite LCD TV (which also carries live scuba transmissions of the Blue Caves underwater world), CD/DVD player, large fully equipped kitchen. Pool, aromatic herbal garden with fountains, traditional village-style oven and BBQ, olive groves. Free extras include hydro-massage, an observatory, standing earth binoculars, mountain bikes, canoes, kayaks, snorkelling and fishing equipment. Rating *****; 100-680 € per villa per night, depending on the season. Open all year. www.bluecavesvillas.gr.

Volímes

Volímes is the largest of the island's hill villages, composed of three hamlets, with some of the best-preserved buildings on Zákynthos. Lower and Middle Volímes have grown together and are an obligatory coach stop to buy hand-made carpets, tablecloths, cheeses and honey. Upper Volímes lies a bit further east, off the main through road, and has kept its traditional farming character.
Buses: up to 2 a day to/from Zákynthos town (out via Macherádo and Pigadákia, back via Katastári). The Skinári bus (up to 4 a *week* also stops in Volímes).

Places of interest

Moní Ágios Andréas: The 4WD track to this abandoned monastery leaves from Lower Volímes. Frescoes from the church are now housed in the Post-Byzantine Museum in Zákynthos town. More details with Walk 20, pages 164-167.

Moní Ágios Geórgios Krimnón: on the road from Middle Volímes to Anafonítria and the Shipwreck; built in 1535. A defence tower was added later to protect the monks. The word 'Krimnón' means 'of the cliffs' — presumably the original church was built near the cliffs; the current building is in a pine grove. The ruins of an ancient castle that once protected the area from pirate raids can be seen nearby. On the left are the residential quarters, in the middle the round defence tower, and on the right a small church in the Venetian style. There is a twin-headed Byzantine eagle in the central aisle of the church, and Byzantine and post-Byzantine icons line the walls. A path below the monastery leads

The Blue Caves

to the **cave** in which **St. Gerasímos**, patron saint of Kefaloniá, lived as a hermit.

Shipwreck viewpoint (Navagio): Reached via a signposted side road 100m north of Ágios Geórgios Krimnón, this is *the* iconic view of Zákynthos — the wreck of a cigarette smugglers' ship dating from the late 1970s, partly buried in sand. The best view is from this cliff-hanging perch 100m above the cove, but on calm days there are also boat excursions from Skinári (via the Blue Caves) and Pórto Vrómi to the beach and wreck itself.

Beaches

Diapóri Beach: a small white pebbly outcrop near Ágios Andréas Islet; no facilities.

Shipwreck Beach: a white pebbly beach near several caves and the famous wreck. Only accessible by boat, no facilities.

Anafonítria

The village is in a key location, near the Shipwreck, Pórto Vrómi and Moní Anafonítria — so the main road is lined with tavernas and shops selling everything from souvenirs to local produce. It's worth stretching your legs by walking through the old village centre and up to the windmill above.

Buses: up to 8 a day to/from Zákynthos town (routes vary).

Places of interest

Moní Anafonítria: About 1km west of the village, this is one of the most visited monasteries on the island, both because St. Dionýsios spent his final years here as an abbot and because the icon of the Virgin is attributed with miracles. (It was a miracle

that it was even found: it was on a merchant ship from Constantinople which was wrecked below the village, and found by fishermen). A small church was built to house the statue; in the 1400s the monastery was added. The impressive bell tower was originally built for the monks' defence against pirates. Although the monastery has long been abandoned, the church (with many frescoes still intact) is still used for mass by the villagers.

Moní Spiliótissa: located near the quiet agricultural village of **Orthoniés** east of Anafonítria (served by the Volímes bus from Zákynthos town). This small monastery (16th century) isn't always open, but worth a visit for the wonderful mountain landscape. Opposite is the large cave (*spiliótissa*) where an icon of the Virgin was found.

Beaches

Pórto Vrómi (north inlet): reached from Anafonítria, a small white-pebble beach from where you can swim to a 'blue cave'. There's a harbour, too, where you can catch an excursion boat to the Shipwreck or to the Blue Caves at Cape Skinári. Facilities.

Mariés

It's worth wandering the stone-paved streets of this largish village below the Vrachíonas peak. Mariés is named for two Marys — Magdalene and Klopa: legend has it that they broke their sea journey to Rome at Pórto Vrómi, from where they told the inhabitants the story of Jesus. Walk 19 (pages 160-163) is easily reached by car from here.

Buses: up to 8 a day to/from Zákynthos town (routes vary).

Places of interest

Maria Magdalena: The large 16th-century church in the village square has a stone cross, an impressive altar screen and some good icons. The saint's day is celebrated on 22 July with a large festival.

Beaches

Pórto Vrómi (south inlet): reached from Mariés, a small pebbly beach on the south side of the high outcrop that splits this beach in two. The crystal-clear water gives the lie to the ancient name *'Vrómi'* ('dirty' — referring

The Shipwreck — the most photographed motif on Zákynthos

View over the steep coastal cliffs

intricately carved iconostasis.

Venetian wells: a footpath opposite the square leads to several cisterns built by the Venetians to provide a reliable source of water for the local area. Unfortunately they are not as well preserved as those at Agalás.

Lákkos Venetian Watchtower: a small but quite well preserved tower, only accessible on foot or by 4WD (see Walk 18, page 156).

Beach

Almirás Bay: a small pebbly beach at the base of precipitous limestone cliffs; no facilities. Only accessible on foot or by 4WD vehicle (see Walk 18).

Kampí

A small traditional village at the edge of 300 metre-high cliffs — a favourite spot to watch the sunset from one of several tavernas. Walk 17 (pages 152-155) is based here.

Buses: none direct; Éxo Chóra buses stop at the *turn-off* to Kampí on the main road.

Places of interest

Kampí cross: a white cross stands on the hillside above the main crossroads — a memorial to the Zakynthians who were sent to their deaths over the Schíza Cliffs during the Greek Civil War.

Mycenaean cemetery: halfway between the Sunset Taverna and the cross monument; several sculpted tombs (see Walk 17).

Folk museum: with displays of traditional domestic and agricultural paraphernalia.

Food and drink

Taverna Kálas (at the Kampí road junction, near the village centre): an alternative to the

to the nearby bitumen upwellings in the sea). Facilities.

Sténtis Beach: reached from Mariés, a small pebbly beach at the base of limestone cliffs; no facilities.

Éxo Chóra

A small village with a pretty, plane-shaded square, base for Walk 18 (pages 156-159).

Buses: up to 8 a day to/from Zákynthos town (routes vary).

Places of interest

Ágios Nikólaos: The village church is impressive, with a lovely wooden ceiling and 'panorama' tavernas, set in a traditional stone building surrounded by trees. Delicious local variations on a range of Zakynthian and Greek dishes. Rating ****. Open all year for lunch and dinner; €€.

Sunset Taverna (at the view-point): set in the shade of pines, with fantastic views to the sheer chalk Schíza Cliffs and the sea; both grills and oven roasts, meat and fish. Rating **; open in summer for lunch and dinner; €€.

Cross Tavern (at the monument): higher up the hill and an even better place from which to watch the sunset — the terraces seems to hang out over the sea. Both grills and oven roasts, meat and fish. Rating **; open in summer for lunch and dinner; €€.

Loúcha and Girí

Small hamlets on the Vrachíonas foothills. From Girí (where there is still a little stonemason's workshop) you can visit the Black Cave (see under Kallithéa, page 67).

Places of interest
Moní Iperagáthou: See page 68 and Walk 15, pages 144-147.

Food and drink
Kafenió of Loúcha: *Beware — there are two!* This one is in the village square opposite the church. It's a little family-run restaurant set on the veranda of a traditional stone house, over-looking a farmed valley. The food (meat dishes, *no fish*) is delicious. Amazingly, even if you find it closed, the family will open up and cook a meal for hungry hikers... If you ask, they will show you the loom on which the mother weaves a range of rugs

and cushions. Rating ****; open for lunch and dinner during the summer; €.

Ágios Léon

A large village on the main road, profiting from its proximity to both the mountains and nearby swimming spots — plenty of places to eat, drink and stock up (petrol station, too).
Buses: up to 8 a day to/from Zákynthos town (routes vary).

Beaches
Limniónas: reached from Ágios Léon — not a beach, but a rocky outcrop with steep cliffs and two 'blue caves' into which you can swim. The sea is deep blue, cold and clear. Facilities include a taverna on the cliff.

Pórto Róxi: reached from Ágios Léon — a rocky outcrop with a rugged, lunar-like landscape. Excellent snorkelling; facilities. (See Walk 16, pages 148-151.)

Korakoníssi Islet: a rocky outcrop and islet (see Walk 16, pages 148-151). There is an arch/cave on the islet; the sea is deep, cold and blue — excellent for snorkelling. No facilities.

Food and drink
Pórto Limniónas Taverna: located at the sea inlet and harbour of Limniónas, with sea caves and the most amazing turquoise sea, offset by pine trees. Delicious local food (meat and fish) served indoors or on an outdoor balcony. You will find it very hard to leave this paradise — bring swimming things, snorkel and mask! Rating *****; open all day for lunch, dinner and drinks, from Easter until Oct.; €€.

Car tour 4: GENERAL ISLAND TOUR

Zákynthos • Bóchali • Tsiliví • Plános • Gerakári • Alikés • Katastári • Ksígia • Makrís Gialós • Míkro Níssi • Ágios Nikólaos • Cape Skinári • Volímes • Shipwreck • Mariés • Éxo Chóra • Ágios Léon • Limniónas • Pórto Róxi • Ágios Léon • Kilioménos • Pantokrátora • Lithakiá Ágios Sóstis • Pórto Koúkla • Lithakiá • Lake Kerí • Marathiá • Kerí

I have summarised the one-day island tour that I take with visiting friends, to give a snapshot of the island. All the sights (save for Pantokrátora) are described in the previous tours; see page references. This tour misses out Cape Gérakas, covered in Car tour 1.

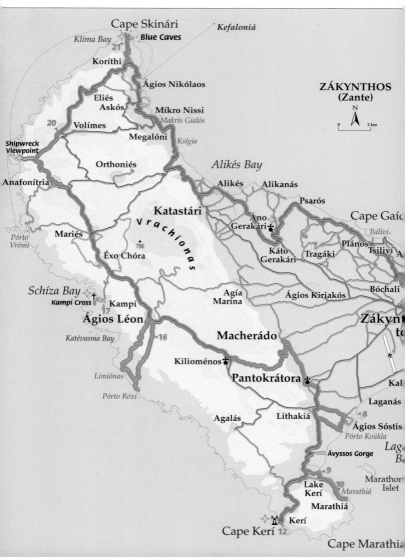

Suggested car touring route

122km/76mi
Walks en route: 8, 9, 10, 12, 16, 17, 20, 21

From Zákynthos town drive up to **Bóchali** (2km; see page 42) and visit the castle. Continue down to **Tsiliví** and **Plános** (page 62), then follow the road up to **Gerakári** (11km; page 64). Stop here at the church, to take in the panoramic views of the island.

Drive down past the salt flats in **Alikés** (page 65), up to **Katastári** (19km; page 66), and along the main road to **Ksígia** (29km; page 70) — a good place to stop for a 10-minute walk down to the mineral-rich beach for a swim. Continue along the coast up to the northernmost point of Zákynthos at **Cape Skinári** (49km; page 72), and swim in the Blue Caves while enjoying the view to Kefaloniá.

Then drive over the mountains, through **Volímes** (page 73) to stop at 'Navagio' — the vertiginous **viewpoint over the Shipwreck** (61km; page 74), taking a 10-minute walk along the peninsula.

Shipwreck Beach — below the viewpoint and only accessible by boat

Drive down the west coast, stopping to look across to the memorial cross at Kampí (page 76). Beyond **Mariés** (page 74) and **Éxo Chóra** (page 76), turn off at **Ágios Léon** (page 77) to the inlet at **Limniónas** (81km; page 77) to have a swim at the turquoise sea caves.

Follow the road past **Pórto Róxi** (page 77) and loop back up to **Ágios Léon** (88km). Then drive south, stopping briefly to view the intricately carved bell tower at **Kiloménos** (page 68). From here drive down the mountains, enjoying panoramic views over the island.

Head along the foothill villages to **Pantokrátora**. The road bypasses this large village, but it is worth stopping to view the 13th-century Byzantine Saviour of Pantokrátora monastery and church for which the village is named, with frescoes and painted door casings.

Continue to **Lithakiá** (100km; page 59), then drive down to **Ágios Sóstis** (page 58) to swim with turtles in summer and see the ancient olive trees near **Pórto Koúkla** (shown on page 116). Return to **Lithakiá** (110km), then go on to **Lake Kerí** (page 60), where you can see the bitumen springs, and along the **Marathiá** peninsula, for a swim or short walk.

Finally, make a final stop at **Kerí** (122km) and end the day by watching the sunset at Kerí Lighthouse.

79

● Walking

Greece is one of the most biodiverse countries in Europe. Most people think of sun, sea and sand, but due to its geographical location linking Europe, the Baltic, Asia and Africa, it is also a country of snow-capped mountains and deep gorges; it has wildernesses large enough for wolves and bears to roam, vast lakes with flamingoes and spoonbills, forests with vultures and much, much more.

As an island, Zákynthos is unusual in that it has both mountains and lowland plains as well as the expected beaches and sea. There is no substitute for seeing all this on foot. Car touring can take you close to nature, but only by walking can you truly enjoy the complete countryside experience. Zákynthos is particularly well endowed with nature's blessings, boasting several rare and unique animal and plant species. At almost any time of year flowers and trees provide a kaleidoscope of colour.

This book describes **22 day walks**, with many variations. They are split into two groups: Walks 1-11 are situated within the National Marine Park of Zákynthos; Walks 12-22 are spread across the rest of the island. No matter where you are staying, all the walks are easily accessible and can be completed in a four-hour round trip or incorporated into a day's outing. Some of the walks are 'out and back', but the majority are circular. To complete the 'loops' I have had to include some stretches on tarmac. These are usually quiet country roads, where you are unlikely to encounter much traffic. However do remember that on celebration days the areas around the beaches, churches and monasteries will be packed with locals.

It would be unusual while walking if you did not see another person all day. Even in the more remote areas you will come across women collecting greens and herbs, goatherds, farmers tending their groves, terraces or livestock and, at specific times of year, bird hunters. All the people you meet will appreciate a greeting — 'hello' (*yassas*), 'good morning' (*kalimera*) or 'good afternoon' (*kalispera* or, if you can get your mouth around it, *kalo apogyevma*) ... and you may even be asked to stop for coffee or to try a local delicacy!

View from Cape Marathiá (Walk 10, Alternative route A)

Quick-glance walk map

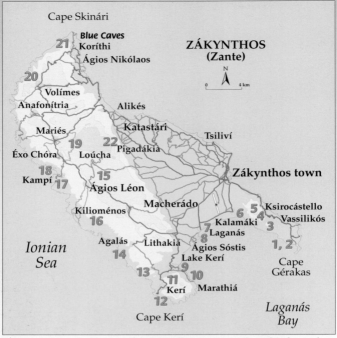

Cape Skinári

Blue Caves
21 Koríthi
Ágios Nikólaos

**ZÁKYNTHOS
(Zante)**

N
0   4 km

20

Volímes
Anafonítria   Alikés

Mariés   Katastári   Tsiliví

19   22 Pigadákia
Éxo Chóra   Loúcha

18   15   **Zákynthos town**
Kampí 17   Ágios Léon

Macherádo   Ksirocástello

Kilioménos   6   5   Vassilikós
16   4   3
             7 Kalamáki
Agalás   Lithakiá 8 Laganás   1, 2
Ionian   14   Ágios Sóstis
Sea   13   Lake Kerí   Cape
           9   10   Gérakas
         11
       Kerí   Marathiá
        12   *Laganás*
Cape Kerí   *Bay*

This map shows the location of the 22 walks, starting at Cape Gérakas and running in a clockwise direction. This skeletal map is only meant for orientation; for more detail, please see the fold-out map inside the back cover.

How the walks are described

Each walk is presented over four pages.

The first section gives planning and route information which should let you judge whether the walk is within your capabilities.

While most of the headings are obvious, do pay special attention to '**Protection status**'. This lists the protection zones you will cross in the walk, so when planning, please check the National Park Visitor Rules for that area (see pages 14-15).

There are two protection categories: National Marine Park and Natura 2000 Specially Protected Areas. There are two Natura protection zones on the island — one lies within the National Park itself, while the other encompasses the land mass 100 metres inland from the sea along the west and north coasts.

The heading '**Alternative routes**' allows you to lengthen or shorten the walk according to your energy, interests and time constraints; under '**Additional suggestions**' there are tips on nearby sites of interest or swimming spots.

The 'Walking notes' are very straightforward, with numbered points that correlate with the 3D sketch map (read more about these maps under 'Navigation and maps' on page 84). Following the 'Walking notes' there is an optional reading section divided into six categories, where I have highlighted points of interest that you might expect to see and experience on the walk.

The second section continues and illustrates these points of interest:
• Geological rock types and formations to look out for;
• Habitat types you will encounter;
• Plant species that are in flower or fruit at different times of the year. I have interpreted season months as December-February (winter), March-May (spring), June-August (summer) and September-November (autumn). Please remember that many of the flowering plants overlap two seasons, and it is possible to find plants such as rock roses and broom in flower out of season, due to the mild winter climate on the island;
• Cultural or heritage sites that lie along the walk or nearby;
• Agricultural practices you are likely to see;
• Wildlife, from invertebrates to vertebrates (split into reptiles and amphibians, birds and mammals) and, in some instances, a summary of sea life as well.

When to walk
The climate between late **September to early May** is perfect for walking on Zákynthos, when temperatures are mild.
In **winter** it is possible to complete three to five walks per week on average, but you must be prepared for strong winds and heavy rainfall which can last two-three days and occasionally entire weeks. On windy days choose walks in areas sheltered from the prevailing wind. On potentially rainy days, select walks with a quick return route in the event of a heavy downpour. If you plan to walk following heavy rainfalls, do so with caution as it can be very muddy!
While continuous sunshine is practically guaranteed from **June to August**, it is far too hot for any lengthy walking activity — even in the early mornings and late evenings. In the heat of the summer only attempt the shortest version of any walk or a walk graded 'easy' — but even then, be extremely cautious in the sunshine. The strength of the sun should never be underestimated; you can be burnt at any time of year without the appropriate protection.
Generally, **May and September** are also too hot for long walks or walks with any hill-climbing during the daytime, except on overcast or rainy days. It is possible to do some walks around sunrise or sunset.
To help with walk planning, you can find out weather information and/or sunrise/sunset times for Zákynthos by logging on to www.interhellas.com/weather/weather-in-Zákynthos.html.

Grading and timing
I found **grading** the walks quite difficult, as some people who can walk all day on the flat without tiring may find even short uphill sections very strenuous. Others

Laganás Bay from the Gérakas headland, with chamomile (Anthemis sp) *in the foreground*

who experience no problems on prolonged climbs may nevertheless feel that a three-hour walk is quite long enough.

At the start of each walk description I have tried to give a good indication of what to expect, but if you read through *the complete walk description* before setting off you will have an even better idea. Some walks are very long, others involve steep climbs, so be sure to choose those that are within your capability. There are suggestions on how to shorten or lengthen the walks, so that you can adapt them to your ability, preference and time constraints. You do not need to be an expert or habitual walker to complete most of the walks in this book, but a reasonable degree of fitness and stamina is necessary. The given **timings** do not include any lengthy stops for picnics or extensive bird watching, plant identification or photography.

Allow for these when arranging your outing and also take into account the weather. Hot sun, driving rain and strong winds can affect your rate of progress. Check the walking notes frequently to avoid missing turn-offs or landmarks. After testing one or two walks you will be able to adjust the timings to your own pace.

It is never advisable to walk alone, and this is especially true for women. If you must go alone, carry a mobile and a loud whistle to use as a distress signal in case of an accident. Whether you are alone or in a group, *do* inform a responsible person where you are going and what time you plan to be back.

Navigation and maps

Navigation along the tracks followed in these walks is generally straightforward; this is fortunate, because at present most walks are *not signposted,* as all roads and land are on **private property**.

I apologise in advance for any mishap this may cause and hope that the presence of walkers will encourage locals to allow signposts to be erected. In the meantime, *do* follow my written instructions at all times.

For those of you with **GPS**, coordinates are given in decimal degrees (Datum WGS84) for all the numbered waypoints on the walks and many intermediate points as well; see tables starting on page 176.

Anyone with any experience of walking in Greece will realise that standard **maps**, both commercial and military, are woefully inaccurate. They do not include all roads, and different maps show different roads.

Using satellite imagery, I have created **my own map of Zákynthos**, with the aim of better indicating the starting points for the walks and outlining the routes. This fold-out map, at a scale of 1:87,000, is at the back of the book. Despite the rather small scale, I believe it is the most accurate map available.

But printed beside the route descriptions, I felt it would be more effective to give the walker a 3D visual impression of the walk in the form of detailed sketches. These hand-drawn 3D maps are *not accurately to scale;* moreover, the maps were drawn up to be easily compared with the walking notes, so *compass points are approximate and are seldom orientated with north at the top.*

The maps were correct at the time of compilation, but as more of the countryside is exploited,

new tracks or roads may appear. All the tracks and paths followed in my walks are highlighted with red dots; alternative or connecting routes are shown in bright blue dots. I advise you to keep to these routes: in regions of deep gorges and precipitous cliffs or mountain peaks it is not sensible to strike off into the unknown.

Equipment checklist

Below is a list of suggested seasonal and year-round recommendations.

All year round
• **sun protection** (suncream, sunblock, sunhat, long-sleeved shirt and sunglasses);
• **comfortable lightweight walking boots with ankle support**. Sandals are not good for walking, as plant seeds or stones can get caught in them, or you could stub a toe.
• **water** — at least 1 litre per person — 2 litres when walking in hot weather or for the more strenuous routes. While you will often pass springs and wells on the walks, it is not advisable to take on their water, as they may be stagnant or contaminated from dumps, leaking sewage or chemical run-off from crops or olive production;
• **warm jacket and trousers** if climbing at high elevations — just in case it gets cool;
• **high-energy food**, like nuts, chocolate or cereal bars, to keep your stamina up;
• **mobile phone**, in case of emergencies. Make sure it's charged. The **emergency number in Greece is 112**;
• **compass or GPS** — just in case you get lost!
• **wristwatch, torch and spare batteries**: keep an eye on the time

Laganás Bay from Marathiá (Walk 11)

relative to the distance you have walked, and always be aware of sunset time, so that you don't get caught out in the dark — but take a torch for backup just in case you do!

• **first-aid kit** for emergencies (plasters for blisters, headache tablets, a small bottle of antiseptic and cotton wool in case you get scratched, mosquito repellent and antihistamines in case you get an allergic reaction if you get bitten);

• **swimwear**: on this island you are never very far from the sea!

• **optional extras**: notebook, identification guides, binoculars, camera, fold-up seat or towel, snorkel and mask, Dog Dazer (see under 'Potential hazards' below).

In winter (October to April)
• **warm clothing** (and you'll need some warm clothing for the evenings in May and September as well);

In winter and the 'shoulder seasons' (September to May)
• **waterproof clothing** (and be prepared for abrupt changes in weather conditions).

Potential hazards

Dogs are kept on most properties, though the fiercer ones are almost always chained up or fenced in. Dogs left to run loose (or abandoned), although noisy, lively and curious, are generally harmless. If dogs worry you, take an ultrasonic 'Dog Dazer' (available from Sunflower Books at www.sunflowerbooks.co.uk).

There are **snakes, scorpions** and **stinging insects** on the island, so be careful when out walking — avoid disturbing rocks, stones and logs. If you are bitten or stung, do not panic, *none of the species is life-threatening*. Just go directly to the hospital to receive the appropriate treatment in case of an allergic reaction.

There are many **wild berries, ripe tubers, mushrooms** and **toadstools** on the island from October to April. While some are edible, many are highly poisonous to humans, so don't be tempted to pick — or even *touch* — any of them.

Deep **gorges**, precipitous **cliffs**, rocky shady **overhangs**, **caves** and **derelict buildings** should all be treated with care and caution no matter how tempting. There are frequent **rockfalls** due to unstable soils and earthquakes.

Although it is illegal, **bird-hunting** is a regular practice on the island from September to April. When walking be aware of where hunters are (they don't stray far from their cars) and listen out for their dogs and guns; whenever possible, keep out in the open. If in doubt, holler out to let them know you are in the vicinity!

Country code

This code of conduct is intended for everyone wishing to explore the island, but especially for walkers — to minimise the disturbance to ecosystems, habitats, plants and animals, on both cultivated and uncultivated landscapes. Please keep in mind that all land (including most roads and tracks, and land within the National Park) is privately owned. It is therefore essential to have respect for land-owners' property (buildings, crops and livestock) at all times. This Country code complements the 'Visitor Rules' of the National Marine Park (see pages 14-15), and I suggest that you use the two together. Please:

• Be aware of where you are, and if in the National Park make sure you comply with their regulations.
• When parking, make sure you never block a gateway, road or track.
• Camp only in designated camp-sites or with the landowner's permission (note that camping and bivouacking are prohibited in the National Park region).
• Always close gates or fences securely behind you.
• Do not stray from tracks (especially if on a motorbike, moped, quad-bike or 4WD) — or paths, tracks and field edges if walking. Erosion is a major problem throughout Zákynthos due to frequent fires and heavy winter rains, so please do not add to it by taking short-cuts or making off-road diversions.
• Drive or walk quietly through farms and hamlets.
• Do not light barbecues, fires or throw away lighted cigarette ends; fire is always a major hazard in countryside that is always parched during the summer months
• Take your litter away with you.

• Protect all wild or cultivated plants; do not pick wild flowers (have an identification book to hand, sketch or take photos); never cross cultivated land, and do not remove vegetables or pick fruit, almonds or olives — as these are clearly someone's livelihood (and could have been sprayed with poisonous chemicals…).
• Do not be tempted to pick and eat wild berries, tubers or mushrooms.
• Do not approach, disturb, frighten or use flash photography on amphibians, reptiles, mammals or birds, on land or in the sea.
• Do not enter caves with bats, approach birds' nests or overturn stones, rocks and logs, as you could cause the animals to abandon offspring or habitats vital to survival.
• If you get stung or bitten (bee sting, scorpion sting, snake or dog bite), remain calm and go directly to the hospital for the appropriate treatment.
• Protect water sources: water is a precious commodity on Zákynthos, and many island residents collect spring water for drinking and cooking. When attending to 'calls of nature' keep well away from springs or streams and bury (or take away) all paper.
• Walkers: do not take risks! It is never advisable to walk alone, and you should always tell someone where you are going and when you expect to return. Remember that any route could become dangerous after storms. If you are lost or injured you may have to wait a long time for help. Take a mobile phone with you in case of emergency. Never stand on the edge of cliffs or sit under overhangs, as there are regular rock falls from erosion and earth tremors.

Walk 1: Gérakas headland trail (Municipality of Zakynthíon)

Distance/time: just over 4km/2.5mi; about 2.

Grade: moderate; ascent of about 100m/330ft between points (1-6) and corresponding *eroded* descent between points (6-9).

Equipment: see pages 85-86.

Travel: The walk is about a 30-minute drive (16km/10mi) out of Zákynthos town. Take the road via Argássi and Vassilikós village. At the crossroads for Pórto Róma continue straight on for Gérakas. Park along the road, in the restaurant car park or at the Wildlife Centre (paid parking).

Suggested time of year: any, but between June and August only attempt as an early morning (after the protected beach opens at 07.00) or late evening walk (before the beach closes at 19.00).

View of the white and red cliffs at Gérakas from the Kanónia bunker

Protection status: National Marine Park: F1 Protected Natural Landscape of Mount Skopós and Vassilikós; P2 Nature Protection Site of Gérakas. Natura 2000 Specially Protected Area: Site code GR2210002.

Alternative routes

1) At the first T-junction (3), turn left; follow the track about 160 m to a viewpoint over Gérakas.

2) About 20 m after turning right at the first T-junction (3), turn left on a path. Follow this up the hill for 200 m, then head west for 30 m on an overgrown path. Once on the ridge, turn left for 50 m to the cannon bunker (8) — or turn right along the ridge, passing a field after 40 m and arriving at point (6) 80 m further on.

3) At the right of the well (4), turn left (ducking under a fence) on a small path annd climb to (5).

4) Continue past the well (4), to join the main Gérakas road.

Additional suggestions: The sandy sea turtle nesting beach of Gérakas is worth a visit. Remember to sit within 3-5 metres of the sea to avoid disturbing the incubating nests under the sand. You can sunbathe, cover yourself in clay, or swim and explore the submerged reefs full of sea life.

Walking notes

From the **parking area/NMPZ guard station**, follow the tarmac road 50 m, to the top of **Gérakas Beach**, and turn right on a motorable track (**1**). This heads through bushy *garrigue* habitats bordering cultivated land and after about 300 m leads past an amazing **view** (**2**) to a cluster of weathered sea clay pinnacles. Continue a further 580 m, up to a T-junction (**3**) and turn right along a cobbled track, after 220 m passing an old well (**4**) on the left. Some 90 m past the well, turn left through a metal gate. Follow this track through woodland for about 350 m (past three right turns), to an olive grove (**5**). Continue to a **T-junction** (**6**) on the ridge, where the track turns right and a footpath leads left.

Follow the path to the left, through a **field** (**7**), securing the gate behind you. Continue over a hillock to a **cannon bunker** (**8**),

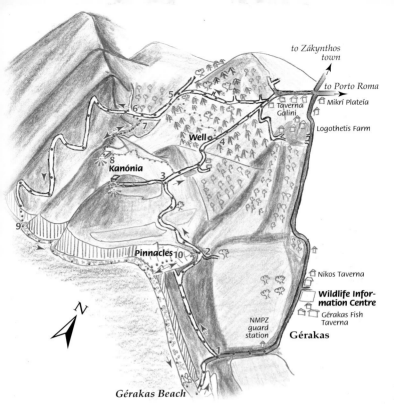

with a panoramic view from left to right of the Peloponnese, open ocean and Laganás.

Then retrace your steps to (**6**) and turn left on the eroded track. This winds 700 m down the cliff, through a small olive grove, then becomes a gully and drops to a **shingle beach** (**9**). To complete the loop back to Gérakas, turn left along the beach. Some 950 m along, you can divert to explore the **sea clay pinnacles** (**10**) seen earlier. Some 350 m past the pinnacles, you reach Gerakás Beach. Turn left and walk 150 m up the wooden walkway and on the tarmac road back to the start.

GEOLOGY

The white and red Ionian Zone sea cliffs of Gérakas were created as a result of tectonic processes and worldwide sea level changes. During the Pleistocene, about six million years ago, Gérakas was part of an open marine, relatively deep sea clay basin, on top of which a sedimentary cover of calcareous sandstone strata was laid during the subsequent Pliocene. Increasing tectonic instability during the Holocene caused rotation, repeated uplift, and erosion activity — leading to the formation of the terraces that you see today.

HABITATS

Scattered stone pine trees tower above the typical Mediterranean *maquis* and bushy *garrigue* habitat bordering the track and paths. The area of 'Kanónia' is primarily a *garrigue* habitat with

89

many flowering annuals in spring. The coastal cliffs are comprised of a degraded olive-carob *(Olea-Ceratonia)* habitat; look out for the striking carob bean pods. Gérakas forest is a unique habitat on the island for its combination of cypress and stone pine trees.

PLANTS
Spring

Kanónia is an amazing place to visit between March and May, when it is full of flowering plants, including several orchids such as bee, bumblebee, early spider, yellow ophrys, eastern yellow ophrys, sawfly, bug and tongue orchids. The tongue orchids can be found flowering under bushes lining the track in early May. There are also Barbary nuts, Spanish and black widow irises. Rock roses dominate the

From top to bottom, left to right: weathered sea clay pinnacles; hillside cypress and stone pine forest backing Gérakas Cove; heather; stone pine cones; early spider orchid

landscape until early June, producing pink and white flowers, with each flower lasting for just one day.

Summer

Only a few species flower in the dry summer heat, with thistles and rock roses being prevalent in early summer. Thyme flowers throughout the region in August, while sea lavender can be found flowering among the clay pinnacles.

Autumn

In September the towering sea squill and mullein are in flower. October is full of the heady scent of heather (pink) and common smilax blooms (yellow-white), contrasting with the berries of the lentisc (red), myrtle (blue) and wild strawberry (red) trees. The discoid fruit of the wild pear tree is also ripe at this time.

Winter

From mid-October onwards, cyclamen flower under bushes and throughout the Gérakas forest. Other flowering plants include *Romulea*, field marigolds and chamomile. All sorts of mosses, lichen and fungi also thrive in the forest. During this period you can collect the falling stone pine cones to extract the edible pine nuts.

CULTURE

Kanónia derives its name from the Nazi occupation during the Second World War. Several cannon bunkers were built in these hills, which could fire cannons up to a distance of 20 miles. The cobbled track running along the base of Gérakas forest was built during the Second World War to access the cannons and German living quarters. The roadside well at point (4), built in the 1930s, was once a flowing watercourse which ran down to Gérakas and was an essential part of local living, providing water for drinking and cleaning.

AGRICULTURE

This region has been subject to frequent burning to clear land for crops and the cultivation of olive trees. Even Gérakas forest is not natural — the cypresses and stone pines are believed to have been planted in the 16th century during the Venetian occupation of the island as a source of resin and building materials. The region would have been previously forested by Aleppo pines, similar to those found in the western region of the island.

WILDLIFE
Invertebrates

Kanónia is a haven for invertebrate species, due to the regularity at which the region is burnt, which in turn creates a host of additional habitat niches for occupation. Praying mantis are regularly sighted here, in addition to rose chafer and cockchafer beetles and a variety of butterflies and moths.

Reptiles and amphibians

During the morning and early evening it is easy to spot lizards, especially Balkan lizards (green and brown). Four-lined snakes are very common to this region, and in spring Hermann's tortoises can be observed in the grassy knolls below the road adjoining Gérakas forest. Green marsh frogs can be found in damp areas.

Birds

The contrasting habitats of the open scrub and closed forest canopy mean that a huge range of birds can be sighted — including golden orioles, turtle doves, rollers and blackbirds, as well as a range of warblers, finches and swifts. Raptors that frequent the area include kestrels and buzzards. Owls are very common to this region, especially barn, tawny and scops owls (the last easily recognised by its 'toot'-like call).

Mammals

Rabbits, hares, rats and mice are the most common mammals you are likely to see evidence of between Gérakas forest and the pinnacles. The eastern hedgehog (white belly) is also a resident, as are sand martens. Pipistrelle and myotis bats may be encountered.

From top to bottom, left to right: the old well at point (4); wild pear tree in a ploughed field; cockchafer beetle; Hermann's tortoise; whinchat

Walk 2: Gérakas–Dáphne trail (Municipality of Zakynthíon)

Distance/time: 4.2km/2.6mi; about 1.5 to 2 hours *each way*.

Grade: moderate; there are no hills to climb, but the pebbly coastline means that shoes with good ankle support are essential. Also be prepared to walk in the sea at one point during the walk.

Equipment: see pages 85-86.

Travel: Start at either Dáphne or Gérakas. From Zákynthos town, head towards the cape and turn right at the Dáphne sign beyond Ksirocástello (12km/7.5mi; 20min), or continue an additional 4km/2.5mi; 10min) to Gérakas (car parks at both start points).

Suggested time of year: any, as from June to August you can stop for more swims to cool off during the day. But *never* attempt this walk in a strong southerly wind; large waves will block the route.

Protection status: National Marine Park: F1 Protected Natural Landscape of Mount Skopós and Vassilikós; P1 and P2 Nature Protection Sites of Dáphne and Gérakas. Natura 2000 Specially Protected Area: Site code GR2210002.

Alternative route: You can combine this walk with Walk 1 (the Gérakas headland trail), by joining Walk 1 at A (Walk 1, point 1) or B (Walk 1, point 9).

Additional suggestions: A snorkel and mask are essential accessories to this walk, as extensive submerged reefs and seagrass *(Posidonia)* habitats exist between Dáphne and Gérakas, which are within the protected (no boating) Maritime Zone A, and are therefore full of a wide range of sea life including starfish, anemones and fish. If lucky, you may spot a sea turtle or two swimming or sleeping on the seabed! Be sure to visit the Thematic Sea Turtle Exhibition in the hills above Dáphne Beach (see page 50).

Coastal cliffs between Gérakas and Dáphne

to Vassilikós road

to Gérakas &
Vassilikós road

hne/Mélla
Beach

Gérakas
Beach

Walking notes

I describe this walk with Gérakas as the starting point.

From the **Gérakas car park/ NMPZ guard station**, follow the tarmac road 150 m to the top of the loggerhead nesting **beach** (**1**). Take the wooden walkway onto the beach and down to the **water's edge** (**2**), to avoid walking on any unmarked sea turtle nests.

Turn right, walk about 85 m to the end of the sandy beach, and climb over a small rock-pile (**3**). Continue walking for a further 250 m, then turn right, heading up the beach and into the region of the **clay pinnacles** (**4**). Explore them with care, being careful not to dislodge the clay formations. Then return to the beach and continue along the coastline. About 660 m further on, after leaving Gérakas cove, you will come to an area of **exposed reefs** (**5**), a good swimming and snorkelling spot. Continue along the coast; after 1.7 km you pass a second region of visible **reef** (**6**), then enter **Dáphne cove**, from where you can see the sandy loggerhead nesting beach of Dáphne/Mélla opposite. Continue following the coastline around the cove for just under 700 m, passing under a striking **cliff-overhang** (**7**); this is subject to regular rockfalls, so do not rest here!

After a further 600 m you arrive at **Dáphne/ Mélla Beach** (**8**). Stop for a rest and swim in the submerged reefs, before walking back to Gérakas — the same way, or by linking up with Walk 1 from point B.

GEOLOGY

The Gérakas coastal cliffs form a series of Pliocene-Pleistocene age layers of laminated marls alternating with calcareous sandstones (rich in easily visible shellfish fossils) and seams of siltstone and Shelley limestone. These deposits were formed as a result of a variety of environments such as low-energy deep waters, high energy shallow waters, fluvial, lacustrine and brackish water seas. Then, between the Late Pliocene and Quaternary, the differential layers were subject to dipping, folding, faulting activity and vertical uplift.

HABITATS

The coastal cliffs are composed of a degraded olive-carob (*Olea-Ceratonia*) habitat, interspersed with stands of juniper. The pebbly coastline comprises a habitat of stony driftline vegetation. There are pockets of sea lavender habitats on both exposed rock and exposed erosive clay regions. The numerous (seasonally running) river beds cutting through the hills support a range of riverside reed habitats. In the sea the most noticeable habitat is Neptune's seagrass (*Posidonia oceanica*) occupying the sandy seabeds between the rocky reef habitats.

From top to bottom, left to right: rock fossils; coastal juniper; small-flowered tongue-orchid; star of Bethlehem; rock samphire

ing (living parasitically) on the flowering thyme. The succulent-leaved sea rocket flowers into the summer, along with species such as sea holly, sea medick, sea spurge, plantain, thistles and caper. Sea lavender can be found in flower on exposed coastal rocks and loose clay. Chaste trees also flower at this time.

Autumn

Tall white-flowered sea squill is found along the coastal cliffs of the degraded scrub habitat. Other noticeable scrub species include plants with berries — juniper, lentisc, smilax and joint pine. Among the flowering species are mullein, spiny chicory, arums and prickly saltwort. Both rock samphire and golden samphire flower during this period. The feathery stems of various rushes and common reeds are highly visible too.

Winter

In winter rock samphire, gynandirises, dandelions, arums, star of Bethlehem and sea spurge can be found in flower.

PLANTS
Spring

Due to the rich mixture of habitats, from scrub to reedbed to driftline, a vast array of flowering plants can be seen. Scrub-flowering species include broom and rock roses; coastal species include knotgrass and sea rocket, lotus, spurge, pinks, plantago, medick, vetch, stock, and star of Bethlehem. There are orchids, too, among the scrub: tongue, pyramidal, bee, sawfly, spider, bug and yellow ophrys. Look also for flowering rushes.

Summer

Despite this being the driest time, broomrape can be found flourish-

CULTURE

This walk provides good views of Peloúso Islet and its monastery ruins. Peloúso once belonged to the priests of the Catholic order of Saint Fragkískos (Francisco), who inhabited the castle above Zákynthos town. In the late 1700s this order built a monastery on the island, around a church dating from 1533 and dedicated to the Virgin Mary Evangelístria. It was abandoned and its irreplaceable library was looted after the 1893 earthquake. After the 1953 earthquake only a couple of walls from the original structure were left standing.

AGRICULTURE

The coastal hills are devoid of agriculture, despite being regularly subject to deliberate burning by locals. Once mature stands of carob and wild olive trees existed here. In previous years, such as during the food shortage when the island was occupied during the Second World War, the carob beans were an essential food resource; they were used within the staple diet to make soups and bread. Today Greeks do not use carob, though in other parts of the world it is used as a chocolate substitute.

WILDLIFE
Sea life

Sea weeds such as seagrass, sea fern and sponges can be found, while invertebrates include shellfish such as whelks, limpets, mussels, tube worms and barnacles. Other invertebrates of the region are anemones, sea urchins, sea cucumbers, starfish, jellyfish, crabs and octopus. Among the fish species are pipefish, pearly razorfish, dog fish, pollack, gobys, gurnards, rays and sea horses.

Reptiles and amphibians

You are most likely to spot lizards on this walk — Balkan green lizards, Balkan wall lizards and Moorish geckos. With luck you might see leopard, four-lined or grass snakes too.

Birds

Passing species include individual grey and purple herons, red-backed and lesser grey shrikes, Cory's shearwaters and black-winged stilts. There are also yellow-legged gulls and lesser black-backed gulls, as well as cormorants and shags. You might

From top to bottom, left to right: ruins of Our Lady of the Annunciation Monastery (Panagía Evangelístria) on Peloúso; carob leaves and blossom; red-star starfish; dogwhelks; black-winged stilt

also spot common sandpipers, pipits, little stints and kingfishers here. Off the coastal cliffs, in the scrub and around the pinnacles, you might find finches, buntings, warblers, flycatchers, larks, blue rock thrush, shrikes, wagtails, sparrows, swifts and martins. Eleanora's falcon, common kestrel, marsh harrier and common buzzards hunt in this region due to the exposed scrub habitat and good ridge lift created by air rising against the cliffs.

Mammals

There are black rats, woodmice, brown hares, beech martens and pipestrelle and European free-tailed bats.

Walk 3: Dáphne hills trail (Municipality of Zakynthíon)

Distance/time: 3.5km/2.2mi; under 2h.
Grade: easy — mostly level, with a very gentle ascent of 50m/165ft from (13) back to the start (1).
Equipment: see pages 85-86.
Travel: The walk is about a 20-minute drive (10km/6.5mi) out of Zákynthos town. Take the Vassilikós road via Argássi and after Ksirocástello village turn right at the sign for Dáphne. Follow the tarmac road up a hill and past an old quarry, then take the second fork to the left (signed 'Sea Turtle Thematic Exhibition'; park in the free car parking area.
Suggested time of year: any, but only attempt as an early morning or late evening walk between

View from the Dáphne hills towards Gérakas

June and August.
Protection status: National Marine Park: F1 Protected Natural Landscape and P1 Nature Protection Site of Dáphne. Natura 2000 Specially Protected Area: Site code GR2210002.
Alternative routes: Several variations are possible, if you want to make the walk longer:
1) You can lengthen the walk by about an hour if you turn left at point (10) and walk 1 km down to Dáphne/Mélla Beach and then leave by the Dáphne road climbing the hill for about 750 m, to rejoin the walk at point (14).
2) The walk can be also be made longer by combining it with Walk 2 (the Gérakas–Dáphne trail) at point (A).
3) You could join Walk 4 (the Ksirocástello trail) at (3), which corresponds to (A) in Walk 4.
Additional suggestions: Visit the Sea Turtle Exhibition (see page 50) before or after the walk; perhaps take one of the NMPZ guided tours, to see the sea turtle tracks from the previous night; you can also see these tracks or the nests (often over 100 of them) from the concrete road to Dáphne between points (14) and (2).

Walking notes

From the **exhibition (1)**, walk 175 m down the road and turn right at the junction (2). Remain on the tarmac road; pass the sign for Sekánia after 30 m (3). Just 20 m further on, turn right on a smaller tarmac road (4). After about 300 m you pass a house on your right and then go through a set of gates, beyond which are several dwellings including a **farm (5)** and a renovated **chapel**. Continue along the main, partly concreted track for 400 m, pass-

ing mature **oak woodland (6)** on your right, until the track forks (7). Turn right down a dirt track through ancient moss-clad **olive groves** from where there are views to the Peloponnese. Continue for about 300 m along this track, ignoring several turn-offs. When the track becomes tarmac, you pass some **occupied dwellings (8)** and descend after 70 m to a **T-junction (9)**, where there are the ruins of several **old dwellings** and a **church**. Turn

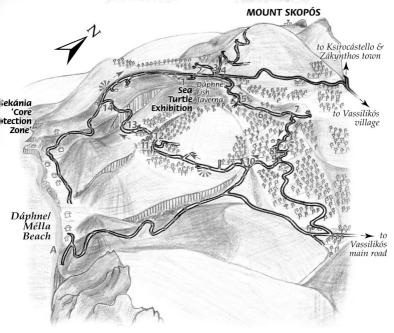

right here and follow the main concrete road for Dáphne/Mélla Beach for 270 m, turning right on a track at the next fork (**10**). Keep to this track, past all turn-offs for some 130 m; then, at a fork (**11**), descend left into an **olive grove**. After 25 m, at a gap in the line of **carob trees** (**12**), cut across the field traversing the gorge and 25 m along join a track. At the fork after 130 m (**13**) veer left and continue downhill for 300 m, until you join the concrete road (**14**). Turn right and follow this 1.25 km back to the start, with views over Sekánia Beach and to the church on Mount Skopós.

GEOLOGY

Dáphne, while in the Ionian Zone, has rock types corresponding to those of Ágios Sóstis, Mount Skopós and Gérakas. The east coast of Dáphne is overshadowed by a precipitous cliff, composed of metamorphosed dolomite limestone rock (black-grey colouration) that has been subject to intensive tectonic activity — thrusts, folds and reverse faults. Triassic seams of carbonates, evaporites of gypsum and metamorphic psammites can be found within the surrounding Pliocene calcareous sandstone and Pleistocene sea clay strata.

HABITATS

This walk leads through a range of habitats. First, there is a hillside carpeted primarily in kermes oaks. Such forests are rare on Zákynthos, having been cleared for agriculture — you will see the results of this as you continue the walk into the olive groves. Keep an eye on the roadside vegetation which hosts a variety of interesting flowering species, especially orchids in spring. At Dáphne you will see the remains of what were once embryonic shifting dunes behind the sea turtle nesting beach, now lost under sunbeds.

97

PLANTS

Spring

Orchids are abundant, with species such as pyramidal, bee, bumblebee, early spider, yellow ophrys, eastern yellow ophrys, sawfly, bug and tongue orchids. Other flowering plants to look out for include 'love-in-a-mist', tassel hyacinths, broom, white and pink rock roses, star of Bethlehem, tree heath, clovers, black widow irises, Spanish iris, gladioli, gageas, cytinus, buttercups, celandines, verbascum, arums and asphodels.

Summer

Due to the humidity created by the oak forest, fringe habitats include flowering species such as honeysuckle, capers, yellow star thistles, Christ's head thistles, galactites thistles, hawksbeards, geraniums, larkspurs, *Ptilostemon, Helichrysum,* wild onions, wild parsley, anthyllis, thyme and broomrape.

Autumn

This is the best time to see heather, myrtle and wild strawberry trees in flower. Keep an eye out for mullein, oleander and sea squill, too. Later in the season, you will also see the berries of the scrub trees. Look out for the acorns of the kermes oak, which stand out against the small holly-like leaves. The chaste tree is in flower during this period: in the past, its leaves were thought to preserve chastity; today it is used in eye medicines.

Winter

Species include cyclamens, anemones, Algerian irises, field marigolds, hyacinthellas, gynandiris, friar's cowls, annual daisies, spiny chicory and scented mayweed.

CULTURE

On the road to Dáphne, there is an arched bridge. This was built during British rule in the 19th century, in an effort to improve road conditions. Many such bridges were built during this period, and three remain in operation on the Vassilikós road to this day, integrated into the Zákynthos road network system. The bridges are characterized by their arches. The stonework is composed of large carved stones bordering the openings, with elaborate protective parapets adorning the upper regions.

AGRICULTURE

Traditional charcoal manufacture is a dying art in Greece. The pyres are built in spring. The ground is cleared, and logs are

From top to bottom, left to right: rock seam with marly limestone; the kermes oak woodland in the Dáphne area; broom; woodcock orchid; Barbary nut

stacked to form a stable base. This is covered with brushwood, which in turn is totally covered with soil to exclude air. The pyre is lit and monitored 24 hours a day for several days, to ensure that the wood doesn't ignite. Once the process is complete, the soil is removed, exposing the smouldering charcoal. It is doused in water to cool, drained and dried on a rack. It is sold in local markets for barbecues.

WILDLIFE
Invertebrates
Species include sand digger wasps, paper wasps, hornets, *Argiope* spiders, predatory ground beetles, rose chafer beetles, *Cataglyphis* ants, harvester ants, darters, dragon-flies, crickets, cicadas and bees. Among the butterflies are pale clouded yellows, painted ladies, admirals, as well as scarce and common swallowtails.

From top to bottom, left to right: abandoned dwellings in the hills above Dáphne; charcoal burning; garden spider; Balkan green lizard; little owl

Reptiles and amphibians
Snake species that might be seen on this walk include Balkan whip snakes, leopard snakes, Balkan green and wall lizards, Moorish geckos, and snake-eyed skinks. Among the amphibians are the green toad, common tree frog and green marsh frog.

Birds
Coastal birds include common sandpipers, common kingfishers, yellow-legged gulls, grey herons, shags and blue rock thrushes. Both owls and raptors have been seen, most frequently scops owls and common buzzards. Other birds that you might see include tree pipits, swifts, goldfinches, greenfinches, Cetti's warblers, olive-tree warblers, olivaceous warblers, Sardinian warblers,

ravens, quails, house martins, buntings, robins, pied flycatchers, red-rumped and common swallows, wrynecks, red-backed shrikes, spotted flycatchers, black-eared wheatears, golden orioles, great tits, sparrows, black redstarts, whinchats, stonechats, serins, turtle doves, redwings, fieldfares, blackbirds, thrushes and hoopoes.

Mammals
Species in the region include woodmice, hedgehogs, brown hares, rats, beech martens, pipistrelle and myotis bats.

Walk 4: Ksirocástello trail (Municipality of Zakynthíon)

Distance/time: 5.5km/3.4mi; about 2-2.5h.

Grade: moderate-difficult linear, walk, with an ascent of about 130m/425ft between points (3-6) and, on the return an ascent of 55m/180ft between (10) and (6); corresponding descents.

Equipment: see pages 85-86.

Travel: The walk is about a 20-minute drive (10km/6.5mi) out of Zákynthos town. Take the Vassilikós road via Argássi and after Ksirocástello village turn right at the sign for Dáphne. Follow the tarmac road up a hill and past an old quarry, then take the second fork to the left (signed 'Sea Turtle Thematic Exhibition'; park in the free car parking area.

Suggested time of year: any, but in summer only attempt the walk in early morning or late evening.

Protection status: National Marine Park: F1 Protected Natural Landscape and A1 Stricty Protected Area of Sekania: Site code GR2210002. *Be aware that access is prohibited to the internationally important sea turtle nesting beach of Sekania.*

Alternative routes: Here are three ideas for a longer walk:
1) Combine this walk with Walk 3 (Dáphne hills trail).
2) Make one long linear walk from Gérakas to the Ksirocástello hills (but you need to be dropped off/picked up at either end).
3) It is also possible to link up with Walk 5 (Mount Skopós trail), although the existing footpath is now overgrown. Turn right at the plateau, then cut off on the track up into the hills.

Additional suggestions: You can go for a swim at Kamínia Beach directly below Ksirocástello. For something cultural, visit the Nemorósa Folklore Museum in Vassilikós village or the National Park's Sea Turtle Exhibition near Dáphne, with photographic displays of the region's flora and fauna, as well as three-dimensional sculptures of turtles and videos of sea turtle behaviour taken in Laganás Bay.

Walking notes

From the **exhibition** (**1**), walk 175 m down the road and turn right at the junction (**2**). Remain on the tarmac road; pass the sign for Sekánia after 30 m. Immediately after this, two adjacent

View towards Banána Beach and Vassilikós from the Ksirocástello hills

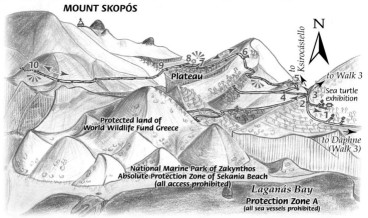

MOUNT SKOPÓS

Plateau

Protected land of
World Wildlife Fund Greece

National Marine Park of Zakynthos
Absolute Protection Zone of Sekania Beach
(all access prohibited)

Laganás Bay

Protection Zone A
(all sea vessels prohibited)

N

to Ksirocástello

to Walk 3

Sea turtle
exhibition

to Dáphne
(Walk 3)

tracks go off left (**3**): a gated track leads down into olive groves, the other up into **scrub vegetation**. Follow the uphill track for 280 m and, at the next junction (**4**), turn sharp right to continue uphill. After 190 m you pass through an **olive grove**, and veer left at a junction, ignoring the turn-off to the right (**5**). Continue uphill for 675 m, until the track levels off before descending, with views across Laganás Bay and down through the valley to Sekánia. Pass a gated right turn (**6**) and continue about 380 m down into a **valley full of olive trees**. At the **plateau** (with stunning

views of the east coast of Vassi-likós and across the sea to the Peleponesse), ignore two right turns 50 m apart (**7-8**) that lead down the east slopes of the hills. Instead, follow the track as it continues round the valley, after another 380 m descending through a dried-out **riverbed** (**9**). Follow the track for another 570 m, to where it ends (**10**), and enjoy panoramic views of Laganás Bay. There is a small hunters' path leading off the track, which you could follow a further 200 m, until it peters out. After enjoying the views, retrace your steps to the exhibition.

GEOLOGY

This area is in the Ionian Zone and includes Triassic evaporites and Plio-Pleistocene sediments (sea clays and calcareous sand-stones) made from fragments of organic skeletal material that have been reworked as a result of high-energy tectonic uplifts, erosion and folding. Seams of gypsum evaporites, dolomites, limestone psammonites, conglomerates of blue marls, Shelley limestone, fine silty clays and sandy marls also exist. Heavy winter rains and regular fires have caused extensive erosion in this region.

HABITATS

The semi-natural habitats occur primarily in the F1 Zone of the walk, which is on the west side of the hills. Because the area is regularly burnt, the represen-tative habitat, olive-carob, is highly degraded. There is a patchwork of thorny burnet, heather and thyme *phrygana* mixed with a riverside-type vegetation of reeds, rushes and sea barley which thrives near natural springs, along seasonally flowing streams and where clay is heavily saturated with rainwater.

From top to bottom, left to right: sandstone with gypsum seams; river vegetation; autumn crocus; anemones; pink butterfly orchid

PLANTS

Spring

Look out for orchids along the grassy regions among the olives on the plateau (7). There are butterfly, giant, bumblebee, sombre bee, early spider, yellow ophrys, eastern yellow ophrys, bug, sawfly, pyramidal and tongue orchids here. Look out also for cytinus, Barbary nuts, field scabious, field marigolds, lesser celandines, asphodels, hairy flax, mullein, larkspur, gladioli, broom, vetch, clovers and wild onions.

Summer

In this region you will find rock roses in flower until early summer and thyme in late summer. Broomrape is parasitic on the thyme, so the flowers of this plant — often mistaken for orchids — will also be abundant. Other flowering plants that might be seen in this area during the summer season include thistles, grasses, reeds, rushes, wild asparagus and wild carrot. In late summer the large carob beans are also ripe.

Autumn

Oleander will be in flower along the streams, as well as the distinctive white plumes of the reeds. More typical flowering plants at this time include cyclamens, heather, satureja, saffron, sea squill and mullein. Also the flowers and berries of smilax, wild strawberry and myrtle might be spotted.

Winter

During winter several species of plant can be found in flower here, including Algerian irises, white autumn crocuses, anemones, annual daisies, hyacinthellas, Bermuda buttercups and friar's cowls. Wild mushrooms might also be found in more sheltered damp areas.

CULTURE

The entire Vassilikós peninsula was once owned by the Greek Orthodox Church, which rented out land for farming. Today most of the land is privately owned. During the Byzantine era pirates frequented Zákynthos, so the inhabitants of this region lived in the hills to keep out of danger. The ruins of such dwellings can still be found today near a well built at the source of a natural spring on the east-facing slopes above the modern village; there are also the ruins of the 16th-century Ág. Geórgios chapel.

AGRICULTURE

On the east side, these hills are carpeted in olive groves, with some stands of ancient trees. Though sections of the west side of the hills have also been converted into olive terraces, most of this region remains undeveloped. Small herds of goats and sheep can be found grazing here, as well as ducks and geese. Some locals still use donkeys to take produce to market at Zákynthos town early in the morning during the summer.

WILDLIFE
Invertebrates

Invertebrates that you might see in this region include digger wasps, paper wasps, carpenter bees, hornets, *Argiope* spiders, garden spiders, ladybird spiders, predatory ground beetles, rose chafer beetles, scarab beetles, dragonflies, darters, lacewings, cockchafers, Roesel's bush crickets, Egyptian grasshoppers, scorpions, harvester ants, cataglyphys ants, and praying mantis. Among the butterflies are clouded yellows, graylings, scarce swallowtails, admirals, cleopatras and painted ladies.

Reptiles and amphibians

Common lizard species include Balkan green lizards, Balkan wall lizards and Moorish geckos. Snake-eyed skinks and Hermann's tortoises might be seen too. There are also Balkan whip snakes, Montpelliers and four-lined snakes in this area. The stream attracts green toads and green marsh frogs.

Birds

Among the birds there are house martins, swifts, pipits, goldfinches, greenfinches, Cetti's warblers, olive-tree warblers, olivaceous warblers, Sardinian warblers, ravens, quail, buntings, flycatchers, chaffinches, blackbirds, red-rumped swallows, tits, wheatears, golden orioles, black redstarts, sparrows, whinchats, common stonechats, woodcocks, European serins, turtle doves, redwings, fieldfares, hoopoes, thrushes and blackbirds. Birds of prey can be seen, too: buzzards, kestrels and short-toed eagles. Owls include the European scops owl and barn owl.

Mammals

This region has brown hares, hedgehogs, rats, dormice, pipistrelle, myotis and long-eared bats.

From top to bottom, left to right: donkey at Ksirocástello; the ancient hills well; darter; hedgehog; kestrel

Walk 5: Mount Skopós trail (Municipality of Zakynthíon)

Distance/time: 4.7km/3mi *(excluding detours)*; about 2-2.5h.
Grade: moderate, with an ascent of about 250m/825ft between points (1-6) and corresponding descent.
Equipment: see pages 85-86.
Travel: The walk is located about a 10-minute drive (6km/3.8mi) out of Zákynthos town. *Note: a 4WD vehicle is advised.* Take the Vassilikós road through Argássi. Just 20m after crossing a stone bridge, turn right (where 'Theodorítis Taverna' is signed to the left). Follow this dirt track 1.5 km up the mountain, to park at an abandoned quarry (1).
Suggested time of year: any, but only attempt as an early morning/late evening walk in summer. (But note that the Byzantine church of Panagía Skopiótissa is only open on one day a year: the Virgin's celebration day, 15th August.) Spring is the best time for fritillaries, orchids and other flowering plants.
Protection status: National Marine Park: F1 and F1' Protected Natural Landscape of Mount Skopós and Vassilikós. Natura 2000 Specially Protected Area: Site code GR2210002.
Alternative routes: There are several variations :
1) You can raise the grade of the walk by starting at the base of the mountain (A), thus climbing some 400m/1300ft — adding 1.5 km each way and making the walk 1-2h longer.
2) From Panagía Skopiótissa (6), follow the track for about 150 m, until it ends at a grassy knoll beneath a rock (B) with a 280° view to Kefaloniá, the Peloponnese, Vassilikós and Peloúso Islet in Laganás Bay.
3) From turning (C) just below Panagía Skopiótissa (6), follow a hunters' path some 230 m, to the peak of the mountain (D), which will afford you views of the loggerhead nesting beaches of Kalamáki and Marathoníssi.
4) When returning from the mountaintop, you can walk down the other side to Vrondónero and Kalamáki by turning left at point (5), via the working quarry. *It is a good idea to arrange to be collected!*
Additional suggestions: A good time of day to do this walk is in the evening, to reach the top in time for sunset and walk back down the hill in the twilight. That way you will see a range of day and night time wildlife.
You could also arrange to visit the Byzantine church of Panagía Skopiótissa on the 15th of August, to enjoy the festivities with the locals and admire the church interior, decorated in wood, silver and gold.

Walking notes

At the abandoned **quarry** (1), first enjoy the **view** across to the Peloponnese. Then follow the dirt track up the mountain. After the first set of bends you will have **views** (2) of Vassilikós and Banána beach, as well as the cypress and oak forest carpeting the hillside beneath you.

View to Mount Skopós and the Byzantine church

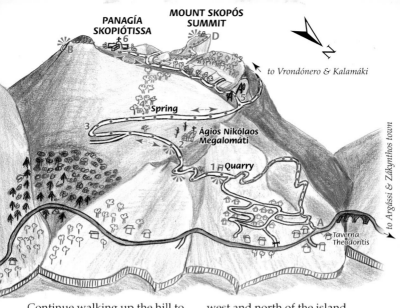

Continue walking up the hill to the next bend, about 1.2 km from the start (**3**): if you look behind you here, you will see the abandoned church of **Ágios Nikólaos Megalomáti**. Some 290 m further on, you come upon a wooded area where holm oaks shelter a natural **spring** (**4**). Some 500 m further on, at a track junction (**5**), there is a **panoramic view** towards the mountains in the west and north of the island. Turn left and follow the track for 210 m, ignoring all turn-offs, to a gated entrance lined with stone walls. Go through the gate and walk another 440 m up to the Byzantine church of **Panagía Skopiótissa**, surrounded by the ruins of a **Venetian fortress** (**6**). Now you have two choices (see Alternative routes 2 and 3 above) before returning the same way.

GEOLOGY

Mount Skopós borders both the Ionian and Apulian zones. It is composed of a number of rock types including marly limestones, Shelley limestone, coarse conglomerates with limestone pebbles, metamorphosed limestone dolomites, sandstones, mudstones, bluish marls, marly sandstones and alluvial sediments. There are also seams of gypsum evaporites and marble (a metamorphosed rock formed from limestone). There are two limestone quarries on the mountain, of which one (on the west side) remains operational.

HABITATS

Post-fire, regenerating *garrigue* scrub habitat is the most noticeable vegetation type on Mount Skopós. But several pockets of interesting habitats can be found, like the cypress and kermes oak forest carpeting the east face of the mountain and the semi-natural meadows by both the derelict church and the Byzantine church of Skopiótissa, which in spring host many wild flowers. Finally there are the stands of ancient holm oaks: although they are already diminished, still more are being lost to fire, logging and agricultural encroachment.

105

PLANTS
Spring

March to May is the best time of year to visit this mountain for flowering plants. Over 15 orchid species flourish in the meadows and under the scrub borders — pyramidal, giant, dense-flowered, bumblebee, woodcock, horseshoe, early spider, sombre bee, yellow ophrys, Reinhold's bee, eastern yellow ophrys, sawfly, bug, Italian man, butterfly, four-spotted, lax-flowered, tongue and long-lipped tongue orchids (look for them in the meadows near the two churches). Look, too, in the holm and kermes oak forests, for solitary violet birds-nest orchids. In April a small population of fritillaries (*Fritillaria messanensis*, particular to the Ionian Islands), can be found on the mountain-top. Other spring-flowering plants include: campions, yellow star thistles, Christ's head thistles, mallow-leaved bind-weed, *Malcomias, Euphorbias*, gynandirises, broom, grape hyacinths, gladioli, star of Bethlehem, wild onions, wild asparagus and asphodels.

Summer

Noticeable species include ferns, thorny burnet, chaste trees and elm, flowering thyme and parasitic broomrape.

Autumn

The fruit of the scrub vegetation is noticeable — carob, wild olive and figs. The acorns of the kermes and holm oak trees are ripe. Among the plants in flower are friar's cowl, heather, sea squill, autumn squill and autumn crocuses.

Winter

Cyclamen, anemones, mullein, ivy, moss, and toadstools and mushrooms are some of the species that might be seen.

CULTURE

Near the summit of Mount Skopós is the rebuilt (in 1966) Byzantine-style church of Panagía Skopiótissa; the surrounding monastery, now in ruins, was a fortified Venetian outpost. The church is famous for its icon of the Virgin Mary, which was brought to the island in 1435 from Constantinople. Pilgrims still climb up here on the saint's celebration day to kiss the icon. On the east side of the hill below Skopiótissa are the ruins of the 12th-century Ágios Nikólaos Megalomáti church; sections of the arches and tiled mosaic floor are still intact. (For more details of both churches, see page 50.)

From top to bottom, left to right: the operational limestone quarry on Mount Skopós; holm oak; Italian man orchid; crocus; black widow iris

AGRICULTURE

Ancient terraces can be seen on many parts of the mountain — for instance below the abandoned mine, by the derelict church, and by the Byzantine church of Panagía Skopiótissa. Today, farming — mostly olive groves and vineyards — is restricted to the upper part of the mountain, opposite the telecommunications pylons. Unfortunately, the expansion of these farming practices is a threat to the remaining trees in the ancient holm oak woodlands. These trees are also seasonally felled to supply the islanders with firewood.

WILDLIFE
Invertebrates

Due to the diversity of habitats and elevation of the mountain, a range of species can be found, including dragonflies and darters, rose chafer beetles, green beetles, myriad beetles, soldier beetles, tumbling flower beetles, Egyptian grasshoppers, Roesel's bush crickets, great green bush crickets, shield bugs, weavil beetles, frog hoppers, spiders, *Cataglyphis* and harvester ants, hornflies, and scoleaid wasps. Butterflies include clouded yellows, common blues, common and scarce swallowtails, marbled whites, red admirals, painted ladies, etc, while moths such as the tiger moth can also be sighted.

Reptiles and amphibians

Mount Skopós, being relatively undisturbed by humans, provides a good habitat for reptile species. Snakes include four-lined snakes, Balkan whip snakes, Montpelliers; among the lizards there are Balkan green lizards, Balkan wall lizards and Moorish geckos.

Birds

Bird species include common, Alpine, and pallid swifts, Cetti's warblers, olivaceous warblers, crows, white wagtails, yellow wagtails, blackbirds, goldfinches, greenfinches, bullfinches, whinchats and wheatears. Due to the presence of a good population of prey reptile species, raptors are likely to be sighted, among them the common and long-legged buzzard, common and lesser kestrel and the short-toed eagle.

Mammals

By day, brown rats and doormice can be heard in the underscrub, while at night bats (pipistrelle and miniopterus) are abundant.

From top to bottom, left to right: the Byzantine church of Panagía Skopiótissa; Zakynthian onions; common blue butterfly; Balkan whip snake; buzzard

Walk 6: Vrondónero trail (Municipality of Laganás)

Distance/time: 9.2km/5.7mi; about 2-3h.

Grade: easy-moderate, with an ascent of about 150m/495ft between points (6-8) and corresponding descent between (10-12).

Equipment: see pages 85-86.

Travel: The walk location is about a 15-minute drive (7km/4.3miles) out of Zákynthos town. Follow the signs for Kalamáki, then drive through the village and park above Crystal/Kalamáki Beach (1).

Suggested time of year: any, but only attempt as an early morning/late evening walk in summer.

Protection status: National Marine Park: P3 Nature Protection Site of Kalamáki; F2 Protected Natural Landscape of Kalamáki. Natura 2000 Specially Protected Area: Site code GR2210002.

Alternative routes: There are quite a few variations possible on this walk:

1) If you do the walk between November and May (when there are no sea turtle nests on the beach), you can start the walk on the beach (A). After 425 m, at the riverbed, climb slope (B) for 40 m into a field and walk 200 m along its seaward edge, to join the track leading out of the farm just after point (3).

2) At the fork at point (6), veer right up the lower slopes of Mount Skopós to explore two ruined churches (C and D).

3) The track heading right at the fork at point (6) leads up Mount Skopós, from which you can combine this walk with Walk 5.

4) At point (9), stay on the tarmac road for 200 m until it forks (E), then turn right to explore another church ruin about 500 metres away (F).

5) Extend the walk by about two hours: at the junction at point (9), continue 2.4 km to the end of the tarmac road; at the main Kalamáki road, turn left for 3.7 km to Crystal Beach.

6) Visit Hipsolíthos Rock (G) to enjoy views over the bay; between April and August you may spot a sea turtle swimming, basking or surfacing for air.

Additional suggestions: Take a dip in the sea at Vrondónero or Kalamáki — and you might be lucky enough to swim with a loggerhead sea turtle.

View from the ruined church of Ágios Andréas towards Laganás Bay

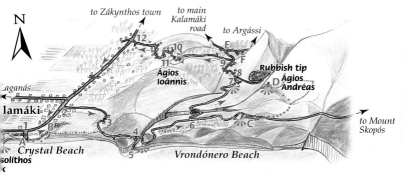

Walking notes

From the **car park** above Crystal/Kalamáki Beach (**1**), turn right and follow the road 1.25 km back into **Kalamáki village**. About 130 m before the left turn to Laganás, turn right along a tarmac road (**2**). After 250 m this becomes a dirt track and, 200 m further on, leads through a **farm** (**3**). Follow the track around a hill for just under 1 km, until it forks (**4**), where you can turn right to visit **Vrondónero Beach** (**5**), shown on page 57.

Otherwise, continue on the track for just over 1 km, to the next junction (**6**). Turn left and follow this track up the hill for 850 m, remembering to stop to enjoy the views across Laganás Bay. At the next junction (**7**) veer left to a tarmac road (**8**) and turn left. Follow this road for about 830 m, then turn left on a concrete track (**9**) which swings left. After 250 m turn right and continue for 150 m (now on a dirt track) through **two farms**. On the far side of the hill you join a concrete road (**10**). Walk 400 m down the road, veer left at a small junction and descend steeply for 150 m, to pass **Ág. Ioánnis** (**11**). Now follow the tarmac road 500 m, down to the main Kalamáki/Zákynthos road (**12**), turn left, and walk 2.2 km back down down through **Kalamáki village** to the car park.

GEOLOGY

This area, along the boundary of the 'Ionian thrust' separating the Apulian and Ionian zones, was subject to large-scale faulting and thrusting, hence the striking shapes and composition of the cliffs. It is geologically rich; the eastern part of Vrondónero Beach is dominated by dolomite rock, from which a permanent waterfall flows out of the cliff face. The foothills are of Pliocene calcareous limestone and Pleistocene sea clays, while the multi-coloured stones on the beach are evidence of limestone conglomerates, marls and evaporites.

HABITATS

There is typical reed bed vegetation alongside the spring behind Kalamáki Beach and the seasonally flowing rivers. At point (6) there is a large area of tall humid grassland made up of various reeds. Here and around the spring are orchid-rich habitats, in particular tongues. Thorny burnet *phrygana* is another dominant habitat of this region. The sandy and stony beach habitats support different plant species. There is also the erosive sea cliff vegetation, large sections of which are dominated by sea lavenders.

From top to bottom, left to right: waterfall emerging from limestone at the back of Vrondónero Beach; Juncus *reedbed; mullein; eastern tongue orchid; hyacinthella*

St. John's wort, spurge, lavender, vetches, gagea, clovers, medicks, lotus, mallows, lentisc flowers, wild pear tree, mulberry, fig and hellebores.

Summer
Several species can be found in this region throughout the summer, including wild onions, rock roses, thistles, cottonweed, sea lavender, fleabane, wild radish, yellow wort, thyme, wild asparagus, sea holly and broomrapes.

Autumn
In autumn, flowering species include scabious, mullein, spiny chicory, chaste tree, myrtle and smilax. The berries of the myrtle, smilax, *Rhamnus* and lentisc are visible later in the season.

Winter
Many plants flower throughout the winter and into spring —for instance annual daisies, anemones, Algerian iris, sedges, *Prasium*, mallow-leaved stork's-bill, lesser celandines, dandelions, buttercups, friar's cowl, hyacinthella, Bermuda buttercups, catchflies, fruit tree blossoms, field marigolds and several toadstool species.

CULTURE
Several churches may be visited on this walk (C, D, F and 11), the histories of which are vague. Of most interest is the Byzantine-style church of Ág. Andréas (D) on the foothills of Mount Skopós, built in the shape of a cross, with a central dome, monastery ruins and surrounding drystone wall (still intact). Kalamáki itself, hidden from the tourist strip, is a traditional Greek village, with its own church and local school.

PLANTS
Spring
Between March and May, the spring behind Kalamáki Beach and the humid grassland are rich in orchid species including the woodcock, bumblebee, horseshoe, Gottfried's, yellow ophrys, eastern yellow ophrys, early spider, crescent, sawfly, loose-flowered, bug and tongue. The tongue orchids may be found by the spring behind the beach and nestled among the tall humid grassland above Vrondónero Beach. Other species include asphodels, Barbary nut, gladioli, borage, mullein, honeywort, bellium, broom, Egyptian

AGRICULTURE

The area between Kalamáki and Laganás is a highly fertile alluvial plain and has been converted into agricultural land, with olive groves, vegetable crops and orchards of lemons and oranges. At Vrondónero, herds of goats and sheep graze the hillsides, as well as poultry. The quarry on Mount Skopós and the rubbish dump on the neighbouring mountain dominate the landscape. The dump is filling the cavity of an old quarry; when full, it will be re-landscaped.

WILDLIFE
Invertebrates

Due to the region being fairly damp, with watercourses and springs, a large range of dragon-flies, darters, lacewings and ant lions is likely to be seen. There are also scorpions, digger wasps, oriental hornets, bees, *Cataglyphis* and harvester ants, grasshoppers, praying mantids, stick insects, garden spiders, glow-worms, burrowing carabid beetles and predatory ground beetles. Some butterflies you might see are graylings, blues, coppers and scarce and common swallowtails.

Reptiles and amphibians

Hermann's tortoises can be found in the undergrowth of the scrub vegetation lining the meadows. Lizards include Greek *Algyroides,* Balkan wall and green lizards, snake-eyed skinks and Moorish geckos. Among the snakes are Balkan whip snakes, four-lined snakes, Montpelliers, leopard snakes and grass snakes. You are likely to see — or at least hear — amphibians too, such as the green toad, green marsh frog and common tree frog.

From top to bottom, left to right: Ágios Andréas, the Byzantine-style church on the foothills of Mount Skopós; cockerel; Egyptian grass-hopper; grass snake; reed warbler

Birds

Reed warblers, swifts, gold-finches and plovers are found here. Due to the coastal location, species like cormorants, shags, sandpipers, common kingfisher, grey heron and night herons might also be seen. Several sea-gull species, such as the yellow-legged seagull, frequent the area due to the rubbish dump. Among the raptors are buzzards, marsh harriers, lesser kestrels and red-footed falcons.

Mammals

There are hedgehogs, beech mar-tens, rats, mice and pipistrelle, *Nyctalus sp.* and long-eared bats.

Walk 7: Kalamáki sand dune trail (Municipality of Laganás)

Distance/time: 2.7km/1.7mi; about 1.5-2.5h.

Grade: easy; there are no hills, but you will be walking on sand, which can be tiring.

Equipment: see pages 85-86.

Travel: The walk location is about a 20-minute drive (10km/6.2mi) out of Zákynthos town. Take the road to Kalamáki, then follow the signs for Laganás, along a straight road running parallel to the coast. You will pass the Zákynthos Airport runway on the right and sand dunes on the left. The walk starts about 1km further along this road. Park opposite the Ileara Hotel (before the Zante Beach Hotel).

Suggested time of year: any.

Protection status: National Marine Park: P3 Nature Protection Site of Kalamáki; F2 Protected Natural Landscape of Kalamáki. Natura 2000 Specially Protected Area: Site code GR2210002.

Important note: The National Marine Park of Zákynthos asks that you use only the designated trail for this walk — to avoid further eroding these already fragile sand dune habitats. Also, please do *not* use the path running along the dunes fronting the beach, as it is a fragile shifting dune system which often has incubating loggerhead turtle nests in summer.

Alternative routes: If you want to remain on the beach, you can walk along the water's edge from Hipsolíthos Rock (by the Crystal Beach Hotel; see map page 109) to the natural fishing harbour of Ágios Sóstis (beyond Laganás; map page 117). It is a 6.2 km walk lasting some 2h. From the beach you will see the sand dune systems, tourism development, traditional fishing boats — and possibly a few sea turtles.

Note: The dunes change shape constantly due to winds, so the most visible routes are those made by the last vehicles. By all means, *do* explore other routes shown on the map, but be prepared to get lost for a while!

Walking notes

The walk begins opposite the **Ileara Hotel**. There are two gated entrances, about 100 m apart, leading into the **dune forest**; take the entrance on the left (**1**), opposite the bus stop sign. Follow this

The Kalamáki–Laganás sand dune system of Laganás Bay

concrete path for about 340 m (ignoring all turn-offs), until it curves to the right (**2**). Continue almost due south towards the sea for 50 m, until you have passed a **small dune** on your left and a **concrete water pump** (**3**) on your right. You will see a **second concrete water pump** 50 m to your left: turn towards it, looping round the dune to head due north for 40 m, until you join a track (**4**) heading right (northeast) through the dunes.

After about 160 m, follow the track as it bends left, ignoring any turn-offs (these change throughout the course of the

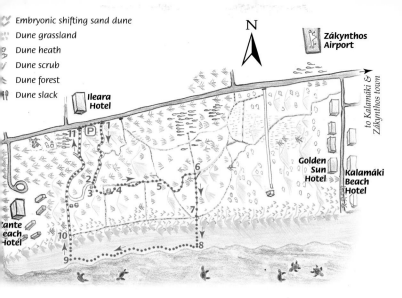

- Embryonic shifting sand dune
- Dune grassland
- Dune heath
- Dune scrub
- Dune forest
- Dune slack

Ileara Hotel

Zákynthos Airport

to Kalamáki & Zákynthos town

Golden Sun Hotel

Kalamáki Beach Hotel

Zante Beach Hotel

year, based on the most recent vehicle use of the dunes). After about 400 m, at a junction (**5**), veer right and follow the track as it loops back north for about 120 m. At the 'crossroads' (**6**) turn right on the track heading south. After 170 m you come to the **beach** (**7**), where there are wooden posts and a 'no entry' sign for vehicles. From here, walk the 50 m straight down to the **water's edge** (**8**) and head west along the beach, staying within 5 m of the sea, as there are unmarked sea turtle nests above this line. After 660 m (80 m short of the Zante Beach Hotel) you will see a **concrete path** (**9**) which ends at the top of the beach (**10**). Walk up the beach and follow the path 640 m back to the main road (**11**), then turn right for 100 m, back to the Ileara Hotel.

GEOLOGY

Prior to the 1970s, the Laganás sand dunes were a natural barrier separating a fresh water lake, Lake Makrí, from the sea of Laganás Bay. Laganás is in the pre-Apulian Zone, and is under-lain with Oligocene alluvial sediments of soft calcareous mudstone, marls, evaporites and silty-sand, while the sand dunes are set on fossiliferous marine clays. Winter rains are retained as 'slacks' by the underlying clays, forming natural underground reservoirs. Landowners extract this water to supply the neigh-bouring hotels.

HABITATS

All sand dune systems are highly dynamic and fragile ecosystems. The Laganás dunes are about 4km in length and 500 metres in width, with heights from 0.5 to 5 metres. They comprise six major, highly fragmented, stable dune habitats: dune forest (Aleppo and maritime pines, eucalyptus); dune scrub (olean-der, lentisc); dune slacks (reeds, rushes); dune grassland (grasses, *Euphorbias*); dune heath (rock roses, thyme); and beach front embryonic shifting sand dunes (sea daffodils) — altogether sup-porting over 100 plant species.

PLANTS

Spring

Due to heavy winter rainfalls, the dunes provide an ideal habitat for spring flowers, such as bellardia, asphodels, clovers, medicks, lotus, and wild asparagus — as well as rushes, reeds, cottongrass, cotton reed and grasses. The damp regions of the dunes and under-scrub also form an ideal habitat for orchids, including the Roman orchid, dense-flowered, sombre bee, early spider, crescent, bug, tongue and lax-flowered orchids. On the drier, raised dunes, rock roses and thyme-leaved fumana are among the flowering species. Within the dune forests, acacia and false acacia flower.

Summer

Despite being one of the driest months, August is the time to visit the fore-dunes between Laganás and Kalamáki — where white sea daffodils carpet the region. This species is protected by the Marine Park, as its populations are being reduced due to people picking the flowers or digging up the bulbs. Other plants that are in flower at this time include sea spurge, sea medick, sea holly and thyme.

Autumn

The pink flowers of oleander in the dune scrub and thyme-leaved fumana in the dune heath are most noticeable during this season. Other flowering plants include fleabane, sea squill and the autumn ladies'-tresses orchid. The fruit of wild pear, fig, lentisc, smilax and myrtle can be found in the dune scrub. Look out, too, for the mature cones of the Aleppo and maritime pines.

Winter

Species include *Euphorbias*, anemones and celandines.

From top to bottom, left to right: water seepage from saturated clay substrate; embryonic shifting sand dunes; maritime pine cone; sea daffodil; thyme-leaved fumana

CULTURE

In the 1970s many Greeks began emigrating abroad to find work. As an incentive to boost the economy, the Greek Government introduced tourism. Zákynthos is a mass tourism success story, from which Laganás literally emerged from the sand dunes in the late 1970s, to support the island's expanding tourism industry. The island receives over 500,000 visitors each year between May and October, of which over 60 per cent stay in Laganás. The official church, mayor's and police offices are actually based in Pantokrátora village, five kilometres away.

AGRICULTURE

In the region behind the sand dunes, Lake Makrí once extended as far as Zákynthos town. It was drained in the 1970s to build the airport and create agricultural land. This region comprises a highly fertile, alluvial rich flood plain, that often floods in winter due to the heavy rainfall. Vegetable crops, and fruits such as watermelon and fruit orchards are cultivated. The dunes themselves are under threat of destruction due to continued illegal extraction of sand for building material.

WILDLIFE
Invertebrates

Invertebrate species include darters, dragonflies, snails, Egyptian grasshoppers, mole-crickets, spiders, scorpions, oriental hornets, ants, praying mantis, ant lions and glow-worms, as well as several different beetle species such as rose chafers. Among the butterflies, clouded yellows, red admirals, graylings and swallowtails can be seen.

Reptiles and amphibians

Between April and early August the most visible reptile is the population of loggerhead sea turtles *(Caretta caretta),* which use the shallow, warm waters off Laganás as mating grounds in spring and to mature their eggs prior to egg-laying in summer. Other reptiles include pond terrapins, Balkan wall and green lizards, Moorish geckos, snake-eyed skinks and Montpellier snakes. Among the amphibians are green toads, common tree frogs and common marsh frogs, which inhabit the dune slacks and Laganás canals.

Birds

Raptors include the marsh harrier, buzzards and lesser kestrel. Barn owls, little owls, scops owls and eagle owls use the dunes as feeding grounds. Other bird species are the Spanish sparrow, moustached and Cetti's warblers, ringed plover, red-rumped swallow and thrush nightingales. Coastal species include sandpipers, curlew, egrets and kingfishers. Flocks of about 100 mute swans occasionally inhabit the flooded farmlands during cold winters.

Mammals

There have been sightings in the dune regions of beech martens, brown rats, eastern hedgehogs, brown hares, pipistrelle and European free-tailed bats.

From top to bottom, left to right: Laganás, with a sea turtle in foreground; lemon tree; common tree frog; mating loggerhead sea turtles; marsh harrier

Walk 8: Ágios Sóstis olive trail (Municipality of Laganás)

Distance/time: 5.9km/3.7mi; about 2-3h.

Grade: easy, only a gentle ascent of about 50m/165ft between points (13-14) and corresponding descent between (14-16).

Equipment: see pages 85-86.

Travel: The walk is about a 25-minute drive (12km/7.5mi) out of Zákynthos town. Take the Kerí road as far as Lithakiá. Turn left at the crossroads and follow the signs to Ágios Sóstis Port, where you can park (1).

Suggested time of year: any — including summer, because there is shade from the olive trees and you are just by the sea for a refreshing swim! Autumn and winter are a great time of year to walk this area, to experience the olive harvest.

Protection status: National Marine Park: T3 Tourism Development Zone. Natura 2000 Specially Protected Area: Site code GR2210002.

Alternative route: To avoid the sometimes-impassable shingle coastline between points (2) and (3), climb the steps to leave the beach at point (2) and follow the tarmac road left along the waterfront. Follow the road as it bends right and leads 175 m inland past a ceramics shop to road junction (A). turn right here; then, within 90 m, take the first turning to the left. Continue along this road for 250 m, ignoring any turn-offs, to rejoin the walk at point (B) and continue on to point (9).

Additional suggestions: Start the walk at sunrise, to watch the fishermen returning from a night's work in their traditional boats (but bear in mind that they don't go out on nights when the moon is full, as the fish stay too deep). Visit the nearby ruins of Sarakína Mansion (also a brilliant location for orchids) or other mansions and churches in nearby Lithakiá village. If there is a northeasterly wind, take a swim at Ágios Sóstis Port Beach between May and July, and you will find yourself in the company of twenty or more sea turtles! Alternatively you can take a boat trip from here to see the turtles or visit Marathoníssi Islet.

Walking notes

From **Ágios Sóstis Port** (**1**) walk 430 m past Cameo Islet and round the headland to **Ágios Sóstis village** (**2**). Continue along the coast for 1.6 km, past the **Pórto Koúkla** headland, until you reach the shingle beach of **Kamínia** (**3**). Here follow a path up the **cliff** (**4**) and join a tarmac road (**5**). (If you miss the path, follow the track up from Nostos Bar, 100 m further along, and turn left when you reach the tarmac road.)

Walk 135 m up the road, and turn right at the fork (**6**). At the end of the road (after 120 m), turn left on the main Pórto Koúkla road (**7**). Rise over a hill, ignoring a

The ancient olives near Pórto Koúkla

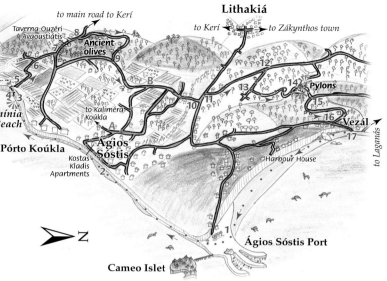

Lithakiá

to main road to Kerí

Taverna Ouzéri
Avgoustiátis

Ancient
olives

to Kerí   to Zákynthos town

Pylons

Vezál

nínia
Beach

to Kaliméra
Koúkla

Pórto Koúkla

Ágios
Sóstis

Kostas
Kladis
Apartments

to Laganás

Harbour House

Ágios Sóstis Port

Cameo Islet

tarmac turning left after 400 m, then turn right after a further 50 m (**8**). Follow this road 570 m, past **ancient olives**. At the next road junction (**9**), turn left. Walk 720 m to the end of this road (ignoring all turn-offs) and turn left on the main Lithakiá / Ágios Sóstis road (**10**). Just 30 m further on, turn right (**11**) on another tarmac road.

After 310 m take the first right turn, again on tarmac (**12**). After 130 m the tarmac ends; turn left here on a dirt track (**13**), heading gently uphill for 400 m. At the crest of the hill, turn hard left on a dirt track taking you in a clockwise direction past some **pylons** (**14**) **with panoramic views** of the region. After 100 m descend a steep concrete track for 100 m, to a tarmac road (**15**). Turn right and descend for 450 m to the main road (**16**). Turn left, walk 260 m down to the **beach** (**17**) and turn right along it for 630 m, back to Ágios Sóstis Port.

GEOLOGY

The island's south includes a long, continuous section of Miocene clays, marls, psammonites and sandy material, overlain with Pliocene calcareous sandstones capped with gypsum evaporites. Cameo Islet and Ágios Sóstis sea cliffs are sandstone, the hills by Sarakína Mansion gypsum. This region falls in the pre-Apulian Zone, affording panoramic views of the Cretaceous limestone formations of Marathoníssi Islet and the west coast and Plio-Pleistocene sandstone formations of Peloúso and the east coast.

HABITATS

Along the sandy and shingle beaches there are the sparsely vegetated cliffs, characterized by their geological strata (sandstone and sea clay) and dominated by sea lavender due to their proximity to the sea. In other places the cliff vegetation exhibits a mixture of *maquis* and *garrigue* composed of grasses and legumes, due to the proximity to agricultural land. There are several seasonally flowing watercourses, hence riverside reed, rush and sedge vegetation are also present.

117

From top to bottom, left to right: clay sea cliffs; sea lavender on sea cliffs; Bermuda buttercup; lax-flowered orchid; narcissus

PLANTS

Spring

The plant species that characterizes this region is the Bermuda buttercup; this is because it is one of the few plant species resistant to the agricultural chemicals used on the olive trees. From the beginning of March until early May, the orchids in the area include giant, bumblebee, early spider, lax-flowered, and long-lipped tongue orchids — although to find orchids you must seek out pockets of land that are not subject to chemicals, as these destroy the fungi on which the orchids depend to grow. Other flowering species include poppies, love-in-a-mist, St. Bernard's lily, wild asparagus, asphodels, vetch, fumitory, hyacinths, poppies, gladioli, wild almond and star of Bethlehem.

Summer

In summer a range of species can be found along the coast and on fringe habitats — the hottentot fig, sea spurge, century plant, chamomile, sea holly, rock samphire, sea lavender, Christ's head thistle, yellow star thistle, yellow bartsia, broomrape, *Pterocephalus*, prickly sow thistle, wild onion, thyme and pimpernels.

Autumn

Several species can be found in flower, such as capers, spiny chicory, sea squill, thyme-leaved fumana, mullein, oleander, autumn crocuses, common smilax and scabious.

Winter

Species include cyclamen, anemone, narcissi, jonquils, rose of Sharon, friar's cowl, annual daisies, buttercups, Syrian thistles, celandines and hyacinthellas.

CULTURE

The traditional settlements of this area are found along the hills on the main road leading through Pantokrátora and Lithakiá. The region hosts a number of architecturally important churches and mansions from the Venetian period, such as Lithakiá's 17th-century Faneroméni Church adorned with important works of Christian art. Country mansions include the baroque-style Sarakína Mansion, the decorative 19th-century Malouchou mansion and the Messala mansion in 'Seven Islands' architectural style, restored after the 1953 earthquake.

AGRICULTURE
This region is literally covered in olive groves. In some places, such as near Ágios Sóstis — between points (7-9) — you will see large olive trees that may date back to medieval times. Ágios Sóstis is a natural harbour, in which you will find a number of traditional Greek fishing boats. The Zákynthos fishing fleet includes about 250 vessels, of which 10 are trawlers; the rest are coastal fishing boats that use nets, trawl lines, latches or slashes.

WILDLIFE
Sea life
Sea turtles frequent the shallow sea here. The sea bed is primarily sandy with Neptune's seagrass. Starfish, crabs, flounder and peacock worms can be found. In the rocky areas between Cameo Islet and Ágios Sóstis, there are eel, sea urchins and anemones.

Invertebrates
In the pockets of semi-natural vegetation, there are Egyptian grasshoppers, froghoppers, shield bugs and scarab beetles. A large variety of butterflies can also be found, including the scarce swallowtail. Moths, such as the quite large emperor moth, can be seen resting along the clay sea cliffs of the region.

Reptiles and amphibians
Balkan wall lizards, Balkan green lizards, Greek *Algyroides,* Peloponnese slow worm and snake-eyed skinks can be found inhabiting the verge-side vegetation. Moorish geckos may be seen in the nooks and holes of the old olive trees. Snakes are fairly common, especially in the grassy meadows — Montpelliers, grass snakes and four-line snakes.

*From top to bottom,
left to right:
Sarakína Mansion;
fishing boats at
Ágios Sóstis harbour;
Neptune's seagrass
(Posidonia ocea-
nica); emperor moth;
hoopoe*

Amphibians such as the green toad and green marsh frog live in the seasonally flowing rivers.

Birds
Birds include goldfinches, Cetti's warblers, olivaceous and olive-tree warblers, tawny pipits, flycatchers, hoopoes, swallows and tits. You might also spot kestrels and marsh harriers. Owls can also be seen, especially in the boughs of olive trees — scops owls, barn owls, tawny owls or little owls.

Mammals
There are eastern hedgehogs, dormice, rats and bats (pipistrelle, *Nyctalus sp.* and *Plecotus sp.*)

Walk 9: Lake Kerí trail (Municipality of Laganás)

Distance/time: 5.2km/3.2mi; about 2-2.5h.

Grade: easy-moderate, with one gentle ascent of about 50m/165ft between points (6-9) and corresponding descent between (10-11). It is possible to shorten the walk to avoid climbing any hills (see alternative routes).

Equipment: see pages 85-86.

Travel: The walk is about a 30-minute drive (17km/10.5mi) out of Zákynthos town. Take the Kerí road via Lithakiá. At the signpost for Lake Kerí, turn left off the main road. Follow the road 1.1 km down to the sea, turn left, and park in the tarmac parking area 80 m further on (1).

Suggested time of year: any, but only attempt in early morning/late evening in summer.

Protection status: National Marine Park: Y and Y' Nature Protection Site of Kerí; F3 Protected Natural Landscape of Kerí. Natura 2000 Specially Protected Area: Site code GR2210002.

Alternative routes: Here are two ways to shorten the walk.

1) At point (4) continue following the track around the edge of the lake a further 360 m to point (A). To return to the car, you can turn right at point (A) on a tarmac road cutting 300 m across the lake. Or you can walk another 80 m down to the sea and walk back along the beach front for 300 m. This reduces walking time by about 1 hour 20 minutes.

2) At points (6) or (8) on the main Kerí road, turn left and follow the road about 1 km back to Lake Kerí village. This will reduce the walk time by about 50 minutes.

Additional suggestions: From Lake Kerí you can hire a boat to explore the sea caves of the Kerí peninsula or Marathoníssi Islet, but please keep in mind that the beach visible from Lake Kerí is one of the six protected sea turtle nesting beaches and is in Zone A2 (Nature Protection Site of Marathoníssi) and Boating Zone B of the National Park where mooring/beaching of boats is prohibited by Greek law.

Walking notes

From the **parking area (1)**, walk across the tarmac road signed 'to beach' and follow the dirt track edging the lake/marsh (keeping the lake/marsh on your right). You will pass an apartment block

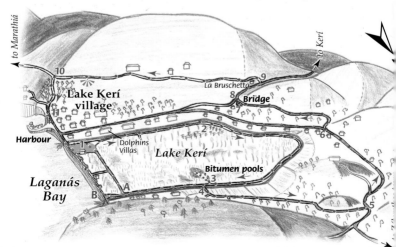

View of Lake Kerí fishing village from the Marathiá headland

with a dolphin painted on the side after 150 m and, 750 m further on, *Cladium* **reedbeds (2)**, which in spring host bog orchids — the only site at which this species is found on Zákynthos. Continue a further 640 m, to a first **pylon** on the lake side of the track (**3**). If it's not flooded after rains, turn right here and follow a raised track into the lake. You will see the machinery used for extraction and come to a dead end at the **natural bitumen pools**. Do not follow any other paths leading into the lake, as the whole region is unstable.

Return, turn right and, after 20 m, at a road junction (**4**), turn left on a tarmac road, away from the lake. After 160 m, bend left with the road, ignoring the right turn to a house. Continue 460 m through olive groves to the end of this road, where it joins the main road to Kerí (**5**). Turn left and follow the main road 620 m, past the turning for Lake Kerí (**6**). Keep on the main road for another 500 m, then cross a **bridge (7)** and ignore a second turning for Lake Kerí which comes up at once (**8**).

Some 310 m further up the hill, turn left at a junction signposted for Marathiá (**9**). Enjoy the **panoramic views** of Lake Kerí and Laganás Bay as you walk along this road. After 1.1 km, turn left down a steep concrete road (just before Villa Meltemi; **10**). After 350 m you'll reach **Lake Kerí fishing harbour and village (11)**, from where it's just 150 m back to the parking area.

GEOLOGY

Lake Kerí is one of the few 'pitch pools' (natural tar/bitumen up-wellings) in Greece (two other sites are in the maritime region of Laganás Bay). Bitumen forms as a result of the breakdown of organic matter during the laying of limestone strata, and upwellings occur only along tectonic fault lines. The lake is in the pre-Apulian Zone; its basin is composed of Upper Miocene clays, marls and evaporates covering Lower Pliocene marly limestones. Wildlife is often accidentally trapped in the waterlogged tar pools in spring.

HABITATS

Once, before the roads were built, Lake Kerí was a transitional freshwater/brackish saltwater lake — with freshwater from groundwater and hill runoff to salt water where the sea once mixed with the lake. Among the several important habitats are open water, tar pools, sedge beds, marshy grassland, *Juncus* rush swamp and reed beds — in particular the *Cladium* reed beds dominated by the giant reed, the common reed, the great fen sedge and the bug orchid.

PLANTS
Spring
Flowers include the large cuckoo pint, borage, honeywort, field marigold, common fumitory, vetch, clovers, grape hyacinth, prickly poppy, winter wild oat, and bedstraw. One orchid species, the bog orchid, can be found at Lake Kerí, primarily in the region of the *Cladium* reedbeds (unlike lax-flowered orchids, bog orchid flowers have white speckles). At this time of year look out also for the sharp rush, which has brownish flowers in a dense rounded inflorescence. In the surrounding area, giant, pyramidal, bee, bumblebee, horseshoe, eastern yellow and yellow ophrys, spider, sombre bee, Grecian spider, bug, milky, butterfly and tongue orchids may also be seen.

Summer
Because of the lake, many species thrive here in the summer, such as the yellow flag iris, *Galactites* thistle, pale bugloss, prickly saltwort, mullein, bunias, dorycnium, buttercup, grass poly, scarlet pimpernel, coris and wild carrot. Water mint can also be found; its oils are used in bath mixtures to improve blood circulation. The eucalyptus gum tree also flowers and bears fruit during the summer months; it is an invasive species introduced from Australia. Look out for the silvery plumes of the giant and common reeds — the common reed is shorter.

Autumn
There is stink aster, annual mercury and rock samphire in flower.

Winter
In winter a range of species can be seen in flower, among them the blue hound's tongue, crown daisy, sun spurge, mallow-leaved stork's-bill, large disk medick, vetch, plantain and lesser celandines.

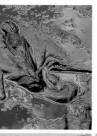

From top to bottom, left to right: squacco heron trapped in a natural tar pool; Lake Kerí mixed reed bed habitats; Cladium *reedbed; pyramidal orchid;* Galactites *thistle*

CULTURE
Since at least 500 BC, records (including the histories of Herodotus) have documented ships being brought to Lake Kerí's natural 'pitch pools', where the hulls were waterproofed with tar. In the 1880s, the tar pools were exploited commercially: tar was exported for the shipbuilding industry. However, since the 1900s the tar has been restricted to local use on the island (primarily for road surfacing), since the cost of export exceeded the low profits to be made from such limited natural assets.

AGRICULTURE

The Lake Kerí wetland is small, with a low water-table, so cannot be used for fishing or fish-farming. Up until 10 years ago, Lake Kerí and the surrounding region was used as a grazing marsh for domestic livestock such as cattle, sheep and goats. Because of the lake's peat bogs, the region is highly fertile, and hence the lake perimeter is constantly being encroached upon and lost to agricultural practices like vineyards and vegetable crops.

WILDLIFE
Invertebrates

The lake is an ideal habitat for invertebrates, and you will easily spot damselflies, darters, several species of dragonflies, paper wasps, freshwater crabs, water boatmen, frog hoppers, mole crickets and black water snails.

From top to bottom, left to right: tar extraction pumps; orange grove; common dragonfly; four-line snake; purple heron

Reptiles and amphibians

The most noticeable reptiles are the terrapins — either European pond terrapin, Balkan terrapin or red-eared terrapin. They bask in the sun on the banks of the peripheral water channels, though you will only be aware of their presence by the splash they make as they dive into the channels for safety! You may also see Greek *Algyroides,* Balkan green lizards, Balkan wall lizards, four-lined snakes, Balkan whip snakes, Montpellier snakes and grass snakes. Amphibians include green toads, common tree frogs and green marsh frogs.

Birds

You might catch a glimpse of great reed warblers, Richard's pipits, grey herons, purple herons, night herons, squacco herons, egrets, wood sandpipers, little stints, reed buntings, black-headed buntings, common snipe, black-winged stilts, wrynecks, yellow wagtails, greenfinches, Cetti's warblers, stonechats and bee-eaters.

Mammals

In the fringe habitats, brown rats and eastern hedgehogs can be found, while — due to the wealth of invertebrate species — this is an ideal feeding ground for bats (European free-tailed, long-eared and *Plecotus sp.*). In the river channels, eel and small fish such as fry can be seen, as well as gut algae — an indicator of water contamination.

Walk 10: Marathiá coastal trail (Municipality of Laganás)

Distance/time: 8.2km/5mi; about 3-4h.

Grade: moderate-strenuous; ascent of 100m/330ft between points (1-4 and B-7) and 250m/825ft between (7-8); descent of 100m/330ft between (5-7 and 7-B) and 250m/825ft between (9-1).

Equipment: see pages 85-86.

Travel: The walk is about a 35-minute drive (17.5km/11mi) out of Zákynthos town. Take the Kerí road via Lithakiá. Then, 0.8km after the sign for Lake Kerí, turn left at the sign for Marathiá. After 2.6km, park near the second taverna (Botsalo Taverna; **1**).

Suggested time of year: from September to May; it is too hot to attempt this walk in summer.

Protection status: National Marine Park: F3 Protected Natural Landscape of Kerí. Natura 2000 Specially Protected Area: Site code GR2210002.

Alternative routes: 1) At junction (7), if you follow the track straight on for 130 m, it splits. The track ahead ends abruptly after 190 m at precipitous limestone cliffs (B), giving coastal views above an azure sea, where you may even spot a monk seal. As an out-and-back walk, this saves an hour and involves less climbing.
2) If you turn left at the fork 130 m after junction (7), the track zigzags for 760 m down to the sea (A). An eroded footpath (care needed!) then leads down to the rocks, from where you can swim. About 100 metres to your left you will find a small sea cave.

Additional suggestions: After the walk, refresh yourselves while enjoying a view of Laganás Bay from Taverna Botsalo. Or perhaps walk seven minutes down to Marathiá Beach — a stony beach with fantastic marine life (take your snorkel and mask!). You could also take a trip to Marathoníssi Islet from here.

Walking notes

From Botsolo Taverna, just before **Marathiá Beach** (**1**), follow the tarmac road for 360 m, then turn sharp right uphill on a concrete road (it may be signed 'Marathia Mt Skopos'; **2**). Follow this for 500 m, past a sign for 'Villa Grades', to a T-junction (**3**). Turn left uphill, past **olive groves** and **old wells**, enjoying **views** of Marathoníssi Islet and Laganás Bay. After 200 m ignore a left turn

Precipitous limestone cliffs of the Marathiá region

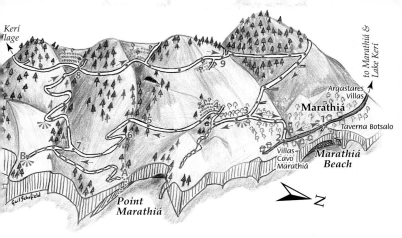

below new stone houses. Some 140 m further up, pass a **memorial** to Agios Dionysios on your left, where the concrete road becomes dirt track. Keep sharp left on this track 150 m further on, past a track joining from the right (**4**). After 310 m the track rounds the headland, and 430 m further on passes a **gorge** (**5**). The track then zigzags down the hillside, after 1 km passing a **view** (**6**) of a sea-carved arch on the opposite cliffs. Another junction comes up after 770 m (**7**). Turn right and follow the track uphill, passing another **gorge** after 450 m and an old **stone**

building on your left after 1.4 km. After just under 2 km you meet a well-used crossing track (**8**). Turn right, ignoring a track leading uphill, and continue around the hill, passing ancient dry-stone walled **olive terraces**. Ignore a concrete road on your left after 410 m and a right turn downhill 250 m further on. After just over 1 km you join a track leading down the mountain at a small **shrine** (**9**). Follow this 1.4 km down the mountainside, ignoring four left turns. When you arrive back at the first T-junction (point **3**), turn left, back to the start.

GEOLOGY

Marathiá is at the southern tip of the west Zákynthos mountain chain and lies within the pre-Apulian Zone. This region is characterized by marly limestone of the mid-late Pliocene and Eocene and flysch dated to the Oligocene age. The many caves and arches have been carved as a result of wave action and seismic activity. You may detect a 'rotten egg' smell near the caves or at Marathiá Beach, due to natural sulphurous springs seeping through the geological rock crust along tectonic plate fault lines.

HABITATS

This walk leads through several habitats of European importance, including *phryganas* dominated by dense, low, cushion-like shrubs like thorny burnet. There are *garrigues* of rock rose (*Cistus*), thyme and sage-dominated habitats. Cliff vegetation includes isolated pockets of Egyptian St. John's wort and stunted growths of juniper. Regenerating Aleppo pines grow across all the hillsides, while the gorges contain mature pines mixed with carob, wild olive, oak and wild strawberry trees.

125

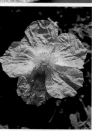

From top to bottom, left to right: the 'Bow of Marathiá' limestone arch (in the foreground); thorny burnet habitat; rock rose (Cistus species); milky orchid; black bryony

PLANTS
Spring
Spring is the best time of year to visit this region where, initially, flowering gorse carpets the hillside in yellow, followed by the mauve sage and then the white, pink and yellow flowers of the rock roses. Between March and May, orchids can be found growing under olive trees, in scrub and along verges; species include: giant, bumblebee, crescent, yellow ophrys, eastern yellow ophrys, Grecian spider, sawfly, milky, pink-butterfly and scarce tongue-orchids. Other flowering species include plantago, fumana, Barbary nuts, phlomis, fritillaries, tassel hyacinths, medick, black bryony and the toadstool-like plant cynomorium.

Summer
In early summer capers and wild onions flower, the buds of which are edible. Common fleabane, a rather nauseous-smelling plant, is in flower, too. Flowering thyme dominates the hillsides, while on the coastal cliffs shrubby ptilostemon, Egyptian St. John's wort and two species of sea lavender peculiar to Zákynthos (*Limonium zacynthium* and *Limonium phitosianum*) can be found in flower.

Autumn
The berries of the scrubs and trees are the most noticeable feature of this period, with the red lentisc berries, blue myrtle berries and the red wild strawberries. Wild blackberries are around, too — though edible, they are very seedy.

Winter
Cyclamen and crocuses carpet the ground layer under the scrub in early winter and are replaced by anemones and Algerian irises later in the season.

CULTURE
This region is a Protected Natural Landscape within the National Park — partly because of the habitats and geology, but also because Stone Age tools of the mid-palaeolithic period (200,000-35,000 years ago) have been found. The traditional method of drystone-walling the olive terraces is not only decorative, but it slows the drainage of rain-water to irrigate the trees, while also preventing soil erosion.

AGRICULTURE

The most noticeable crop in this region is olives. The initial part of the walk leads up through well-maintained groves. Along the outer peninsula you will notice old drystone wall terraces, some overgrown with scrub or Aleppo pines, and only a few with young olive trees. Herds of goats are kept in this area, and you will no doubt see or hear evidence of their presence during the walk.

WILDLIFE

Invertebrates

Many species of butterflies can be found, including scarce and common swallowtails, cleopatras, clouded yellows and skippers. Predatory ground beetles, rose chafer beetles, scorpions, stick insects, Egyptian grasshoppers, millipedes, centipedes, spiders, *Cataglyphis* and harvester ants, bees, hornets and wasps comprise a few examples of the wealth of invertebrate wildlife present.

From top to bottom, left to right: drystone wall terrace; kid goats; scarce swallowtail on thyme; Montpellier snake; Cory's shearwater

Reptiles and amphibians

The snake you are most likely to spot is the silvery-grey Montpellier. Other species include the four-lined and Balkan whip snake. Among the lizards are Balkan green and wall lizards, Greek *Algyroides* and Moorish geckos. Snake-eyed skinks can also be seen.

Birds

Olive tree and olivaceous warblers can be sighted among the olive groves. Species include turtle doves, hoopoes, blackbirds and whinchats, stonechats, flycatchers, bee-eaters, woodchat shrikes, wagtails, finches, sparrows, blackcaps, white-throats and swifts. The Eleanora's falcon nests on the precipitous coastal rock crevices of this peninsula. Scops owls and barn owls are common. In spring, hundreds of migrating Cory's shearwater pass these coastal cliffs. Audouin's gulls can also be found along the coastline.

Mammals

Evidence of mammals is sparse in this region, with rats, mice and eastern hedgehogs being the expected species. A variety of bat species, including long-eared, myotis and horseshoe bats, may be sighted flying and catching insects from dusk onwards.

Walk 11: Marathiá hills trail (Municipality of Laganás)

Distance/time: 5.7km/3.5mi; about 2h.

Grade: easy-moderate, with a gentle ascent of about 50m/165ft between points (6-7) and corresponding descent between (5-6).

Equipment: see pages 85-86.

Travel: The walk location is about a 40-minute drive (20km/12.5mi) out of Zákynthos town. Take the Kerí road to Kerí village. About 300 m after entering the village, there is a concrete bus shelter on the left: turn left here, past a war memorial on your right, up a steep tarmac road. Follow this road into the hills for 2km, to the first tarmac road on the left (1); park nearby.

Suggested time of year: any, but in summer only attempt this walk in the early morning/late evening. April is the time to find fritillaries.

Protection status: National Marine Park: F3 Protected Natural Landscape of Kerí. Natura 2000 Specially Protected Area: Site code GR2210002.

Alternative routes: Here are a few variations on this walk:
1) You can reduce the length of the walk (by about 40 minutes) by following the road in between the mountains between points (1-7), thus taking in either the northerly or the southerly part of the trail.
2) At junction (2) you can continue straight ahead and walk to the top of Mount Skopós (A) where, in spring, a wealth of wild flowers (particularly orchids) covers the ground.
3) If you're very fit, you can combine this walk with Walk 10. Point (6) on this walk corresponds to (10) on Walk 10, and (B) corresponds to (8) on Walk 10.

Additional suggestions: It is worth stopping and taking time to explore the streets of the old mountain village of Kerí on foot, to catch a glimpse of rural village life ... the old men sitting outside the local cafeteria, or the women outside their houses doing embroidery. If you visit in winter, you can watch the olive harvest in the surrounding groves.

Walking notes

View of Marathoníssi Islet and Laganás Bay from the Marathiá hills

This walk circumnavigates Mount Skopós of the Kerí region. Start at the tarmac left-hand turning where you parked (**1**): walk along this road for 135 m and, after passing over a hillock, turn left downhill (**2**) on a track leading into the **olive groves**. After 130 m turn hard right (**3**) on a track rising into the pines and rounding the mountain. From the west side of the mountain there are **views** (**4**) to the precipitous limestone cliffs on the island's west coast; from the east side you can take in **views** (**5**) to Marathoníssi Islet and Laganás Bay. After 1.3 km the track starts to

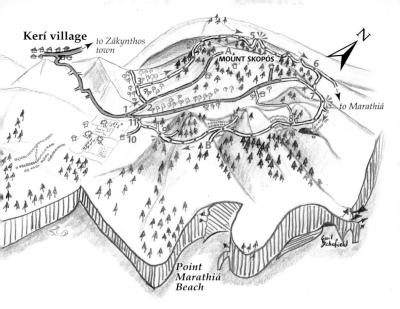

zigzag downhill, and ends after a further 790 m, joining the track leading down to Marathiá (**6**). Turn right and walk uphill for 590 m to the next junction (**7**). Turn left along a track leading out around the coast with **ocean views**. After 480 m, veer right to remain on the track, ignoring a left turn downhill. Some 240 m further on, ignore a concreted right turn (**8**). After another 420 m, at point (**B**), ignore tracks leading downhill and uphill. After this point, *keep on the outer track.* At point (**9**), you enjoy **views** of the precipitous coastal cliffs (look out for monk seals in the sea). As you continue along the track, the hills to your left open up into a fertile **farmed valley** (**10**). At the end of the track (**11**), turn left back onto the tarmac road and the start of the walk.

GEOLOGY

This walk offers panoramic views of the west coast pre-Apulian Zone limestone mountains. The southern section of this range is composed of white limestone rock of the Pliocene and Eocene periods. The mountains in the Laganás Bay area are Vassilikós Mount Skopós, rising to 450m/ 1475ft on the peninsula opposite, Marathiá Mount Skopós (around which you are walking; 400m/ 1315m), Kakávakia (416m/1365ft) opposite point (**9**), and the lowest, Mount Thirío (345m/1130ft), north of point (**4**).

HABITATS

This walk habitat is primarily comprised of mature Aleppo pine *(Pinus halepensis)* forests. The coastal phase of the walk, however, includes scrub habitats of typical Mediterranean *maquis* and *garrigue* interspersed with regenerating juvenile pines — which exist as a direct result of fires over the last 10-20 years. Semi-natural meadows are also a feature of the walk: they have replaced the once-farmed drystone olive terraces built into the mountainsides, which have now been abandoned.

From top to bottom, left to right: limestone rock formation; Aleppo pine; dense-flowered orchid; Ionian fritillary; goat's-beard

PLANTS
Spring
From the beginning of March until early May orchids include: giant, crescent, bumblebee, early spider, yellow ophrys, eastern yellow ophrys, Grecian spider, sawfly, bug, milky, pink butterfly, dense-flowered, tongue and scarce tongue-orchids. Early to mid-April is the time at which the fritillary particular to the Ionian Islands *(Fritillaria mesenensis)* flowers. The best fritillary sites are among the pines at point (5) and on the abandoned olive terraces of the west coast at points (8-9). Be sure to look out for Spanish irises, black widow irises, grape and tassel hyacinths, almond blossom, sage, goat's-beard, valerian and star of Bethlehem.

Summer
In early summer watch for yellow *Helichrysum* and rock roses in the bordering scrub of the abandoned terraces. Common fleabane lines the roads. Later in the summer thyme is in flower.

Autumn
There are mature Aleppo pine cones in the forests and the acorns of the Kermes oak in the scrub habitats — note how different these oak leaves are from those of traditional northern European oaks! There are many carobs in this region, so look also for the mature long green beans of this tree.

Winter
Cyclamen carpet the ground layer of the pine forest floor. You will also see Algerian irises, white autumn crocuses, annual daisies, sage, moss, lichen, toadstool and mushroom species that thrive in the warm, moist island climate.

CULTURE
Recent and visible historical remains are the traditional drystone walls of the olive groves and animal shelters, still in use today. Marathoníssi Islet was historically known as Pórto Ianáta. Two monasteries were built there in the 16th century, one dedicated to the Virgin Mary Odigítrias and another which the Venetians used as a watchtower. Byzantine and post-Byzantine ceramics and tools have also been excavated by archaeologists.

AGRICULTURE

On Zákynthos, about 40 per cent of the land is farmed. Because it is an island, unique varieties of plants have evolved and been cultivated to suit local conditions as a result of centuries of farming. Zákynthos has its own species of melon, onion, olive and grape. Other produce includes wheat, maize, fodder, pulses, potatoes, cabbages, round courgettes, cauliflowers, tomatoes and citrus fruits. In the last 20 years there has been a marked decline in arable land use, resulting in traditional agriculture and horticulture practices being abandoned.

WILDLIFE
Invertebrates

The floor of the pine forest provides a good habitat for a number of invertebrates, where the decomposing pine needles act as shelter and retain moisture. The rocks of the drystone terraces also provide important niches for a range of invertebrate species. If you overturn any stones in search of invertebrates, do so with care, and please replace them in their original position.

From top to bottom, left to right: drystone shelter; sorting the olives; hornet on a thistle; Balkan wall lizard; turtle dove

Reptiles and amphibians

If you walk carefully, you may glimpse snakes and lizards basking in the sun on the track and in the verges. Grass snakes, Montpellier snakes, four-lined snakes and Balkan whip snakes may be seen; Balkan green and wall lizards are in abundance.

Birds

The pine forest is a good place to search for blackbirds, wrynecks, hoopoes, cuckoos, turtle doves and golden oriole. Keep an eye out for buzzards, kestrels, peregrine falcons and marsh harriers. Tawny owls, barn owls and scops owls also frequent this region. Quail, sparrows, blue rock thrushes, firecrests, Sardinian warblers, collared and pied flycatchers are just a few examples of the species that might be sighted in this area.

Mammals

The pine forest is a good place to look for eastern hedgehogs. Bats are also resident in this region, with several caves and overhangs providing good roosting sites for horseshoe bats and myotis bats.

Walk 12: Kerí hills trail (Municipality of Laganás)

Distance/time: 5.7km/3.5mi; about 2-3h.
Grade: easy-moderate; a gentle ascent of about 100m/330ft between points (1-3) and corresponding descent between (9-14).
Equipment: see pages 85-86.
Travel: The walk location is about a 40-minute drive (20km/12.5mi) out of Zákynthos town. Take the Kerí road to Kerí. At the village square, turn right and follow the road towards the Kerí Lighthouse and sunset viewpoint for just over 1km. Park about 100 metres before the taverna, beside a dirt track leading left off the tarmac road (1).

Section of the Kerí trail covered in Aleppo pine forest

Suggested time of year: any, but in summer only attempt in the early morning/late evening. This region is a hive of human activity during the olive harvest in autumn and early winter.
Protection status: Natura 2000 Specially Protected Area: Site code GR2210001.
Alternative routes: There are a couple of possible variations:
1) At point (4), you can turn left down the hill; this will take you straight down to point (9), shortening the walk by 1.7km.
2) At point (7), you can continue straight down the tarmac road. At the end, turn left to reach the village square, point (10).
Additional suggestions: Explore the old alleyways of Kerí village, and visit the main church of Panagía Keriótissa in the lower part of the village. This trail also makes a good early evening walk, after which you can enjoy the sunset at a café adjacent to the Keri Lighthouse (480 m further along the tarmac road from the walk start). It is possible to spot Mediterranean monk seals from here.

Walking notes

From the parking place follow the dirt track (**1**) that leads left off the tarmac road, climbing gradually. Ignore a left turn after some 400 m. After 850 m you come to point (**2**): turn right off the track for 10 m to enjoy the **view of the Mizíthres outcrops**.
Return to the track and continue for 660 m, then take a small left turn (**3**). Stop at the clearing 20 m further on, to explore the **drystone walls**, **natural springs** and **old wine press** outhouse.
Return to the dirt track and keep on for another 210 m, to a fork (**4**), where you turn right.

Ignoring any turn-offs, walk about 1 km to the end of this track, to a tarmac road (**5**). Turn left and follow the road 430 m, with fine views over the valley on your right (**6**). Just before a sharp descent, take the first left turn, a concrete track (**7**). This quickly becomes a dirt track, passing **farm settlements**, **ancient olive groves** and **vineyards**. Keep to this track past all turn-offs for 600 m, until you reach a junction with another dirt track (**8**), where you bend right, downhill, on the main track. After 240 m it becomes tarmac, and a

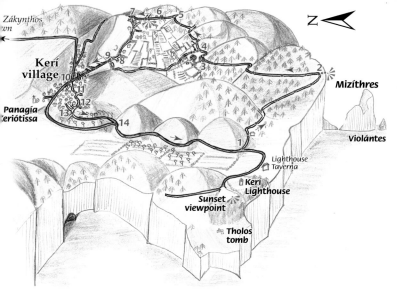

concrete road joins from the left (**9**). Continue straight down the tarmac road, passing a church on the left after 340 m and entering a **paved square** in **Keri village** (**10**) 60 m further on.

Still facing in the direction from which you walked down the hill, turn left at the lamp-post in the centre of the square (just before the main road to the lighthouse) and follow the concrete alley through the village. After 80 m,

opposite a grey house with bay windows, take the first right (**11**); after 20 m go straight on past a left turn (**12**) with a 'no entry' sign. Continue a further 70 m (past three right turns), then veer right on a concrete track (**13**). This becomes tarmac after 130 m and 70 m further on joins the main road from Keri to the light-house (**14**). Turn left for 650 m, past **olive groves** and a **cave** on the right, back to the start.

GEOLOGY

This walk has stunning views of the pre-Apulian Zone precipitous coastal limestone cliffs of the island's west coast — particularly if you visit the Kerí Lighthouse viewpoint. The Mizíthres and Violántes 'dancing rocks' are two parallel rocky outcrops rising from the sea. Their names date back to ancient times, to when Odysseus (Ulysses) returned from the Trojan War and was shipwrecked apparently due to an earthquake (… or possibly inebriation), which 'moved the rocks' at that exact moment …

HABITATS

This walk encompasses a range of habitats, including mature and regenerating pine forests, patches of *maquis* habitat comprising lentisc and broom, as well as *garrigues* and *phryganas* dominated by rosemary, rock roses, thyme, heather and thorny burnet. The grassy clearing at point (3) is a hotspot for herbaceous flowers from autumn through until spring. The precipitous cliffs provide habitats for junipers as well as a number of rare and interesting chasmophytic plants.

133

PLANTS
Spring
A wealth of orchids can be found here, including pyramidal, giant, crescent, bumblebee, woodcock, horseshoe, sombre bee, yellow ophrys, eastern yellow ophrys, Grecian spider, sawfly, bug, milky, pink butterfly, tongue and scarce tongue-orchids. The scarce tongue-orchid is a species particular to the Ionian Islands which can be found in high numbers among the thorny burnet *phrygana* at the Kerí Lighthouse viewpoint. On the sea cliffs the yellow Egyptian St. John's wort flowers can be seen. Other species include friar's cowl, broomrape, hyacinth, hairy flax and much, much more!

Summer
In early summer the rock roses carpet the hills in pink and white flowers, to be succeeded by the purple thyme flowers later in the summer. Thistles, broomrape, fleabane and capers can be found.

Autumn
Cyclamens flower everywhere in wall crevices and in the nooks of ancient olive groves. A species of particular interest which flowers in great numbers here is the autumn ladies'-tresses orchid, which grows in shady grassy knolls. White and purple crocuses, sea squill and spiny chicory can also be found in bloom.

Winter
The hillsides are carpeted in rosemary *garrigue* which, due to the mild climate, flowers at this time of year. You may also come upon rock roses flowering out of season. Lady's bedstraw, scabious, annual daisies and strawberry trees are all in flower, and a wealth of wild mushrooms and toadstools can be found.

CULTURE
The rural region around Kerí village is full of ancient and more recent relics. In a stone-walled field, near the clearing at point (3), there is a disused grape-press outbuilding. On the hillside near Kerí Lighthouse you will see the remains of an ancient stone-built 'Tholos' tomb. Mycenaean tombs can also be found at point (6) in the walk; engravings on them indicate an Eastern influence. The baroque village church of Panagía Keriótissa is believed to have once saved the villagers from pirates. It contains fine wood carvings and icons, and has a huge bell tower which can be climbed for wonderful views.

From top to bottom, left to right: Mizíthres outcrop; pine, juniper and scrub habitat succession; cyclamen; autumn ladies'-tresses orchid; hairy flax

AGRICULTURE

This region has a rich agricultural heritage. There are many olive groves, including several stands of ancient and wonderfully gnarled trees; keep an eye open for these during the walk. In winter, the alleyways of Kerí village are piled high with sacks of olives waiting to be collected for processing. Vineyards are the other major agricultural feature, while fig groves, small vegetable crops for home use, and collections of livestock also characterize the region.

WILDLIFE
Invertebrates

Due to the exposed rocky habitat, crickets such as the Roesel's bush cricket and Egyptian grasshoppers are easily seen resting on rocks. The spring-flowering rock roses, summer-flowering thyme, autumn-flowering heather, and winter-flowering rosemary attract a wide range of caterpillar and butterfly species. Other invertebrates include rose chafers, scarab beetles, shield bugs, lacewings, darters, dragonflies, spiders, ants, bumblebees, ladybirds, and praying mantis.

Reptiles and amphibians

Due to the wealth of invertebrates, snakes and lizards are abundant. Lizards include the common Balkan wall lizards, Balkan green lizards and Greek *Algyroides*, in addition to snake-eyed skinks. Numbered among the snakes are Montpelliers, four-lined snakes and Balkan whip snakes.

Birds

The combination of pine and scrub habitats provides refuge and a vital food resource for migratory birds. Species include hoopoes, turtle doves, redstarts, wheatears, thrushes, whinchats, stonechats, flycatchers, wagtails, finches, sparrows and swallows. Birds of prey such as falcons (for example, kestrels) and buzzards are common, and you might see scops owls, tawny or barn owls perched in the hollows of ancient olive trees. From the sea cliffs, blue rock thrushes might be spotted, as well as seagulls, terns and shearwaters.

Mammals

Mammals include rats, hares, hedgehogs, several bat species (for instance, horseshoe, pipistrelle, myotis and European free-tailed). The Kerí Lighthouse is also a good location to look out for Mediterranean monk seals.

From top to bottom, left to right: roof of a Mycenaean tomb; harvesting the olives; caterpillar; Greek Algyroides; yellow-legged seagull

Walk 13: Kentinária coastal trail (Municipality of Laganás)

Distance/time: 5.9km/3.7mi; about 2-3h.

Grade: easy-moderate, with an ascent of less than 50m/165ft between (1-2) and corresponding descent between (4-5).

Equipment: see pages 85-86.

Travel: The walk is about a 40-minute drive (20km/12.5mi) out of Zákynthos town. Take the Kerí road and about 2km after passing the Lake Kerí turn-off, turn right on a tarmac road signposted to Agalás. About 1.25km up this road, just before a hairpin bend, take the second tarmac road on the left (the first tarmac left turn leads up to a hotel complex). Follow this for 1.7km through a valley. At a fork with a dirt track (A), veer right, still on the tarmac road. Park at the next fork (1), where a tarmac road turns left.

Suggested time of year: any, but only attempt this walk in the early morning/late evening in summer.

Protection status: Natura 2000 Specially Protected Area: Site code GR2210001.

Alternative routes

1) Shorten the walk by about 1.5km/30min by not visiting the Venetian wells: just turn left at (7) and after about 170 m rejoin the walk at (12).

2) Lengthen the walk by 1.7km/1h by following the tarmac road to the right at junction (13); this leads down the seaward side of the cliffs, to a stunning view (B) of Kentinária and precipitous sea cliffs. From here *very precipitous, difficult* steps cut into the cliff lead 500 m down to the sea.

3) You can combine this with Walk 14 (the Agalás coastal trail) at points (9-11) by the Andronios Wells. Or you can expand the loop by 2km: take the road to the right at point (13) and rise over the hills to point (C) which correlates with point (6) in Walk 14.

Additional suggestions: If you return to the main Agalás road by driving back the way you came, you will have a fine view of Laganás Bay and the two islets. About 20 m before the end of the road, an old Mycenaean tomb hides in the bushes. When you finish the walk you could drive the tarmac road over the hills until it also joins the main Agalás road, and then loop back down to the Kerí road.

Walking notes

From the **parking place (1)**, take the main road uphill, into a **valley**. When it levels out (1 km) take the first left, a dirt track (**2**) passing a house set back some 75 m. Ignoring all turns into olive fields, continue 570 m to the next junction (**3**). Descend hard left here for 360 m into a small valley with **drystone walls** and **ancient olive trees**, then follow the track up a small hill to pass an old **stone barn** set off the track (**4**), with fine coastal views. Rounding the hill, you can see the Damianós Caves in the distant cliffs.

Some 330 m from the barn, go straight on at the crossroads (**5**) where tracks lead into olive

Kentinária Islet from the trail

groves. Ignore a turn-off left, but at the next fork (**6**) veer left to continue along the main track for another 330 m, then go right on the tarmac road (**7**). After 340 m you pass an **abandoned workers' dwelling** (**8**). Some 570 m further on, turn left (**9**) to the signposted **Andronios Venetian wells** (**10**). Walk 200 m, past the wells, to the end of this track (**11**), turn left and follow the track some 670 m through **ancient olives**. At the junction (**12**) turn right on the tarmac road, then go left on the dirt track (**13**) almost at once. At the next fork (after about 100 m) keep right (**14**), and follow this track 570 m, to a junction (**15**). Go straight on for 280 m to the next junction (**16**), by a quarry. Go left for 490 m, back to the start (**1**).

GEOLOGY

This walk crosses the divide between two different limestone formations of the pre-Apulian Zone mountain belt of west Zákynthos — the Mount Vrachíonas detrital limestones of the Cretaceous age and the Kerí marly limestones of the late-mid Pliocene and Eocene. There are also seams of Oligocene flysch. Limestone weathers easily, hence the many sea arches, caves and islets, such as Kentinária, that characterize the western coast.

HABITATS

This walk takes in habitats of mature and regenerating Aleppo pine forests, gorges of kermes oak forest, and wild olive and carob *maquis*. *Garrigues* of rock roses, rosemary, thyme and heather fringe the precipitous limestone cliffs. Juniper trees and chasmophytic plants, including sea lavenders and Egyptian St. John's wort dominate the sea cliffs. Kentinária Islet is forested with mature Aleppo pines and juniper habitats.

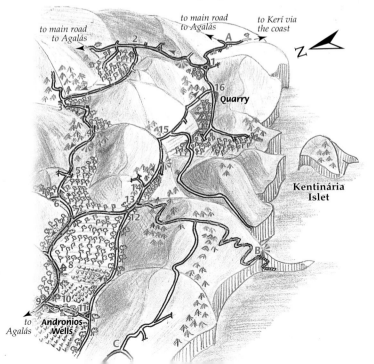

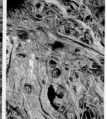

From top to bottom, left to right: limestone cliff overhanf and gorge vegetation; abstract olive trunk formation; field marigold; hybrid orchid; wild mushroom

mallows, capers, sea holly, fennel, thyme, rock roses, broomrape and fleabane.

Autumn

In autumn, heather and satureja carpet the hillsides, interspersed with the towering white-flowered sea squill. Myrtle bushes, wild strawberry trees and common smilax are in flower.

Winter

In winter a wealth of species can be found in flower, including cyclamen (on the ground among the roots and in the crevices of ancient olive trees), Algerian irises, Cretan irises, Barbary nuts, hyacinthella, putoria, *Helichrysum,* annual daisies, Bermuda buttercups, rosemary, spiny chicory, mayweed and field marigolds. There are also several species of lichens and moss that grow on the bark of the olive trees and on rocks. Along the roadsides and in the forests, a variety of mushrooms and toadstools thrive during the warm damp Zakynthian winters.

PLANTS
Spring

In spring the orchid species of the region include man, pyramidal, crescent, woodcock, horseshoe, sombre bee, yellow ophrys, eastern yellow ophrys, Grecian spider, sawfly, bug, Italian man, milky, lax-flowered, pink butterfly and scarce tongue-orchid. Other species that may also be found are asphodels, mullein, love-in-a-mist, hare's-tails, wild carrot, wild asparagus, sage, wild onion, wild parsley, pinks, vetch, clover, violets and fumana.

Summer

During summer, flowering species include campions,

CULTURE

This walk features views to the Damianós Caves and a visit to the 11 Andronios Wells (photograph page 69), built by the Venetians to provide a water source for inhabitants of the region. You will also pass several abandoned dwellings in various stages of disrepair. They were built to house workers during harvesting. The small windows on the north, east and south walls were to keep the house warm in winter and cool in summer. The west face of the house has the front door and large windows to allow in light.

AGRICULTURE

Olive groves are the dominant agricultural feature of this walk, from young crops to mature stands at least 300 years old — especially between points (3-4) and in the valley with the Venetian wells (5 through to 12). Take the time to admire the variety of abstract trunk formations. Around the wells there are vineyards, which are waterlogged in winter — ideal for this crop. There are also pockets of almond trees, cultivated for their nuts.

WILDLIFE
Invertebrates

There are the silky tents of the pine processionary moth larvae, honey bees, praying mantis, butterflies, bush-crickets, cicadas, Egyptian grasshoppers, spiders, predatory ground beetles, rose chafers, dragonflies, shieldbugs, ant-lions, lacewings, hoverflies, thistle gall-flies, bee-killer wasps, hornets and scorpions.

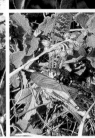

From top to bottom, left to right: abandoned workers' dwelling; almond blossom; praying mantis; Balkan whip snake eating an Egyptian grasshopper; barn owl

Reptiles and amphibians

Due to the *garrigue* and *phrygana* habitats and wealth of invertebrates, there are many lizards and snakes in this area — among them Balkan green and wall lizards, and Greek *Algyroides*. Snakes include the Montpellier, four-lined and Balkan whip. Tortoises may also be seen.

Birds

Birds of prey, including peregrine falcons, kestrels and buzzards, can be seen hovering over the mountains or precipitous coastal cliffs. In spring, rollers, hoopoes and bee-eaters can be found throughout the region. Other species include robins, blackbirds, thrushes, wheatears, warblers and shrikes. Scops owls

might be heard, and barn owls have been reported roosting in the sea caves of this region. Along the sea cliffs, swifts, blue rock thrushes, shearwaters, terns, seagulls and cormorants may also be sighted.

Mammals

Due to the many olive groves in this area, which — especially when cultivated organically — are host to a wealth of insect species, several bat species (horseshoe, myotis and European free-tailed) can be spotted feeding at night. Monk seals inhabit the sea caves of this coastline. There are also dormice and hedgehogs.

Walk 14: Agalás coastal trail (Municipality of Laganás)

Distance/time: 7km/4.3mi; about 3h
Grade: moderate-strenuous, with a descent of about 250m/825ft between points (2-8) and corresponding ascent between (8-14). Sections of this walk form part of an officially signposted route (PD Trail Number 14).
Equipment: see pages 85-86.
Travel: The walk is about a 40-minute drive (24km/15mi) out of Zákynthos town. Take the Kerí road and at the Lithakiá crossroads turn right. Drive through Lithakiá and up the mountain until you reach a fork, then turn left following the sign for Agalás. Drive through Agalás and park by the square (1), beside the school and telephone box.

View of the west coast of Zákynthos from the Agalás trail

Suggested time of year: September to May — it is too hot to attempt this walk during the summer months.
Protection status: Natura 2000 Specially Protected Area: Site code GR2210001.
Alternative routes:
1) You can shorten the walk by 30 minutes by not visiting the Venetian wells; just turn right at (A) and rejoin the walk at (5).
2) You can lengthen the walk by 30 minutes (2 km) by taking the track to the left at point (7); this leads out to the coast and loops back to the main trail below the house, just after point (7).
3) After joining tarmac at point (14), fork right and follow this road 2.6 km to the end, then take a signposted footpath downhill to view the Damianós Caves up close.
4) On joining the road at point (14) turn left; then, after 110 m, take the first tarmac road on the right (signed 'Milon Square'). This leads 440 m uphill, past an old windmill, to a fine panorama.
Additional suggestions: Explore Agalás village and visit the Museum of Zakynthian Nature. It is worth remaining in the area until evening, to enjoy the sunset.

Walking notes

From the square at Agalas, walk east on the road signposted to the Venetian wells (**1**), past the school and soon round a 90° bend to the right — along the gorge ridge. After 650 m, just before the road bends sharp left, look towards the opposite mountain for a **view** (**2**) to the Damionas Caves. 150 m further on, ignore a dirt track to the right (**A**), then a tarmac road to the right after about 350 m. But after 300 m take the *next* right (**3**), 140

a dirt track which leads in 100 m to the **Andrionas Wells** (photograph page 69).
After viewing the wells, follow the track 80 m to a fork and turn right (**4**). Walk 370 m past **ancient olive trees**, to a road (**5**), where you turn sharp left uphill. After 170 m, at the end of the tarmac, continue ahead on a dirt track, past a left turn (**6**). In a further 140 m turn right (**7**), after 50 m passing a house on your left.

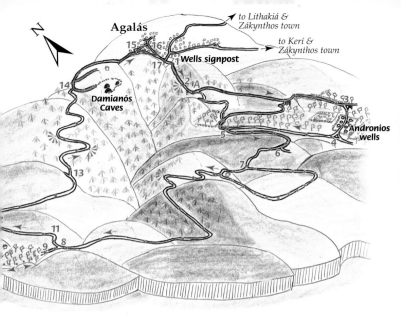

Follow this track 1.2 km down through the pine-forested gorge, across the gorge and then up a small rise where it joins another dirt track (**8**). Turn left down into an **olive grove** (**9**) and walk 130 m diagonally right (NNE), to the **cliff edge** (**10**), for a view along the island's west coast.

Then return to point (**8**) and take the track up the hill, bending left (**11**). Ignore a left turn after 450 m (**12**). 390 m further on, at the next junction (**13**), turn right. Zigzag up the hill on this track for 1.3 km, to a road (**14**). Here, turn left for 480 m, back into Agalás village.

Turn left down a concrete road (**15**) and walk 100 m through the **ruins of old Agalás**, to a tarmac road (50 m in front of the church). Turn right for 170 m to the next junction (**16**) and keep ahead to rejoin the main road (**17**); then return 130 m to the square.

GEOLOGY

This area is part of the pre-Apulian Mount Vrachíonas detrital limestone of the Cretaceous age, interspersed with Oligocene flysch (sediments produced by the erosion of uprising structures). The region is characterized by sea caves: while the entrances to some are visible above the sea, many also begin underwater and it is these that provide refuge for the endangered Mediterranean monk seal. Due to the porous nature of the rock, over the centuries the locals have developed ingenious methods of collecting and storing rainwater.

HABITATS

The primary natural habitat is the Aleppo pine forest. There are some mature stands, but most of the pines are young, regenerating after the last fire. The edges of the forest are composed of rock rose and/or rosemary *garrigue*. Chasmophytic plants, adapted to the water and nutrient-poor habitats of the precipitous limestone cliffs, are also found; several species are unique to Zákynthos.

141

From top to bottom, left to right: the Damianós Caves; regenerating Aleppo pine forest; putoria; eastern yellow ophrys orchid; sea squill with shield bugs

Summer

Numbered among the flowering species during summer are campions, mallows, capers, sea holly, fennel, thyme, rock roses, broomrape and fleabane.

Autumn

In autumn, heather and satureja carpet the hillsides, interspersed with the towering white-flowered sea squill. Myrtle bushes, wild strawberry trees, and common smilax are in flower.

Winter

In winter a wealth of species can be found in flower — cyclamen, Algerian irises, Barbary nuts, hyacinthella, putoria, rock roses, annual daisies, Bermuda buttercups, rosemary, spiny chicory, salvia, field marigolds, catchflies, broom and friar's cowls. A range of ferns, lichens and mosses can be observed growing on the bark of the pine trees or on rocks. Along the roadsides and in the forests, various mushrooms and toadstools thrive during the warm damp Zakynthian winters.

PLANTS
Spring

In spring orchid species of the region include man, pyramidal, crescent, woodcock, horseshoe, sombre bee, yellow ophrys, eastern yellow ophrys, Grecian spider, sawfly, bug, Italian man, milky, lax-flowered, pink butterfly and scarce tongue-orchids. Among the other species you may encounter are asphodels, mullein, wild tulips, tall bearded irises, love-in-a-mist, hare's-tails, wild carrot, wild asparagus, sage, wild onion, wild parsley, cynomorium, pinks, vetch, clover, violets, fumana, flowering lentisc, etc.

CULTURE

The Venetians built a group of 11 wells (photograph page 69) in an area called Andronios, about 2km outside Agalás. These were used to capture rainwater for the local population. It is possible that they also drew water from the Damianós Caves (two shallow caves lying one on top of the other) as part of the same system. Also of interest are the ruins of old Agalás, including old residences, a mansion and an old olive press, which can be visited. The village also has several old churches worth visiting.

AGRICULTURE

The main agriculture of the region is olive groves; young and ancient groves interspersed with vineyards can be found in these fertile valleys. Domestic livestock includes goats, sheep, poultry, rabbits and hens. You may also find groups of beehives in the hills; the honey (made by the bees from wild rosemary and thyme pollen) is collected for domestic use — and for sale to both locals and tourists.

WILDLIFE
Invertebrates

Due to the abundance of pine trees, the large silky tents constructed by the larvae of the pine processionary moth are abundant. The adult has grey-buff wings with dark brown lines and flies between May and July. Other invertebrates include bees, bee beetles, harvester ants, common blue butterflies, swallowtail butterflies, Roesel's bush-cricket, Egyptian grass-hoppers, *Argiope* spiders, etc.

From top to bottom, left to right: sheep; beehives; honey bee; pine processionary moth nest with caterpillars; yellowhammer

Reptiles and amphibians

Among the region's lizards are Balkan green lizards and Balkan wall lizards, snake-eyed skinks, and Greek *Algyroides*. Snakes include the Montpellier, four-lined and Balkan whip snakes. Tortoises may also be sighted in the undergrowth of this area.

Birds

This region has an ideal mix of scrub and trees for many different birds, which can be seen especially during the northern migration in spring. There are rollers, golden orioles, wheatears, Cetti's warblers, Sardinian warblers, hoopoes, yellowhammers, buntings, serins, shrikes, red-wings, rock thrushes, etc. Birds of prey include kestrels, buzzards, hobbys, and peregrine falcons. There are also several owl species. Audouin's gulls and cormorants can be sighted off the sea cliffs.

Mammals

Several mammals may be seen, including the eastern hedgehog and dormice. European free-tailed and myotis bats may be spotted roosting by day in the holes of ancient olive trees or in caves. The viewpoint at point (10) is an excellent place to look out for Mediterranean monk seals; the 12 seals currently inhabiting Zákynthos live in the sea caves of the west coast.

Walk 15: Loúcha monastery trail (Municipality of Artemisíon)

Distance/time: 10.4km/6.5mi; about 2.5-3.5h.

Grade: easy-moderate, with a total ascent of about 100m/330ft between (2-5/6) and corresponding descent from (5/6-7).

Equipment: see pages 85-86.

Travel: The walk is about a 40-minute drive (27km/17mi) out of Zákynthos town. Take the road to Lithakiá, turn right at the crossroads and go to Kilioménos. Turn left in the village square on the main mountain road for Ágios Léon and Mariés. After about 5km, turn left at the sign for Loúcha and follow this road to a T-junction with a windmill and the large Paliomilos Taverna, just before the village. Park here.

Suggested time of year: any, but only during the cooler hours in summer. Moní Iperagáthou's celebration day is 21 November.

Protection status: none.

Alternative route: You can shorten the loop by about 3.5km/1h by taking the first left at point (2) and rejoining at (7). There are also several paved pathways in the village that can be explored.

Additional suggestions: Take time to admire the lovely polygonal bell tower in Kilioménos — a stone-carved structure with engravings around the top of a skull and crossbones, key and lock, etc. Visit the stalagmite cave north-east of the neighbouring village of Girí. Alternatively, go for a swim in the sea on the west coast at Pórto Róxi or at the Limniónas sea caves, both accessible via Ágios Léon Village.

Walking notes

This walk begins on the dirt track about 20 m before the **parking place** (1). Follow this track 2.5 km over the hills, ignoring two right turns and taking in scenic views of the Loúcha valley and the west coast. At a **five-way junction** (2) continue straight on (the third track in a clockwise direction) — or cut up to the pylons for a **panoramic view** towards the monastery (A).

Continue along the track; after 530 m the pylon track rejoins from the left and, after another

2.3 km, down in the valley, you meet a junction (3). Turn left here on a track signposted to the monastery. Ignore any left turns, and after 650 m turn right (4), following the sign 'to the monastery'. Follow this track through the valley for 310 m, then turn right (5) to **Moní Iperagáthou** and its church (see page 68). From the monastery return to the track and continue through the valley, ignoring two left turns (6 and 7). After 870 m, at a junction (8), turn left into another, smaller

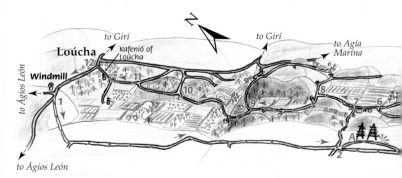

Mosaic of olives, vines and vegetable crops

valley. Follow this past a gated right turn and three turnings left. After a little over 1 km, at a junction (**9**), veer left down the hill, through the cypress trees and after 230 m you will come into the **Loúcha valley**. Follow the track, ignoring a turning right (**10**), for 1.4 km until it becomes a tarmac road (**11**). Ignore the right turn here: keep straight on for 400 m into the traditional stone village of **Loúcha**, soon passing the church on your left. After 220 m you reach the main road (**12**): turn left and walk 660 m up the hill, back to the start.

GEOLOGY

The Loúcha and monastery valleys are underlain by Oligocene substrata, while the surrounding mountains are of pre-Apulian Cretaceous limestone of the Mount Vrachíonas region. The limestone is highly porous, and as rainwater filters through the rocks to the groundwater (rainwater soaked into the underlying rock), it causes erosion and the formation of fissures, caves and sink holes.

Several caves near here have stalactites and stalagmites of calcium carbonate deposits.

HABITATS

The hills immediately behind Moní Iperagáthou are forested by kermes and holm oaks. Most of the rest of the region has been subject to fire, and hence is covered in regenerating Aleppo pine forests, *maquis*, *garrigue* and *phrygana* dominated by rock roses, thyme and thorny burnet. Cypress stands line the cultivated fertile plain, and were probably planted during Venetian rule in the sixteenth century for building material and for extraction of their resin.

Moní
eragáthou

to Kilioménos

145

PLANTS
Spring
Between February and May the following are some of the orchid species that can be found in this region: giant, bumblebee, woodcock, horseshoe, sombre, bee, yellow ophrys, eastern yellow ophrys, Grecian, spider, sawfly, Italian man, milky, lax-flowered, butterfly, four-spotted, man, dense-flowered, horseshoe and scarce tongue-orchids. Other species to look out for are wild asparagus, hare's tail and vetch.

Summer
In the mountains, rock roses, fleabane and yellow *Helichrysum* continue flowering into early summer, and thyme flowers from late summer into the autumn. In late summer look out for the bean pods of the carob trees.

From top to bottom, left to right: limestone rock formation; cypress stand; fungi; sombre bee orchid; hawthorn

Autumn
Flowering heather covers most of the region in early autumn. Wild pear trees are in fruit, and the berries of the hawthorn are out. Wild strawberry trees are in flower, as are wild parsley, vetches and satureja. Fennel is also in flower at this time; its leaves are collected for cooking, and they are also used to prepare olives for eating; here's the recipe: pick some green olives and smash them so that the skins break; put them in salted water and change daily for a week; then make a 7% salted water solution, put in the olives, add fennel leaves and flowers, and cover with one finger of olive oil; after one week or so they should be soft enough to eat).

Winter
Wild mushrooms, Algerian irises, cyclamen and white and purple crocuses carpet the ground. Look in the rock crevices for bedstraw, *Ceterach* ferns, mosses and lichens. Annual daisies and dandelions are also flowering.

CULTURE
The 17th-century monastery of Moní Iperagáthou (see page 68) was the first station of the Allied Military Mission set up to liberate the Ionian Islands from German occupation in 1944. Loúcha mountain village has an old church, a Mycenaean cemetery, and local women who still weave cushions and rugs on traditional looms. The surrounding hills are punctuated with old flour-grinding mills, and the fertile plain is dotted with long-abandoned dwellings still containing stone wells and wash basins.

AGRICULTURE

The fertile plain stretches almost continuously between the monastery and Loúcha, most of it a mosaic of farming — olive groves, vineyards, crops, wheat fields, fig and almond groves. In addition, several herds of goats and sheep, attended by herds-men, graze the surrounding hill-sides. Small vegetable plots are still maintained near old, abandoned dwellings, and free-range chickens roam about.

WILDLIFE
Invertebrates

Many invertebrates can be found in this region, including scarab beetles, cabbage white butterflies, admiral butterflies, bumblebees, pine processionary moths, etc.

Reptiles

Among the lizards of this region are Balkan wall lizards which inhabit the drystone wall crevices, providing them with niches. Hermann's tortoises can sometimes be found, too. Other species include skinks, the four-lined snake, Montpellier snake and Balkan whip snake. Near the many wells by the abandoned settlements you may also find frogs and toads. These wells are filled from the rainwater which is collected in stone rills that feed into them.

Birds

Many different kinds of birds can be found in this area — robins and blackbirds are particularly abundant. Buzzards and kestrels are an almost permanent feature, gliding along the mountain ridges or hovering over the hills. Many owls can be found too, including the barn owl and little

From top to bottom, left to right: traditional dwelling; sheep; scarab beetle; hare; robin

owl. Other species include thrushes, yellow wagtails, sparrows, larks, warblers, dunnocks, black redstarts, black-eared wheatears and fieldfare.

Mammals

Locals claim to have seen the edible dormouse in the oak forests, but it is more likely the common dormouse. The edible dormouse is characterized by a bushy tail — a bit like a squirrel. Typical species of the area include hedgehogs, rats and bats (long-eared, European free-tailed) which inhabit the many limestone caves and crevices of the surrounding mountains.

Walk 16: Korakoníssi trail (Municipality of Artemisíon)

Distance/time: 7km/4.3mi; about 3h.

Grade: moderate, with a descent of 250m/825ft between points (1-10) and corresponding ascent. *Note: be prepared to deal with unchained dogs on this walk.*

Equipment: see pages 85-86.

Travel: The walk is about a 30-minute drive (25km/16mi) out of Zákynthos town, and starts on the road for Pórto Róxi, near Ágios Léon. Take the Kerí road out of town and turn right at the Lithakiá crossroads. At the fork for Agalás, veer right for Kilioménos and, in that village, turn left for Ágios Léon. On entering Ágios Léon, opposite the petrol station, turn left on a tarmac road signposted for Pórto Róxi. Follow this road until the tarmac road forks after 1.3km (1); park here.

Suggested time of year: October to March — it is too hot to

Arch on the southern part of Korakoníssi Islet

attempt the full walk during the spring and summer months.

Protection status: Natura 2000 Specially Protected Area: Site code GR2210001.

Alternative routes: There are several variations that you can make on this walk:

1) The walk can be shortened by driving further along start of the walk (tarmac, then track).

2) You can arrange to be dropped off at (1) and collected at (10), so you do not have to walk back. There are also two alternative routes to Korakoníssi from Kilioménos: one, a tarmac road, leads to (7), the other, a dirt track, to (9) (see the fold-out map). If you can be dropped off and collected, you can join one of these to make an extended linear walk or create a circuit out of the two alternatives from Kilioménos. This would extend your walk to about 12km/7.5mi; about 3-4h, with a 500m/1650ft descent from Kilioménos and a 250m/825ft ascent to the Pórto Róxi road.

3) It is also possible to walk along the coastal track from point (9) towards Agalás, joining Walk 14 (Agalás coastal trail) at point (12).

Additional suggestions: If you do not feel fit enough for this walk, you can do the whole route in a 4WD (or by bike). *Do* explore Korakoníssi, including the arch and old drystone buildings. It is a fantastic location for snorkelling and swimming.

Walking notes

From the **parking spot** by the fork in the road (1), turn left. This section of road becomes a dirt track after about 500 m. Follow the track (sometimes tarred) through a cultivated valley. After about 460 m cross a small **bridge**

(2) and continue past several turn-offs.

Just over 1 km further on, at a fork by a **pine wood** (3), veer right and continue along the track, past several **dwellings**. After another 1 km track

148

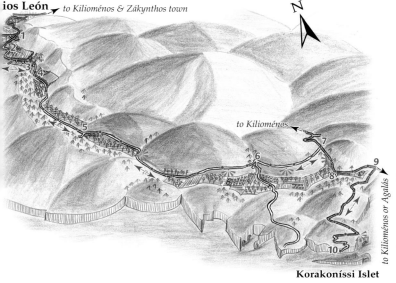

to Kilioménos

to Kilioménos or Agalás

Korakoníssi Islet

descends a small hill; you pass a **well** (**4**) and then several fields of **olive groves**.

After another 360 m ignore a turning to the right (**5**), and continue following the main track through a valley. When you reach the next junction after just under 1.5 km (**6**), continue straight on, but at the following junction, 420 m further on (**7**), turn right on the tarmac road.

Walk 220 m downhill and follow the road as it veers left at the next fork (**8**). After 260 m, at the next junction (**9**), follow the road to the right until it ends about 1.4 km further on. Then continue 280 m down a track to the sea and **Korakoníssi Islet** (**10**). Explore the islet and swim in the sheltered waters before returning to the start.

GEOLOGY

Korakoníssi Islet is composed of the pre-Apulian Mount Vrachíonas detrital limestone of the Cretaceous age. An anticline (fold) runs through this section of coastline, the intensive pressure of which has resulted in the 'giants' step'-like forms on the islet and some other unusual iron-rich dolomite formations. The southern part of the islet is dominated by a huge arch; it was probably once a cave, but eventually collapsed as a result of sea erosion and seismic activity. The surrounding cliffs are carved with sea caves and arches.

HABITATS

Patches of Aleppo pine forest — both mature and regenerating — can be found in this region. The primary habitats are *garrigue* and *phrygana*, including communities of rock roses, thorny burnet, thyme and rosemary. Along the precipitous limestone cliffs, a number of chasmophytic plants can be found, including Egyptian St. John's wort and sea lavenders. Korakoníssi Islet has an interesting mix of vegetation including juniper stands, *phryganas* and succulent rock plants, some of which are specific to the Ionian chain.

149

From top to bottom, left to right: limestone formations at Korakoníssi Islet; autumn squill; Helichrysum; scarce tongue-orchid; Algerian grape hyacinth

PLANTS
Spring
In March, scarce tongue-orchids can be found growing along the entire length of this trail. Other orchid species that may be found include include eastern yellow ophrys, yellow ophrys, butterfly, sawfly, sparse-flowered and bumblebee orchids. Fritillaries peculiar to the Ionian Islands can be spotted growing in large numbers in the Aleppo pine forests. Other flowering species include thorny burnet, stinking iris (on Korakoníssi Islet), Algerian grape hyacinths, tassel hyacinths, poppies, lentisc, celandines, glasswort, wild carrot, wild asparagus, sage, broom and asphodels.

Summer
In summer, flowering species include thyme, broomrape, fumana, rock roses and fleabane. On Korakoníssi Islet flowering sea lavender can be found all over the rocks.

Autumn
In autumn, the flowers of heather, satureja and wild strawberry trees cover the hills. Sea squill and verbascum flowers tower above the scrub layer. The berries of myrtle bushes, lentisc, common smilax and wild strawberry trees are also abundant.

Winter
In winter flowering rosemary carpets the precipitous sea cliffs. Later in the season Egyptian St. John's wort turns Korakoníssi yellow with its abundant flowers. Other flowering species include cyclamen, Algerian irises, Cretan irises, hyacinthellas, *Helichrysum*, Bermuda buttercups, rosemary, spiny chicory, field marigolds, annual daisies, catchflies and friar's cowls.

CULTURE
Despite the remoteness of this walk location, the ancient olive stands in the rich red-soiled fertile valleys adjacent to Korakoníssi testify to the fact that this region has been farmed, and most probably inhabited, for many hundreds of years. This is supported by the presence of drystone dwellings, domed drystone storage huts, established wells and drystone walls and terraces. Earlier inhabitants would have been self-sufficient,

supplementing their produce with edible wild plants, berries, mushrooms, birds, fish and cockles from the rocky shores.

AGRICULTURE
Olive groves, of various ages, are the most noticeable crop in this region; they were traditionally planted alongside the gullies to obtain the maximum amount of rainwater for irrigation. Vineyards are also present in the area. Herdsmen can still be seen, watching as their goats and sheep roam freely across the hillsides. Rabbit-farming is also quite common in the area. The most noticeable sign of any human presence is that of hunters and their dogs — after birds and hare.

WILDLIFE
Sea life
When looking into the clear waters around Korakoníssi Islet, sea urchins are immediately obvious. Other sea life here includes dogwhelks, smelt, mullet, pipefish, starfish and eels.

Invertebrates
Among the invertebrates are the pine processionary moth, Egyptian grasshoppers, bees, hornets, bee beetles, rose chafers, velvet mites, centipedes, harvester ants, swallowtail butterflies, Roesel's bush-cricket, wolf and garden spiders.

Reptiles and amphibians
Lizards include Balkan green lizards and Balkan wall lizards, snake-eyed skinks and Greek *Algyroides*. Numbered among the snakes are Montpellier, four-lined, cat and Balkan whip snakes. Tortoises may also be sighted in the undergrowth. In the sea, look out for basking sea turtles, some of which over-winter here and feed on the seagrass beds.

Birds
This is a good place to look out for birds migrating north in spring. Birds include hoopoes, rollers, golden orioles, wheatears, rock thrushes, warblers, redwings, blackbirds, etc. Among the birds of prey are kestrels, long-legged buzzards and Montague's harriers. There are also tawny and Eurasian scops owls. Seagulls, shearwaters and cormorants can be sighted off the sea cliffs.

Mammals
There are eastern hedgehogs, dormice, myotis and European free-tailed bats. Dolphins or the elusive Mediterranean monk seals may be sighted in the sea.

From top to bottom, left to right: drystone shelter; sheep with lambs; sea urchins; striped dolphin; yellow wagtail

Walk 17: Kampí coastal trail (Municipality of Elatíon)

Distance/time: 9.5km/6mi; about 2.5-4h.

Grade: easy-moderate, with three ascents of about 50-75m/165-250ft each (2-4; 8-10; 6-4) and corresponding descents.

Equipment: see pages 85-86.

Travel: The walk location is about a 45-minute drive (27km/17mi) out of Zákynthos town. Take the Kerí road and turn right up into the mountains at the Lithakiá crossroads. At the fork for Agalás, veer right for Kilioménos. At the T-junction in Kilioménos village, turn left and drive north through Ágios Léon. About 2km after Ágios Léon, turn left at the sign for Kampí. Drive down the hills for 2.5 km and into the village. Park near the square and church (1), by the signpost for the Kampí sunset.

Suggested time of year: any, but in summer only attempt the walk during the cooler hours of the day.

Protection status: Natura 2000 Specially Protected Area: Site code GR2210001.

Alternative routes: There are several variations:

1) You can extend the walk by 30 minutes (2 km return) by visiting the signposted Kampí Mycenaean cemetery (A) and taking in the views of Schíza Bay from the Memorial Cross (B).

2) You can extend the walk by 2 hours (5 km return) by turning right at point (9) and right again at point (C), to visit the Limniónas sea caves.

3) The walk can be reduced by 3 km (about 1.5 h, with an ascent/descent of about 100m/330ft) by making it a linear ('out and back') walk between Kampí and Katévasma Bay — from point (1) to (8) and back.

Additional suggestions: After the walk, visit the Kampí Museum, Mycenaean cemetery and memorial cross. Then drive back into Ágios Léon, and from there follow the signposts for Limniónas inlet, to see and/or swim at the sea caves and experience the beautiful turquoise sea. On leaving Limniónas, follow the tarmac road that forks right and leads around the coast to the Pórto Róxi inlet, set along a rugged rocky peninsula with more unusual limestone geology. You can return directly to Ágios Léon from Pórto Róxi to complete the loop.

Limniónas inlet and one of the sea caves (Alternative route 2)

Walking notes

From the starting point on the main road, facing **Kampí church** (1), turn left and follow the main road out of the village. Ignore the first (private) right turn, just past the church; 250 m along, take the *second* tarmac turning right (2). After 280 m, at a junction, with a small **chapel** on the right (3), veer left on a track lined with dry-

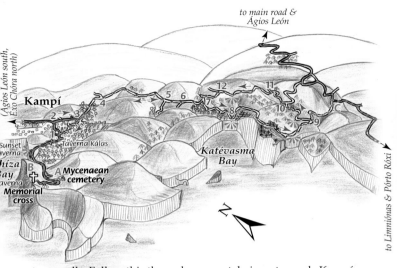

stone walls. Follow this through a valley for 1.9 km, continuing straight on at the next three junctions (**4**, **5**, **6**). At the T-junction (**7**), turn right and follow the track 850 m through a valley, to the stunning **viewpoint at Katévasma Bay** (**8**).

Continue on the track for another 1.5 km to the next junction (**9**), where you turn left uphill. After 620 m, at the next junction (**10**), turn left again and walk 1.3 km through the hills, enjoying the coastal views towards Kampí. Keep to this track, ignoring turns to the left after 360 m and 510 m, then a turning right 40 m further on (**11**). At the next fork (**12**), turn left and descend 700 m into the valley, back to the junction at point (**7**).

From here retrace your steps to the fork in the road by the small chapel (**3**), veer left, and walk 270 m along a paved road through **old Kampí village** to the church and square in Kampí.

GEOLOGY

The precipitous white cliffs and surrounding hills of this region are composed of the Mount Vrachíonas region detrital limestone of the Cretaceous age. During the walk it is worth stopping to view the precipitous cliffs of Schíza Bay at Kampí and, later, the rock formation at Katévasma (which, literally translated, means 'straight down') Bay — where a fault line has resulted in the dipping, folding and vertical uplifting of the rocks. Nearby Limniónas inlet has several limestone sea caves that swimmers can explore.

HABITATS

Due to the frequency with which these hills are deliberately burnt, *garrigue* and *phrygana* vegetation are the primary habitats — although in areas that have not been burnt for at least five years new growth of young pine trees speckles the hillsides. Pockets of *maquis* may be found in sheltered hollows, in gullies or where hills join. Along the cliffs, or on hills separated by deep gorges, mature Aleppo pine forests are the dominant habitat.

153

From top to bottom, left to right: view of precipitous sea cliffs from the trail; gorge forested with Aleppo pines; Cretan irises; bumblebee orchid; sea stock

PLANTS

Spring

In spring, broom, sea stock and rock roses carpet the hills of this region. Orchid species can be found on the verges of cultivated land, in abandoned meadows and sheltered under scrub vegetation; among their number are dense-flowered, crescent, bumblebee, woodcock, funeral, horseshoe, sombre bee, yellow ophrys, eastern yellow ophrys, Grecian spider, sawfly, Italian man, lax-flowered, pink butterfly, four-spotted and scarce tongue-orchids.

Summer

In summer, the hills are carpeted with flowering thyme, broom-rape, capers and fleabane.

Autumn

In autumn, heather and satureja carpet the hillsides, interspersed with the towering white-flowered sea squill. Myrtle, lentisc, the wild strawberry tree and common smilax flower and produce berries during this period.

Winter

Rosemary flowers carpet the hillsides and cliff edges during the winter months. Other species include hyacinthellas, narcissi, mayweed, annual daisies, field marigolds, Bermuda buttercups, spiny chicory, cyclamens, and catchflies. In winter both Algerian irises and Cretan irises can be found (the two species are very similar but can be distin-guished by leaf width; the former have a width of 7-15mm, while the latter are less than 3mm wide). Mushrooms flourish after heavy rainfalls in winter, and local people can be found searching the scrub of this region for edible delicacies.

CULTURE

Kampí is a small, traditional mountain village built at the edge of the 300-metre-high cliffs of Schíza. It has one of the most prominent landmarks on Zákynthos — a giant memorial cross honouring the resistance fighters during the civil war who were sent to their deaths over the cliff edge. This cliff is also the site of an ancient Mycenaean graveyard with several engraved tombs. Kampí village also has a small and interesting folk museum with domestic and agricultural paraphernalia.

AGRICULTURE

During the walk you will notice many beehives, the honey of which can be found for sale in the village of Kampí. The hills of this region remain mostly uncultivated and are grazed by several herds of goats and sheep. Closer to the village of Kampí, there are vineyards and several olive groves set among drystone walled fields — some of them fairly ancient, dating back about 300 or more years. Drystone walls are a beautiful tradition of the mountain villages and a skill that is almost lost.

WILDLIFE
Invertebrates

Between spring and autumn honey bees are the most noticeable insect, due to the abundance of managed beehives in this region. Other species include bumblebees, wasps, hornets, cicadas, grasshoppers, bush-crickets, predatory ground beetles, bloody-nosed beetles, spiders, scorpions, etc.

From top to bottom, left to right: Kampí's Mycenaean cemetery; free-grazing goats; bloody-nosed beetle; Moorish gecko; kingfisher

Reptiles and amphibians

Among the lizards are Balkan green and wall lizards, skinks, Moorish geckos and Greek *Algyroides*. Snakes include the Montpellier, four-lined, leopard, grass and Balkan whip snakes. Tortoises are also present.

Birds

In spring, the hoopoe, an elegant and distinctive bird, can easily be spotted in this region searching for insect food among the scrub. Other spring and summer migrants include nightjars, turtle doves, wheatears, warblers, whinchats and swifts. Among the resident and overwintering species are robins, blackbirds, thrushes, wrens, dunnocks, wagtails, larks, fieldfare and rock thrushes. Kingfishers can also be spotted in coastal areas. Birds of prey include buzzards, hobbies and kestrels. Seagulls, terns, shearwaters and cormorants can be sighted off the sea cliffs.

Mammals

Land mammals include hedgehogs, dormice, hares, martens and several bat species (myotis, European free-tailed). In the sea, the resident Mediterranean monk seals might be spotted along the coast — or migratory species such as bottlenose and common dolphins.

Walk 18: Éxo Chóra trail (Municipality of Elatíon)

Distance/time: 6km/3.7mi; about 2-3h.

Grade: easy-moderate, with two 50m/165ft descents between points (1-2) and (6-7) and corresponding ascents (2-3; 10-1).

Note: Some tracks may be fenced off at different times of the year, to corral livestock. *Close any fences securely behind you!*

Equipment: see pages 85-86.

Travel: The walk is about a 45-minute drive (29km/18mi) out of Zákynthos town. Take the Kerí road and turn right at the Lithakiá crossroads. At the fork for Agalás, veer right for Kilioménos. In Kilioménos turn left and follow the mountain road to Ágios Léon and on to Éxo Chóra. Opposite Éxo Chóra village square, turn left (signposted for Lákkos Venetian Watchtower) and follow the tarmac road 300 m to a chapel and cemetery. Veer left after the chapel and after another 230 m veer right, passing a left turn. After another 320 m, park opposite the second tarmac turning left (1).

Suggested time of year: any, but only attempt in early morning or late evening during summer.

Protection status: Natura 2000 Specially Protected Area: Site code GR2210001.

Alternative routes: There are two ways to make this walk longer: 1) At junction (9), you could turn left and descend 130m/430ft (40 minutes) to the Lákkos Venetian Watchtower at point (A). Allow an hour to walk back up. Or continue down to Almirás Bay (B) — a total descent/ascent of 250m/825ft: allow an hour down and two hours to climb back up. 2) You could visit Ágios Chará-lambos. Turn left at junction (10), and continue straight along this road to the little church. Allow about 1 hour there and back, with negligible ups and downs.

Additional suggestions: If you have a 4WD vehicle, be sure to visit the Lákkos Venetian Watchtower (A) and drive down for a swim in the sea in the cove (B) beneath the tower. The road to the Charálambos church is tarmac, and it is well worth visiting. Spend some time in Éxo Chóra village, too, to explore the church, square and Venetian wells.

Walking notes

From the junction (**1**), turn left down the tarmac road, which becomes a dirt track after about 350 m. After another 850 m you

Lákkos Venetian Watchtower (Alternative route 1)

will arrive at a junction (**2**). Do not turn left for Kampi; continue down the track for 320 m. About 100 m after passing through an olive grove, turn left on a small path for 40 m, for stunning **views** from the cliff edge.

Return to the main track and walk 860 m uphill, until the track ends in a small **clearing** with a drystone wall ahead (**3**). Bear right down a track surrounded by woodland, keeping the **drystone wall** on your left. About 170 m from the brow, the track

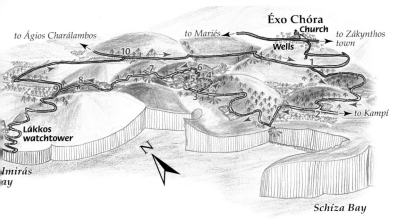

to Ágios Charálambos • to Mariés • **Éxo Chóra** • Church • to Zákynthos town
Wells
10 • 7 • 6 • 4 • 5 • 3 • 8 • 9 • 1 • 2 • to Kampí
Lákkos watchtower
Imirás ay
N
Schíza Bay

ends (**4**). Turn left, passing through a gap in the drystone wall, into a field with olive trees and old buildings. Walk diagonally west up the valley for 110 m, towards an olive tree above a drystone wall. Just before the olive tree there is a large lentisc bush against the wall: turn due north here on a stone footpath (**5**), which becomes clearer after about 10 m. (The footpath starts 20 m before the raised wall in the field.) After 30 m the path meets a raised **drystone wall** on your left. Keep the stone wall on your left for 140 m, until the path becomes a wide dirt track (sometimes fenced for goats). Bear left here (**6**) and follow the track gently downhill. After 180 m the track bends right; 100 m further on, at a fork, veer left to continue on the main track (**7**). Walk 240 m down the track into an olive grove, then follow the track uphill a further 310 m (ignoring tracks into fields at point **8**) until it joins the tarmac road (**9**). Turn right here and walk 1.2 km to a T-junction (**10**). Now turn right and follow the tarmac road up the hill, back to the starting point.

GEOLOGY

This region is representative of the detrital limestone of the Mount Vrachíonas pre-Apulian Zone. Detrital limestone is derived from pre-existing rocks as a result of weathering or erosion. Two fault lines occur in this region, which has led to the uplifting of the coastal cliffs. There is also a groundwater course passing through the area. The limestone was created by billions and billions of shells from tiny microscopic ocean organisms falling to the floor and being compressed over a long period of time to become rock.

HABITATS

This region forms a mosaic of habitats, the most apparent being the regenerating Aleppo pines. Some mature stands have survived, among pockets of cypress trees (introduced by the Venetians for shipbuilding material). There is also *maquis* of carob and kermes oak, rock rose *garrigues* and thorny burnet *phryganas*. Small patches of grasslands on the edge of meadows and in forests support a wide range of flower species.

PLANTS

Spring

The orchid species of this area include Ionian tongue, yellow ophrys, sawfly, pink butterfly, Italian man, bug, Gottfried's, bumblebee, woodcock and four-spot orchids. Among other species in flower at this time are anemones, black widow irises, grape hyacinths, lesser celandines, Barbary nuts, chamomile, field marigolds, Bermuda buttercups, thorny burnet, tree heath and broomrape.

Summer

Several different types of rock roses carpet the sea cliffs in white, pinks and yellow. There is also thyme, on which broomrape can be found living parasitically.

Autumn

Heather and sea squill flower across the region. The many carob trees produce long green beans, and the kermes oak produces acorns at this time. Among other flowering species are lady's bedstraw and myrtle.

Winter

Cyclamen, rosemary, spiny chicory, Algerian irises, hyacinthellas, anemones, annual daisies and *Helichrysum* may be flowering at different times during the winter months. Wild strawberry trees also flower and produce berries here throughout the winter. On the sea cliffs Egyptian St. John's wort can be seen in flower from February until early April. Mushrooms are abundant in this region a few days after heavy winter rainfalls. A wide range of moulds, mosses and lichens can also be found growing on live and dead pine and cypress trees.

CULTURE

Of interest in this area (in addition to the amazingly well-maintained domed drystone shelters) is the Lákkos Venetian Watchtower. This relatively well-preserved tower dating from the 17th century once served as a lookout post to watch for enemy ships. Ágios Nikólaos church in Éxo Chóra village square has a lovely wooden ceiling and wood carvings, as well as paintings and icons worth seeing. On the opposite side of the road from the church, beneath ancient olive groves, there is a cluster of traditional stone Venetian wells; although not as well preserved at those at Agalás, they are worth visiting.

From top to bottom, left to right: limestone rock formation; carob and regenerating Aleppo pine habitat; wild strawberry tree; sawfly orchid; lentisc in flower

AGRICULTURE

There are pockets of cultivation along the cliff edges and in the valleys. The dominant crop is olives, interspersed with vineyards. Beehives can be found throughout the region. Herds of domestic goats graze the wild vegetation on the sea cliffs. Domed drystone huts can be found along the drystone terraces and walls —perhaps once used for shelter from bad weather by herdsmen, they are more likely to provide shelter for livestock today.

WILDLIFE
Invertebrates

The nests of the pine procession-ary moths can be seen on many of the Aleppo pine trees. These burst open in spring, releasing caterpillars which form 'trains' (many caterpillars joined head-to-toe), to reach their preferred food source safely. Other species include garden spiders, violet carpenter bees, honey bees, Egyptian grasshoppers, crickets, cicadas, orange-tip butterflies and fritillary butterflies.

Reptiles and amphibians

Several lizards can be found here, including Greek *Algyroides* and Balkan wall lizards. Snakes include four-lined, Montpellier, Balkan whip and cat snakes. On neighbouring Kefaloniá, the cat snake is known as *ágio fídi* ('holy snake'), as its migration coincides with their Patron Saint's celebra-tion day in August. The snakes are placed on the icons and are believed to be reborn nuns, the 'cross' mark on their heads being proof of this. These snakes are not dangerous, as they have small jaws and very little venom.

From top to bottom, left to right: beautifully preserved domed drystone storage hut; goat; violet carpenter bee; cat snake peregrine falcon

Birds

This region has many birds, including robins, redstarts, golden orioles, chiff-chaffs, stonechats, blue rock thrushes, blackbirds and hoopoes. Among the birds of prey are buzzards, peregrine falcons and kestrels. There are also tawny, barn and scops owls. Sea birds number yellow-legged gulls, herring gulls, shearwaters and shags.

Mammals

There are hedgehogs, dormice, weasels and bats (European free-tailed, myotis, *Nyctalus sp.*); there is also the possibility of sighting Mediterranean monk seals off the coastal sea cliffs.

Distance/time: 6.4km/4mi; about 2.5-3h.

Grade: easy-moderate, with an initial ascent of 200m/660ft between points (1-4) and corresponding gradual descent; most of the walk is on level ground.

Traditional cylindrical drystone building, one of several on the walk

Equipment: see pages 85-86.

Travel: The walk is about a 40-minute drive (30km/19mi) out of Zákynthos town. Take the Katastári road out of town. At the fork for Ágios Nikólaos 4km after Katastári village, remain on the main road, but, 0.5km further on, at the fork for Volímes, veer left and follow the signs for Mariés. After about 3km, turn left on a tarmac road signposted 'quarry'. Follow this road for 2.3km up to the first quarry, and park at the junction some 100 metres further on.

Suggested time of year: any, but only attempt as an early morning/late evening walk in summer. Spring is the best time for sighting cuckoos.

Protection status: none.

Alternative routes: There are three suggestions for lengthening the walk:

1) To see some cylindrical dry-stone buildings up close, extend the loop around the mountain by about 330 m (20min). Turn left at junction (6), to follow the outer edge of the cultivated valley for 130 m, to a junction (B). Turn right and keep on this track (past any small turnings) for 920 m, back to the tarmac road (C). Turn right to rejoin the walk after 280 m, at point (7) .

2) Extend the loop by 1 hour by turning left at point (5) and after about 385 m right at the next junction (A). This takes you down into a cultivated valley. After about 1.5 km take the first right turn; then, about 1.5 km further on, veer right at another junction, to arrive at junction (B) after a further 360 m.

3) Add 8.2km/5mi to the walk (or do this in a 4WD) by circling Líva peak; the two connecting tracks to complete the loop have been shown on the sketch map, but refer to the fold-out map.

Additional suggestions: You can explore the mountains further by visiting the nearby traditional mountain villages of Loúcha and Girí. From Girí you can visit Kakí Ráchi (the 'Bad Rock'; see under 'Culture' on page 174) or the Black Cave on the road down to Kallithéa, which has stalactite (hanging from the ceiling) and stalagmite (towering from the ground) formations.

Walking notes

From the **parking place** at the junction past the **first quarry** (**1**), turn left to walk up the steep hill. Pass the quarry and rise up onto the **mountain plateau**. After 740 m, at junction (**2**), veer right along the unfenced track, to enter a cultivated valley. After a further

330 m, take the first right turn (**3**) and follow this track 750 m up to the **top of Mount Vrachíonas** (**4**). From here you can enjoy panoramic views of the island and can see Mount Aínos on Kefaloniá towering above you in the north. Retrace your steps to junction (**3**) and turn right. Ignoring all turn-offs into fields, follow the track along the edge of the valley. You pass between two small hills and leave the valley, and after just over 1 km reach a junction (**5**). Turn hard right and follow this track for 1.3 km, as it contours around the mountain, with southerly views towards the Loúcha valley. The track leads down into a cultivated valley, where you turn right on a side-track (**6**) and walk about 1 km along the valley's edge until you meet the tarmac road (**7**). Turn right here for 430 m, climbing a small slope back to the start.

GEOLOGY

The west Zákynthos mountain belt is characterized by pre-Apulian Cretaceous age detrital limestone. Mount Vrachíonas is the belt's highest peak at 756m/2480ft. It is surrounded by five other peaks, all above 600m/1970ft, but they are all dwarfed by the 1600m/5250ft peak of the Mount Aínos range on Kefaloniá. A large anticlinal fault configuration begins at the south face of Mount Vrachíonas (between points 5-6) and extends through Girí village and down the east side of the mountain range.

HABITATS

These mountains were probably once entirely covered in pine forests, although today just a few mature Aleppo pines remain, with regenerating pines among the *maquis* and *garrigue* vegetation of lentisc and wild strawberry trees. The most noticeable habitat is that of low-growing impoverished *phryganas* of thorny burnet, rock roses and heather, with tufted grasses nestling between the soil-poor rocks and stones.

From top to bottom, left to right: rugged limestone mountain landscape; impoverished phrygana *and tufted grasses; lesser celandine; giant orchid; mountain anemone*

PLANTS
Spring
The orchids of this region include giant, four-spotted, butterfly, Provence, Italian man, milky, sawfly, eastern yellow ophrys, Grecian spider, woodcock and bumblebee. Other noticeable species at this time are the flowering and fruiting thorny burnet, wild asparagus and kermes oaks, as well as annuals such as verbascum, clovers, black widow irises, catchflies, grape and tassle hyacinths and gladioli.

Summer
Due to the high altitude, several species remain in flower until early summer — among them thistles and the pink and white rock roses. These are followed later by thyme, wild onions, broomrape and fleabane.

Autumn
In this period, heathers and satureja are in flower, while the flowers of the wild strawberry tree, lentisc, smilax, honeysuckle and myrtle mature into berries that flourish throughout most of the winter. Other flowering species include the autumn ladies'-tresses orchid, autumn crocuses, autumn squill and *Arenaria*.

Winter
During winter the rocky ground is initially carpeted with cyclamen flowers, and later with a range of wild anemones in pinks and purples, as well as an anemone with a distinctive yellow centre found only in mountain habitats. Other species you may notice are spiny chicory, celandines, friar's cowl, hyacinthellas, Algerian and Cretan irises and iris-like Barbary nuts.

CULTURE
Throughout the valleys of the Vrachíonas mountain range there are cylindrical drystone buildings which at one time may have been inhabited, but today are used to shelter herds of domestic goats or for storage of agricultural equipment. Mount Vrachíonas is the highest peak on the island and therefore a triangulation point. The peak may also have once been used as a communication point between the residents of Zákynthos and Kefaloniá (using flares or fires), since the peaks of the Mount Aínos mountain chain tower above Zákynthos.

AGRICULTURE

The mountain valleys are cultivated with vineyards and various vegetable crops. There are also herds of domestic goats, watched over by goatherds, as well as a herd of wild mountain goats. The wild herd roams across the Vrachíonas mountain range and has been observed sheltering in the Black Cave below Girí village during bad weather. Due to its limestone, this mountain range is subject to intensive quarrying activity.

From top to bottom, left to right: old domed drystone dwelling; vineyards in the valley floor; blue-winged grasshopper; millipede; cuckoo

WILDLIFE
Invertebrates

In the pine trees, the nests of pine processionary moth larvae are abundant. There are also the caterpillars of other butterfly and moth species, as well as crickets, grasshoppers and cicadas. These three species can be distinguished by the way that they create sound — termed *stridulation.* Crickets scrape their two wing covers against each other, grasshoppers scrape their legs against their wing covers, while cicadas buckle a section of their thoracic plates repeatedly and so quickly that it sounds like a continuous buzz. The different species are triggered to 'sing' at different temperature ranges. Other species in the area are bees, wasps, ladybirds, spiders, beetles, shieldbugs, etc.

Reptiles and amphibians

Reptiles include Balkan wall and green lizards, geckos, skinks, grass snakes, Montpellier snakes, four-lined snakes and Hermann's tortoises.

Birds

The pine forest adjacent to the first quarry is a breeding site for

wrynecks which feed primarily on hairy caterpillars. There are also blackbirds, golden orioles, cuckoos, rock thrushes and fieldfare. Birds of prey include kestrels and buzzards, while among the owl species are the barn owl, scops owl and tawny owl.

Mammals

The limestone caves found in this region support bat roosts for several species, including myotis and European free-tailed bats. Among the other species are eastern hedgehogs, mice, martens and weasels.

Walk 20: Volímes monastery trail (Municipality of Elatíon)

Distance/time: 6.6km/4mi; about 3h.

Grade: moderate, with a gentle descent of about 100m/330ft between 1 and 6, descent to and corresponding ascent from the monastery of about 100m/330ft (7-11), and gentle ascent of 100m/330ft from 12-15.

Equipment: see pages 85-86.

Travel: The walk is about a 45-minute drive (32km/20mi) out of Zákynthos town. Take the Kata-stári road and follow the signs for Volímes. From the main square in Káto Volímes (a three-way junction), keep the school on your left and drive 0.75 km along the main road (past the medical centre left and town hall right). Continue straight through the village (do not turn off for Koríthi) until the road bends 90 degrees left. Opposite this bend there is a parking area (1).

Suggested time of year: September to May; in summer a shorter version may be attempted in the early morning/late evenings.

Protection status: Natura 2000 Specially Protected Area: Site code GR2210001.

Alternative routes
1) Follow footpath (A) 80 m from the monastery; this takes you over a stone wall to the coastal headland, where you can take in the stunning sea views.
2) Shorten the walk by about 1 km by cutting directly down to the monastery at point (9) — or shorten it by about 500 m by going straight down at point (10).
3) Shorten the walk by about 2.6 km, completing the sign-posted 'Volios' hills loop only, and not continuing out to the monastery at point (7).

Additional suggestions: It is worth exploring the old mountain village of Volímes, which has many churches and is the island's handicraft centre. In summer the streets are lined with sellers of lace work, carpets, rugs, tablecloths and linens. If you search carefully, you will find locally handmade goods. The famous Shipwreck is about a 15-minute drive west of the village, while the Blue Caves at Cape Skinári are a 20-minute drive northeast.

Walking notes

From the **parking area** (1), walk 145 m down the tarmac road and take the first right, a dirt track (2). Follow this for 320 m, then veer right at the fork (3). Ignoring any turn-offs, walk 870 m down this track, into a cultivated valley bordered with pine forests, and then up a slope. Ignore a turning left; go sharp right (4). Descend this track 670 m (past several turn-offs) to a T-junction with an **old stone building** on the left and a sign to 'Vigla' and 'Kukuni koifidi' (5). Turn left, ignore a left turn after 50 m (6), and continue

Ágios Andréas Monastery

380 m to the **crest of the hill** (7), with fine views back to Volimes. Ignore a left turn here and a second left after 330 m (8). Follow the partially concreted track 870 m along the edge of the hill and down to a junction (9). Veer right and follow the track 200 m to a field, then veer left and follow the edge of the two fields for 150 m, to the outer wall of **Ágios Andréas Monastery** (10).

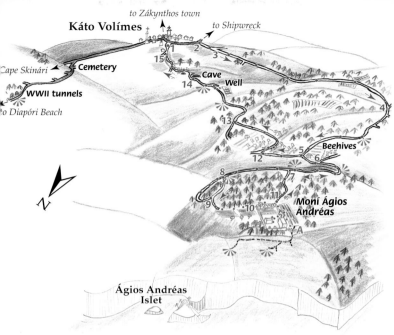

Continue along the edge of the wall for 90 m to the northwest-facing main entrance. *Carefully* explore the ruins of the main building and church, the well, and the garden.

Then leave on the track (**11**) leading directly up the hill in line with the west wall. After 620 m you will be back on the crest (**7**); turn right and follow the main trail back to the '**Vigla**' **signpost** (**5**). Continue straight on here: descend 325 m into a cultivated valley. At a stone wall lined by **almond trees** (**12**), turn sharp right (straight on leads into a field of olives), and follow the track around and up the hill bordering the valley. After 380 m a track joins from the left (**13**). Continue straight on; after 360 m you pass a livestock **cave** on your right (**14**). Keeping the stone wall on your right, after a further 230 m you pass a **barn** and a fenced **well** on your left. Turn right up the track 70 m further along (**15**), reaching the tarmac road and start after 80 m.

GEOLOGY

This region is representative of the detrital limestone of the Mount Vrachíonas pre-Apulian Zone, dating back to the Cretaceous age. There are also seams of flysch, sandstone, limestone conglomerates of pebbles, and Shelley limestone. The islet of Ágios Andréas is hidden behind another, larger outcrop off the precipitous white coastal cliffs situated to the north of the monastery. Kefaloniá's Mount Aínos massif towers out of the sea in the distance.

HABITATS

The primary natural habitat that you are likely to see is scrub *phrygana* of thorny burnet and *garrigues* of rock roses or hairy thorny broom with regenerating pines, interspersed with patches

165

of mature Aleppo pine forest. Behind the monastery is a stand of cypress — probably planted by the monastery occupants in the 17th century during Venetian rule. Bare patches of rock near natural springs make suitable moss and lichen habitats.

PLANTS
Spring
Zákynthos is known as 'the orchid garden', and the rural areas around Volímes support over half of the 55 species known to exist on the island. Among the species are the bumblebee, woodcock, horseshoe, funeral, yellow ophrys, Reinhold's bee, eastern yellow ophrys, sawfly, man, Italian man, four-spotted, and violet bird's-nest orchid. A wealth of additional flowering plants can be found along the borders of scrub and farmed areas, including tree heath, tassel hyacinths, thistles, hare's-tails, chamomile, mullein, asphodels, spurge, irises, celandines, almonds and wild carrot.

Summer
In summer the hills are covered in rock roses and thyme. Wild onions and broomrape are also in flower.

Autumn
At this time of year heather, sea squill, bedstraw, field scabious, wild strawberry trees, arums, biarums and honeysuckle are in flower.

Winter
Due to the dampness and high humidity of the region, many species of edible and inedible mushrooms and toadstools can be found. White edible mushrooms grow in abundance: 15cm (6in) in diameter, they blends in with the surrounding rocks! Cyclamens are in flower everywhere. Also look out for ferns growing in stone walls, and flowering plants such as star of Bethlehem, white and purple crocuses, salvia, sea squill, annual daisies, smooth sow thistles, chicory and wild parsley.

From top to bottom, left to right: limestone rock formation at Ágios Andréas inlet; regenerating Aleppo pine forests; sparse-flowered orchid; wild carrot; mushrooms

CULTURE
Moní Ágios Andréas was built in 1641. A few faded frescoes remain in the ruined church, although the best-preserved examples are on display at the Post-Byzantine Museum in Zákynthos town. There is another monastery to visit nearby: Ágios Geórgios Krimnón (see page 73), as well as several churches in Volímes with early frescoes. The road to Diapóri Beach in the hills opposite Ágios

Andréas has a network of tunnels built by local slave labour during the Nazi occupation.

AGRICULTURE

During the walk you will come across many examples of the farming practices used by the inhabitants of this region, from livestock (including old caves once used to keep the livestock in overnight or during bad weather), to vineyards, fallow meadows, crops of wheat and vegetables, as well as sheltered hillsides with olive and almond groves. There are also beehives with honey made from thyme, rosemary and lavender flowers.

WILDLIFE
Invertebrates

A wide range of invertebrates might be seen during this walk — Egyptian grasshoppers, darters, dragonflies, bumblebees, hornets, crickets, spiders and rose chafer beetles. Butterflies include clouded yellows, wood whites, Cleopatras, swallowtails, fritillaries, graylings, meadow browns, coppers, skippers, and common blues.

Reptiles

You will more than likely hear Balkan wall lizards, Balkan green lizards, skinks or slow worms moving into the undergrowth as you pass by. This region is also rich in snake species, including the four-lined snake, grass snakes, Balkan whip snakes, Montpelliers and maybe even vipers. Tortoises frequent the region, too. You might also see frogs, toads or salamanders; they are supported by many natural springs (look out for mossy patches on wet rocks hidden in the undergrowth, especially near the monastery).

Birds

This is prime habitat for hoopoes, rollers, bee eaters, golden orioles, blackbirds, sparrows, thrushes, wagtails, fieldfare, buntings, finches, shrike, tits, flycatchers, warblers, redwings, larks and wheatears. Birds of prey, including buzzards and kestrels, can be seen gliding and hovering over the hills. Seagulls and cormorants are likely to be sighted flying along the precipitous coastal cliffs.

Mammals

There is a good chance of spotting hedgehogs, mice, rats and weasels. Bats (horseshoe and pipistrelle) are also abundant, due to the many caves and overhangs that exist in this area.

From top to bottom, left to right: cave once used to keep livestock; Ágios Andréas Church; Mediterranean monk seal; painted lady butterfly on a scabious flower; fieldfare

Walk 21: Cape Skinári coastal trail (Municipality of Elatíon)

Distance/time: 12.3km/7.6mi; about 3.5-5h.

Grade: strenuous, with an initial ascent of 50m/165ft between points (1-4), a descent and corresponding ascent of 50m/165ft to the sea and back up between points (6-7), and a 200m/660ft ascent between points (8-11), with a corresponding descent from (11) back to (1).

Equipment: see pages 85-86.

Travel: The walk is about an hour's drive (42km/ 26mi) out of Zákynthos town. Take the Katastári road out of town. At the fork for Ágios Nikólaos, 4km after Katastári village, turn right. Drive through Makrís Gialós, Míkro Nissí and Ágios Nikólaos to Koríthi. At the junction for Volímes in Koríthi village, turn right, following signs for the 'Blue Caves'. Drive about 2.4km downhill to the 'Taverna Fáros' (lighthouse) and signs for tickets to the Blue Caves; park here (1).

Suggested time of year: any, but only attempt as an early morning/late evening walk from June to August, due to the heat.

Protection status: Natura 2000 Specially Protected Area: Site code GR2210001.

Alternative routes
1) You can make it a shorter 'out and back' walk, going 3.7 km each way from point (1) to (6) and back, with the option of walking down to Klima Bay (7), and then returning the same way (770 m each way). This will make a moderate walk of about 3h.
2) The walk can be shortened by just over 1 km (about 30 min) if you turn left at the junction (12) in Koríthi village and follow the main tarmac road back to Cape Skinári and your starting point.

Additional suggestions: After the walk, you can go for a swim in the clear blue sea at Cape Skinári's small beach. It is possible to swim to the Blue Caves from there (or from the windmill), but beware of the strong sea current and busy boat traffic. Alternatively — and more safely — you can visit the Blue Caves (and the Shipwreck) on one of the tour boats from Cape Skinári.

Walking notes

From the **Taverna Fáros** (**1**), walk about 550 m back up the tarmac road, ignoring an overgrown left turn after 450 m (**2**). Then, about

Sea cliffs with Egyptian St. John's wort

100 m before Lithies Apartments, turn right on a dirt track (**3**), bordered on the left by a **dry-stone wall**. Follow this track for about 1.5 km, after which it rises for 200 m through the hills, with views of Kefaloniá just 8.5 nautical miles away. Ignore a track joining from the left here (**4**). Continue along the main track for about 1.4 km, past a juniper and oak **woodland** (**5**). After 750 m the track starts to bend downhill, and you reach a track forking sharp right behind you (**6**). Zigzag 770 m down this track to the sea at **Klíma Bay** (**7**).

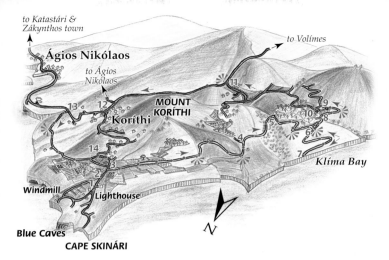

After stopping for a brief break, climb back up the hill to (**6**) and turn right along the track. Keep right on the main track at a turn-off after some 200 m (**8**). Rise into the valley for just over 1 km, past a track leading right uphill (**9**). Some 80 m further on (where a left turn goes to a farm 100 m away), turn right uphill on a concrete track (**10**). This track becomes a tarmac road; follow it uphill for about 1.6 km (ignoring all turn-offs) to the junction with the **main road to Volímes** (**11**). Turn left here and follow the Volímes road for 1.7 km into **Koríthi**. At the junction in the village (**12**), veer right and continue 620 m along the main road — until you come to the third tarmac turn-off left (**13**), just before the gorge. Follow this road (later a track) for 1.3 km around the coast until it rejoins the tarmac road to Skinári opposite Lithies Apartments (**14**). Turn right here, back to the start.

GEOLOGY
Beneath the peak of Koríthi (337m/1105ft), the peninsula of Cape Skinári is the most northerly point on Zákynthos. It is in the pre-Apulian geotectonic Zone and is part of the Mount Vrachíonas Cretaceous detrital limestone formation. This coastline has many inlets and caves, but most famous of all are the Blue Caves ('Galázia Spiliá') off the tip of Cape Skinári — renowned for the brilliant turquoise colour of the sea, which is created by the reflection of the sunlight on the white limestone rocks, purple seaweed and sheer depth of the sea.

HABITATS
On the rocky coastline, Egyptian St. John's wort is the dominant habitat, with small patches of sea lavender. There is also a juniper woodland interspersed with kermes oak and cork oak and fringed with tree heath at point (5). Large patches of thorny burnet *phrygana* cover the coastal hillsides where fires have not occurred. In areas that have been burnt over the last ten years, a *garrigue* habitat dominates, with a mixture of wild strawberry trees, *Anthyllis*, broom and lentisc.

From top to bottom, left to right: coastal limestone rock formation; oak and juniper woodland; tree heath; yellow ophrys orchid; moss-covered tree trunk

PLANTS
Spring
The orchid species of this area include bumblebee, woodcock, yellow ophrys, eastern yellow ophrys, Grecian spider, horseshoe, milky, pink butterfly, four-spotted, sawfly, Reinhold's bee, dense-flowered and several tongue-orchids. Other flowering plants are tree heather, the flowers and berries of black bryony, thorny burnet, annual daisies, chamomile, field marigolds, asparagus, grape hyacinths, asphodels, Barbary nuts and black widow irises.

Summer
During summer, rock roses and *Helichrysum* are in abundance, followed by thyme, broomrape and sea lavender on the sea cliffs.

Autumn
In autumn, the woodland kermes oak acorns and juniper berries are ripe. The wild strawberry tree and lentisc flower and produce fruit. There is also satureja, sea squill, myrtle and common smilax.

Winter
This region includes a habitat of special importance within Europe — a large population of Egyptian St. John's wort which vegetates the limestone sea cliffs and is in full flower between January and April. Other winter-flowering species include cyclamens, Algerian and Cretan irises, anemones, spiny chicory, friar's cowl, Bermuda buttercups and narcissi. There are also mushrooms in the undergrowth, and mosses and lichens growing on rocks and trees.

CULTURE
The highly visible lighthouse at Cape Skinári has warned ships away from this dangerous coastline for over a century. On the west side of the peninsula, there is a derelict building which was once the communications centre for the island. On the east side there is a windmill (shown on page 40) reminiscent of the many windmills that once operated across the mountainous areas of the island to process the once-abundant crops. On the journey up to Cape Skinári, take time to stop and look at the 17th-century Venetian tower at Míkro Nissí.

AGRICULTURE

There is a wide range of crops cultivated in this region, from vineyards and olive groves to fields of wheat and vegetables. Wild pear, almond and citrus trees can be also be found growing in the fields for domestic use. You may also see locals collecting greens and wild asparagus from the field and track edges. Herds of domestic goats can be found throughout the hills of this area, grazing on the semi-natural vegetation, and watched over by their goatherds.

WILDLIFE
Invertebrates

There are several different types of butterflies around, including skippers, swallowtails, whites and yellows, orange-tips and Cleopatras, admirals and painted ladies, fritillaries, blues, coppers and graylings. Other species include bees, hornets, several types of spiders, mites such as the velvet mite (which is widespread in spring), crickets, cicadas, grasshoppers, scorpions and beetles.

Reptiles and amphibians

On warm days at any time of year you may hear or even spot Balkan wall lizards scuttling into the undergrowth as you walk past. Other lizards that may be found include the Greek *algyroides,* the Balkan green lizard, geckos and snake-eyed skinks. Snakes include Balkan whip snakes, Montpelliers and four-lined snakes. You may even be lucky enough to see a Hermann's tortoise too!

Birds

Birds inhabiting the scrub and oak-juniper woodlands may include golden orioles, rollers, hoopoes, bee-eaters, swifts, martins, swallows, pipits, wagtails, larks, wheatears, whinchats, warblers, goldfinches, greenfinches, flycatchers, buntings, sparrows, blue rock thrushes, quail, partridges and turtle doves. Among the birds of prey are harriers, buzzards and kestrels; owls number Eurasian scops owls, tawny owls and barn owls. For sea birds there are shearwaters, shags, slender-billed gulls, yellow-legged gulls and lesser- backed gulls.

Mammals

You may find hedgehogs, mice, and weasels in this area. From twilight on, European free-tailed bats might well be spotted. Monk seals may sometimes be seen in the sea.

From top to bottom, left to right: machinery at an old windmill; wheatfield with poppies; female Balkan wall lizard; bee beetle on a rock rose; bee-eater

Walk 22: Pigadákia hills trail (Municipality of Alykon)

Distance/time: 3.7km/2.3mi; about 1.5-2h.

Grade: easy-moderate, with an ascent of 200m/660ft between points (2-4) and corresponding descent between (6-10).

Equipment: see pages 85-86.

Travel: The walk is about a 20-minute drive (16km/10mi) out of Zákynthos town. Take the road leading through Ágios Kiriakós and Ágios Dimítrios for Katastári village, and at the sign for Pigadákia (and the Vertzágio Museum) turn left. Drive into the village and park by the church of Ágios Pantelémon (1) in Pante-límana Square, near the Vertzágio Museum.

A sage-dominated garrigue *habitat characterizes this walk.*

Suggested time of year: any, but in summer it is best to complete the walk in the early morning or late evening.

Protection status: none.

Alternative routes:

1) You can shorten the walk to 2.3 km, saving about 1 hour (with only a 75m/250ft ascent): turn left at point (3) and walk through the shaded old olive terraces to rejoin the walk at point (6).

2) You can lengthen the walk by about 2.5 km (1 hour). Continue up the track from the chapel (5) for 200 m, to a T-junction (**A**). Turn left and follow this track for 1.4 km, until you reach a scree slope on the left (**B**) with loose white stones and an olive grove 60 m directly below. Cut carefully down the scree on the hunters' footpaths to the olive grove. Bearing ENE (60°), cut down two olive terraces, to a grassy/dirt track (**C**) about 50 m further on. Follow this as it loops left into a clear dirt track (you will have seen this from the terraces). You pass a metal shed and then an old stone house. Turn right downhill at the nearby junction, then go left at the next two junctions (130 m and 40 m further on). After another 110 m, pick up the walk from point (6).

3) Lengthen the walk by 30 minutes by going from point (D) to (E) to visit the lower Vertzágio Cave (100m/330ft additional ascent). Or make the walk 1 hour longer by visiting the higher Vertzágio Caves at (F) — an *additional* ascent of 200m/ 660ft. There is an unmarked footpath to the lower and upper caves; for information, ask for Spíros Vertzágias at his restaurant, Kakí Ráchi, opposite the church.

Additional suggestions: Before the walk, visit the Kakí Ráchi restaurant to see a video of the walk to the Vertzágio Caves, and be sure to visit the Vertzágio Museum. Swim at Alikés or Alikanás, and visit the Alikés salt flats, to see migratory waterfowl.

Walking notes

From **Ágios Pantelémon** church (**1**), opposite the restaurant, turn right along the tarmac road and after 250 m take the first left turn, a concrete (sometimes dirt) track (**2**). Follow the track up the hill

172

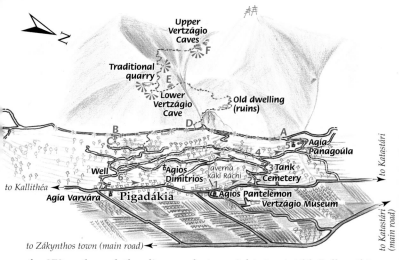

for 370 m, through the olives, and veer right at the junction by the concrete **water tank/building** on the left (**3**). After 160 m, *take note* of a dirt track off to the left (**4**): this is your return route. Then, ignoring all further turn-offs, keep *always uphill* on the main track. After another 550 m, turn off left to the **Agía Panagoúla** chapel (**5**), from where there is a fine view to Kefaloniá, as well as the north, central and southern regions of Zákynthos.

Return 550 m down the track and turn right at point (**4**). Follow this track for 610 m through the olives until you reach a junction with three other tracks (**6**). Take the second turning left here — a concrete track leading down the hill. You will pass several houses, and after 500 m a **well** on your right, followed after 80 m by a **graveyard**. 200 m further down, reach the main road through Pigadakia (**7**). Turn left, walk past **Agía Varvára**, and continue along the road for 500 m, back to the starting point.

GEOLOGY

On this part of the island the central plains join the western mountains. Along a fault line, Cretaceous detrital limestone meets lower-mid Miocene and Oligocene rock strata composed of alluvium, flych, marly limestones, psammonites and gypsum. The 'Bad Rock' sulphur springs beneath the church and around the village formed due to the presence of the ideal rock strata and fault line. Thousands of years of rainwater, permeating and dissolving the rock, carved the Vertzágio Caves into the detrital limestone.

HABITATS

The natural habitat of this region is characterized by *garrigue* dominated with sage, which is collected by locals to make herbal teas. Other representative species include carob, wild strawberry trees and rock roses. Small clearings exist around abandoned buildings and near the upper Vertzágio Caves, where many wildflowers grow in spring and sea squill in winter. The leaves of the sea squill can be twisted into 'cups' to drink the soft water collected in the caves.

173

From top to bottom, left to right: cave and well collecting water filtered through the rock; spiny chicory; man orchid; tall bearded iris; wild gladiolus

Mediterranean lupins, star of Bethlehem, gagea, and tree heath.

Summer

In summer, rock roses and thyme flower. Other species include capers, gladioli, broomrape, prickly pears (an introduced species planted for hedging), wild carrot, common dodder, bindweed, fleabane, hare's-tails, globe thistles, galactites thistles and yellow star thistles.

Autumn

Sea squill, meadow saffron, white and purple autumn crocuses and myrtle are in flower. There are many mature wild strawberry trees in this region, the berries of which are collected by locals at this time. The branches of this shrub were also once collected to make sturdy walking sticks.

Winter

Flowering plants include cyclamen (or sowbread), anemones, hyacinthellas, narcissi, annual daisies, Algerian and Cretan irises, spiny chicory, and friar's cowl. Mushrooms can also be found.

PLANTS
Spring

The orchid species in this area include man, giant, crescent, horseshoe, eastern yellow ophrys, Grecian spider, sawfly, bug, milky and pink butterfly orchids. Flowering sage carpets the hillsides in spring and is collected by locals to make herbal teas. Grape hyacinths and wild asparagus stalks are also collected at this time of year for eating. Among the other flowering plants are the cultivated tall bearded iris (by the Panagoúla chapel), asphodels, celandines, poppies, gladioli, broom, chamomile, Barbary nuts,

CULTURE

The church of Ágios Pantelémon at Pigadákia is built over a spring where 'bad waters' (sulphurous) pour out and flood the church once a year. This water is believed to have natural healing powers. There are other sulphurous springs signposted around the village. The Vertzágio Museum, based in an old building beside the church, houses a variety of artefacts illustrating traditional Zakynthian life and farming practices (see page 67). There is information in English.

AGRICULTURE

The foothills of the Zákynthos mountain range are carpeted with olive groves, some new and some dating back several hundred years. The flood plains of the central and eastern parts of the island are primarily covered in vineyards, from which several commercial wines are produced (visit one of the wineries to see the wine-making process and sample the results). There are also vegetable crops and livestock. Doves are also kept.

WILDLIFE
Invertebrates

Many invertebrates can be found in this region, including garden spiders, cicadas, grasshoppers, bush-crickets, beetles, darters and dragonflies. Butterflies include swallowtails, graylings, blues, coppers, hairstreaks, whites, Cleopatras, brimstones, commas, tortoiseshells, painted ladies and red admirals.

Reptiles and amphibians

Among the vegetated rocks, Moorish geckos and Balkan wall lizards can be found. Common snakes of the region include Balkan whip snakes, four-lined snakes and Montpelliers. In the permanently flowing rivers (those that flow into the sea at Alikés and Laganás), green toads and common marsh frogs may be heard, if not seen!

Birds

Birds include robins, blackbirds, swallows, swifts (which nest in the cave crevices), wagtails, wheatears, sparrows, warblers and pipits. For birds of prey there are common and long-legged buzzards, kestrels and peregrine falcons. Among the ancient olive

From top to bottom, left to right: traditional farm equipment at the Vertzágio Museum; dovecote; bumblebee on sage; horseshoe bats; stonechat

groves, scops and tawny owls might be seen.

Mammals

The caves that speckle the mountains in this area provide shelter for several bat species including long-eared, horseshoe, myotis and *Plecotus sp.*). There are also eastern hedgehogs and weasels. A population of wild goats which grazes the slopes of Mount Vrachíonas also uses the Vertzágio Caves and Black Cave (between Girí and Kallithéa) to shelter from bad weather. This wild herd came about when a goatherd accidentally left behind some new-born goats.

GPS waypoints and intermediate coordinates

Walk 1: Gérakas headland

Wp	Northing	Easting
1	37.707864	20.986530
	37.708224	20.985062
	37.708548	20.984268
	37.708687	20.983407
2	37.709483	20.983377
	37.709806	20.980413
	37.709943	20.979831
3	37.710208	20.978350
a*	37.709298	20.978434
	37.710420	20.978250
4	37.712230	20.977200
	37.713190	20.977410
	37.713040	20.976390
	37.712880	20.975660
5	37.712050	20.975520
6	37.711385	20.974991
7	37.711249	20.975141
	37.710817	20.975640
	37.710595	20.975904
	37.710432	20.976093
	37.710289	20.976173
8	37.710060	20.976363
	37.711587	20.974801
	37.712159	20.974354
	37.712573	20.973901
	37.711926	20.973850
	37.711036	20.973997
	37.710688	20.973733
	37.711473	20.973339
	37.711067	20.973026
	37.710968	20.972836
	37.710631	20.972835
	37.710327	20.972929
9	37.710317	20.972933
	37.708728	20.974836
10	37.708063	20.982889
	37.707489	20.985236
	37.706968	20.986525

Walk 2: Gérakas–Dáphne

Wp	Northing	Easting
1	37.707864	20.986530
2	37.706968	20.986525
3	37.707489	20.985236
4	37.708063	20.982889
b*	37.708710	20.982723
5	37.708728	20.974836
B	37.710317	20.972933
	37.711010	20.972351
	37.711863	20.971603
	37.713314	20.970611
	37.713774	20.968910
	37.713947	20.968142
	37.714191	20.967717
	37.714092	20.966732
6	37.714407	20.964486
	37.716220	20.963855
	37.719010	20.963025
7	37.720038	20.960648
	37.720354	20.958159
8	37.720700	20.955557
C	37.721560	20.954374
A	37.708224	20.985062

Walk 3: Dáphne hills

Wp	Northing	Easting
1	37.729770	20.945988
	37.739370	20.945758
2	37.731231	20.945896
3	37.731742	20.945933
4	37.731946	20.946094
	37.731497	20.947516
	37.731327	20.947534
5	37.731444	20.948012
	37.731322	20.948650
	37.730295	20.949457
6	37.730148	20.950608
	37.730012	20.951762
7	37.730494	20.952634
	37.730682	20.953198
	37.730194	20.953351
	37.729695	20.954419
	37.729294	20.954872
8	37.728519	20.955555
	37.728609	20.955973
9	37.728581	20.956001
	37.727977	20.956333
	37.727584	20.956214
	37.727240	20.955318
10	37.726637	20.956089
	37.725719	20.955360
	37.725635	20.954134
	37.725608	20.953671
	37.725711	20.953397
11	37.726067	20.953258
	37.726223	20.952841
12	37.726469	20.952603
13	37.726322	20.952273
	37.725861	20.952188
	37.725230	20.952068
	37.724933	20.951361
	37.725153	20.950771
	37.724918	20.950165
	37.724226	20.950054
	37.724269	20.949277
	37.724389	20.948734
	37.724742	20.948188
14	37.724427	20.948037
	37.724745	20.947783
	37.724957	20.947164
	37.724810	20.946813
	37.725722	20.945656
	37.726402	20.944781
	37.727315	20.944823
	37.727929	20.944440
	37.729287	20.944557
	37.730126	20.944973
	37.730696	20.945115
	37.730947	20.945642
	37.731302	20.945814
	37.721560	20.954374
	37.732357	20.944358
	37.732218	20.943527

Walk 4: Ksirocástello trail

Wp	Northing	Easting
1	37.729770	20.945988
	37.739370	20.945758
2	37.731231	20.945896
3	37.731870	20.945980
	37.731970	20.943740
4	37.732170	20.943400
5	37.732670	20.945060
	37.733170	20.944760
	37.732840	20.944010
	37.732990	20.943670
	37.733260	20.943280
	37.733610	20.942430
	37.733660	20.941790
	37.733640	20.941580
	37.733590	20.941430
	37.733440	20.941220
	37.733740	20.940870
	37.733910	20.941290
6	37.734840	20.940009
	37.735220	20.939730
	37.735590	20.939690
	37.736350	20.939770
	37.737020	20.940180
	37.737420	20.940550
7	37.737430	20.940550

*a: viewpoint; b: pinnacles

	Northing	Easting
8	37.737750	20.940130
	37.737670	20.939750
	37.737930	20.938970
c*	37.737520	20.938600
	37.737250	20.938330
	37.736870	20.938070
	37.736770	20.938040
9	37.736640	20.937540
	37.736260	20.936650
	37.735260	20.935390
	37.734900	20.935270
	37.734660	20.934880
	37.734270	20.934480
	37.734010	20.934620
10	37.733720	20.933780
d*	37.733170	20.932210

Walk 5: Mount Skopós

Wp	Northing	Easting
A	37.758577	20.939416
	37.757717	20.938211
	37.757349	20.937959
	37.756462	20.936839
	37.756418	20.936282
	37.755984	20.935118
	37.754786	20.934434
	37.753537	20.932840
	37.753011	20.932138
	37.752762	20.932511
	37.752999	20.933726
	37.753027	20.935105
	37.752500	20.935577
1	37.752105	20.935570
	37.752261	20.936735
	37.751818	20.937601
	37.751255	20.937559
	37.751473	20.937412
	37.750889	20.936631
	37.750236	20.936158
2	37.748362	20.935417
3	37.744858	20.936669
4	37.745948	20.934164
	37.746336	20.933507
5	37.747543	20.932328
	37.746780	20.932867
e*	37.745880	20.932927
	37.743023	20.932584
6	37.743380	20.933076
	37.743773	20.933296
	37.744044	20.933549
B	37.743944	20.933817

	Northing	Easting
C	37.743345	20.932559
	37.743240	20.932196
	37.742987	20.931755
	37.742932	20.931782
	37.742797	20.931997
	37.742424	20.932122
	37.742226	20.931990
	37.742074	20.931759
	37.741913	20.931571
	37.741816	20.931468
	37.741830	20.931436
	37.741716	20.931261
	37.741637	20.931135
D	37.741579	20.931036

Walk 6: Vrondónero

Wp	Northing	Easting
1	37.737615	20.906006
	37.737607	20.906023
	37.737629	20.905735
2	37.741639	20.906706
3	37.741144	20.909154
	37.738304	20.910225
	37.738114	20.911228
	37.737943	20.912238
4	37.737859	20.913251
5	37.736853	20.913422
	37.737401	20.914200
	37.738569	20.915311
6	37.739814	20.916028
	37.740443	20.916254
7	37.743511	20.917820
8	37.744305	20.918152
9	37.750575	20.912015
10	37.752268	20.905966
11	37.751615	20.905921
12	37.753180	20.901721
	37.748951	20.904409
	37.747073	20.904629
A	37.737037	20.906412
B	37.737307	20.907734
C	37.740292	20.917143
to D	37.738974	20.918910
to D	37.738998	20.918914
to D	37.738986	20.918934
to D	37.739006	20.919015
to D	37.739042	20.919104
to D	37.739055	20.919216
to D	37.739048	20.919246
to D	37.739101	20.919270
to D	37.739168	20.919232

	Northing	Easting
to D	37.739296	20.919353
to D	37.739401	20.919326
to D	37.739949	20.919635
D	37.740584	20.919468
E	37.752100	20.911899
F	37.752106	20.911898
G	37.736617	20.904511

Walk 7: Kalamáki dunes

Wp	Northing	Easting
1	37.734932	20.879199
	37.734235	20.879381
	37.733223	20.879343
	37.732370	20.879396
2	37.732150	20.879485
3	37.731960	20.879390
	37.731890	20.879540
	37.731960	20.879390
	37.732090	20.880210
	37.731830	20.879900
	37.732160	20.880190
4	37.732160	20.880190
	37.732610	20.881280
	37.732780	20.881510
	37.732910	20.882300
	37.733140	20.883020
5	37.733540	20.884030
	37.733410	20.884530
6	37.733960	20.884920
	37.732690	20.885740
7	37.732410	20.885890
8	37.732432	20.885787
	37.731009	20.881904
	37.730628	20.880743
	37.729897	20.879043
9	37.730099	20.879296
10	37.730416	20.879313
	37.731294	20.879014
	37.732008	20.878550
	37.732749	20.878649
	37.733298	20.878318
11	37.734357	20.878206

Walk 8 Ágios Sóstis

Wp	Northing	Easting
1	37.714809	20.863649
	37.713870	20.861915
2	37.710472	20.857179
3	37.705753	20.852688
4	37.704666	20.850282
5	37.704806	20.850042
6	37.706189	20.849030

c: track into field; d: footpath peters out; e: monastery gates

7	37.707226	20.848068
	37.708315	20.847570
8	37.709688	20.844864
	37.710334	20.846061
	37.711282	20.848038
9	37.710410	20.850119
10	37.715344	20.852843
	37.712503	20.852134
11	37.715534	20.852429
	37.715933	20.852354
	37.716805	20.852162
12	37.717952	20.851713
	37.718038	20.851861
13	37.718224	20.853292
	37.718972	20.853269
	37.720329	20.853247
	37.720844	20.853555
	37.721512	20.853801
14	37.720838	20.854050
	37.721181	20.854109
	37.721351	20.854361
	37.721241	20.854820
15	37.721438	20.855073
	37.720898	20.856311
	37.720819	20.857873
16	37.719522	20.859251
	37.719492	20.859988
17	37.720170	20.862071
	37.716434	20.861737
A	37.710270	20.855156
	37.711075	20.854957
	37.711279	20.853301
B	37.711136	20.852584

Walk 9: Lake Kerí

Wp	Northing	Easting
1	37.683545	20.835201
	37.683123	20.832191
2	37.684636	20.829738
	37.686090	20.826443
	37.687616	20.828827
3	37.686870	20.831562
	37.686822	20.831708
	37.687314	20.832008
	37.687778	20.829101
5	37.689439	20.828137
	37.688272	20.825598
6	37.685528	20.825660
7	37.682073	20.827308
8	37.681817	20.827293
9	37.679852	20.825750

f: junction for B-C

	37.679773	20.828352
	37.679373	20.833746
	37.679228	20.837011
	37.682278	20.836139
A	37.686201	20.835566
B	37.685769	20.836165

Walk 10: Marathiá coast

Wp	Northing	Easting
1	37.669419	20.849843
2	37.668933	20.849358
	37.668576	20.848839
	37.668350	20.848899
	37.667265	20.850972
3	37.666457	20.851881
	37.666706	20.852609
	37.666723	20.852625
A	37.666415	20.853275
	37.665554	20.853290
	37.665082	20.853789
4	37.663134	20.853254
	37.662373	20.853904
5	37.659888	20.850622
	37.658874	20.851992
	37.658008	20.853596
	37.658682	20.853253
6	37.657246	20.855900
7	37.657036	20.855629
f*	37.656290	20.854637
C	37.655069	20.854691
B	37.657026	20.856417
8	37.659298	20.845540
	37.661018	20.848692
	37.661819	20.848959
	37.662894	20.848064
	37.665363	20.846986
9	37.665318	20.845725
	37.664958	20.843699
	37.667149	20.843949
	37.668826	20.844015

Walk 11: Marathiá hills

Wp	Northing	Easting
1	37.661915	20.835404
2	37.663000	20.835950
3	37.663855	20.834951
4	37.668589	20.833565
	37.666272	20.834208
	37.668700	20.841156
5	37.669592	20.840418
	37.668778	20.842033
	37.669305	20.842901

6	37.668826	20.844015
	37.667149	20.843949
	37.664958	20.843699
7	37.665318	20.845725
	37.665363	20.846986
	37.662894	20.848064
	37.661819	20.848959
8	37.661018	20.848692
	37.659983	20.847203
	37.659168	20.847116
	37.659025	20.844785
	37.657632	20.845219
	37.656857	20.845981
9	37.655836	20.845481
	37.655774	20.845206
	37.656456	20.842318
	37.658509	20.841307
	37.660548	20.839470
10	37.660920	20.838501
11	37.661869	20.835504
A	37.667360	20.836938
B	37.659298	20.845540

Walk 12: Kerí hills

Wp	Northing	Easting
1	37.655620	20.810080
	37.653780	20.813693
2	37.651249	20.816834
	37.652795	20.820142
3	37.655240	20.820989
4	37.655087	20.822664
	37.655516	20.825386
	37.659400	20.828765
5	37.661015	20.829356
6	37.661873	20.828466
7	37.662731	20.825197
	37.660938	20.825976
	37.659998	20.823651
8	37.658851	20.822465
9	37.659179	20.820023
	37.660185	20.816124
10	37.660664	20.815994
	37.661010	20.815794
11	37.660461	20.815336
12	37.661046	20.814991
13	37.661043	20.814826
14	37.660551	20.812898

Walk 13: Kentinária

Wp	Northing	Easting
1	37.682224	20.787002
	37.684656	20.788411

	37.686033	20.789941
2	37.687719	20.790692
	37.688490	20.789641
	37.689437	20.788168
	37.690422	20.787364
3	37.691271	20.787396
	37.690365	20.786019
4	37.689642	20.784071
	37.690020	20.783150
	37.691193	20.782607
5	37.691775	20.782213
	37.691828	20.782232
6	37.693045	20.780564
7	37.693081	20.779917
	37.694559	20.779451
8	37.696155	20.778067
9	37.697111	20.776826
10	37.696587	20.775989
11	37.696088	20.774858
	37.695233	20.775963
	37.693944	20.778333
12	37.692137	20.779458
13	37.691973	20.779526
14	37.691499	20.780049
	37.689771	20.780857
15	37.687288	20.783619
16	37.685061	20.783365
g*	37.681235	20.804820
A	37.679873	20.793476
B	37.691155	20.779429
	37.692082	20.778914
	37.690556	20.777573
	37.689161	20.776091
	37.689713	20.775224
	37.688912	20.775569
	37.687302	20.775652
	37.686827	20.775323
h*	37.685371	20.772503

Walk 14: Agalás

Wp	Northing	Easting
1	37.707244	20.776908
	37.706862	20.777497
2	37.704645	20.775019
	37.703826	20.773584
3	37.697111	20.776826
4	37.696088	20.774858
	37.699481	20.775788
5	37.700048	20.772901
	37.698008	20.772852
6	37.698209	20.771249

g: main Agalas road; h: car parking area

7	37.699065	20.770031
	37.699400	20.769726
	37.700098	20.768038
	37.700908	20.765311
	37.699157	20.762763
8	37.699838	20.760820
9	37.699813	20.760311
10	37.700047	20.759588
11	37.701195	20.761422
12	37.703321	20.762695
	37.703058	20.764890
13	37.704125	20.766075
	37.704066	20.767144
	37.704115	20.767460
	37.704535	20.768256
	37.704965	20.769258
	37.707060	20.768402
14	37.707814	20.770114
	37.707779	20.770141
	37.708386	20.772609
15	37.708252	20.773900
16	37.708897	20.774534
17	37.707690	20.775818
A	37.702055	20.774106

Walk 15: Loúcha

Wp	Northing	Easting
1	37.788797	20.725997
	37.787269	20.727538
	37.784634	20.730457
	37.781704	20.737113
	37.778121	20.742149
	37.777938	20.743673
	37.777125	20.744011
2	37.776135	20.744901
	37.776007	20.744833
	37.773511	20.746007
	37.771988	20.747466
	37.769887	20.750664
	37.768963	20.754257
	37.766225	20.757199
	37.765017	20.758788
	37.764837	20.759935
3	37.763692	20.759584
	37.765477	20.760619
	37.768011	20.759730
4	37.769263	20.759479
	37.770633	20.759957
5	37.771392	20.759146
	37.773712	20.757037
6	37.774623	20.755207

7	37.775609	20.753689
8	37.776917	20.752044
	37.777582	20.748447
	37.779731	20.745982
9	37.781982	20.742171
10	37.783776	20.740951
	37.784501	20.739758
	37.784673	20.738723
	37.786507	20.736297
	37.787211	20.734766
	37.788602	20.732245
	37.789616	20.730974
11	37.790090	20.730833
	37.791856	20.728100
	37.792937	20.726583
12	37.793879	20.725514

Walk 16: Korakoníssi

Wp	Northing	Easting
1	37.760600	20.719612
	37.758864	20.719423
	37.754857	20.719375
2	37.753762	20.720049
	37.752346	20.719724
	37.750420	20.719692
3	37.748087	20.723104
	37.745400	20.722908
	37.741467	20.723495
	37.740835	20.724457
	37.738622	20.724749
	37.737071	20.726964
4	37.735193	20.728388
	37.734020	20.729150
	37.732768	20.729975
5	37.730700	20.732054
	37.729251	20.734232
	37.728267	20.735340
6	37.728235	20.736593
	37.727280	20.738059
7	37.726396	20.740117
8	37.725443	20.737697
9	37.723382	20.739616
	37.721886	20.738741
	37.721586	20.737110
	37.720782	20.733159
	37.717457	20.731157
	37.718340	20.729210
	37.718034	20.729191
10	37.717972	20.729055

Walk 17: Kampí coast

Wp	Northing	Easting
1	37.780336	20.685128
2	37.781931	20.686572
	37.780922	20.687117
3	37.779683	20.687610
	37.778836	20.688582
	37.778084	20.690641
	37.777626	20.691814
4	37.775473	20.693104
	37.773901	20.694032
	37.773078	20.694872
	37.771356	20.695791
5	37.769835	20.696390
6	37.768472	20.697490
	37.768207	20.698245
	37.767767	20.697985
7	37.767255	20.697769
	37.766671	20.696615
	37.765540	20.696535
	37.761730	20.698052
8	37.761160	20.697921
	37.759974	20.698633
	37.758351	20.698241
	37.756216	20.696878
	37.754339	20.696887
	37.752198	20.699725
9	37.751662	20.701678
	37.752614	20.701294
	37.753365	20.700707
	37.754332	20.703533
10	37.756068	20.703357
	37.757348	20.705438
	37.758385	20.705888
11	37.759172	20.705341
	37.760442	20.704386
	37.762758	20.704367
12	37.764469	20.702493
A	37.779077	20.679519
B	37.780038	20.678569
C	37.750565	20.704077

Walk 18: Éxo Chóra

Wp	Northing	Easting
1	37.800085	20.680166
	37.798859	20.680856
	37.797704	20.681628
	37.796323	20.681374
	37.794991	20.681808
	37.793474	20.682019
2	37.793059	20.680254

i: viewpoint

	Northing	Easting
i*	37.792978	20.679141
	37.791253	20.678575
	37.792068	20.677315
	37.792767	20.675778
	37.793413	20.675988
	37.793873	20.676213
	37.794517	20.674307
3	37.795539	20.673004
	37.795700	20.673101
	37.795799	20.673334
4	37.796259	20.674507
	37.796301	20.674693
	37.796312	20.674510
	37.796413	20.673935
5	37.796527	20.673675
	37.796584	20.673716
	37.797143	20.673607
	37.797328	20.673486
	37.797425	20.673608
	37.797571	20.673433
6	37.797819	20.673358
	37.798277	20.672961
	37.798304	20.672137
7	37.798152	20.671402
	37.798791	20.667575
8	37.798745	20.666757
	37.799287	20.666478
9	37.800419	20.665766
	37.802017	20.664098
	37.802368	20.666738
	37.802164	20.669677
	37.802431	20.671019
10	37.802395	20.673582
	37.802036	20.674362
	37.802869	20.675660
	37.801837	20.677194
	37.800247	20.678296
	37.800046	20.679820
A	37.797594	20.654585
B	37.796398	20.653931

Walk 19: Vrachíonas

Wp	Northing	Easting
1	37.815407	20.700537
	37.815688	20.700563
	37.815712	20.700569
	37.816363	20.701370
	37.817336	20.704086
	37.818072	20.706066
2	37.817900	20.707109
	37.817360	20.708905

	Northing	Easting
3	37.816594	20.710466
	37.816436	20.708705
	37.816231	20.708480
	37.814731	20.710071
	37.815313	20.708809
	37.815079	20.708814
	37.814254	20.709065
	37.814370	20.708859
4	37.816553	20.710475
	37.815915	20.711218
	37.813947	20.713078
	37.812378	20.717396
	37.811472	20.718379
5	37.810610	20.719821
toA	37.810485	20.721075
	37.810448	20.722651
	37.810546	20.718843
	37.810964	20.715958
	37.809877	20.715574
	37.808384	20.716228
	37.807225	20.713995
	37.807469	20.710733
6	37.807355	20.709818
	37.807617	20.709062
	37.812018	20.702725
7	37.812068	20.701909
toA	37.810485	20.721075
A	37.810448	20.722651
B	37.806840	20.710387
C	37.809602	20.701150

Walk 20: Volímes

Wp	Northing	Easting
1	37.875858	20.653349
2	37.874863	20.652363
	37.875095	20.650678
	37.874551	20.649555
3	37.874456	20.648789
	37.874415	20.646793
	37.874144	20.646214
	37.873245	20.645893
	37.873267	20.644943
	37.872881	20.643069
	37.873291	20.641590
	37.873304	20.640880
4	37.873020	20.639249
	37.873496	20.638970
	37.874551	20.639584
	37.875765	20.640196
5	37.877903	20.640826
6	37.877974	20.640649

	Northing	Easting
	37.878687	20.641058
7	37.879541	20.642799
	37.880199	20.644689
8	37.880644	20.646196
	37.882812	20.645799
9	37.884328	20.644840
10	37.884334	20.644842
	37.884506	20.643524
	37.884231	20.641975
	37.884334	20.641731
11	37.882339	20.641756
	37.880976	20.641794
5	37.877903	20.640826
	37.878500	20.642563
12	37.878886	20.643670
	37.878095	20.645028
	37.878536	20.646208
13	37.878009	20.646993
	37.877479	20.647471
	37.877597	20.648695
	37.876584	20.649642
14	37.876314	20.649774
	37.876002	20.652014
15	37.876007	20.652992
	37.875858	20.653349

Walk 21: Cape Skinári

Wp	Northing	Easting
1	37.929586	20.700649
2	37.929550	20.700584
3	37.925503	20.699958
	37.925514	20.699961
	37.925705	20.697848
	37.925437	20.695265
	37.925366	20.692530
	37.925004	20.689564
	37.923460	20.686771
	37.921918	20.685686
	37.922079	20.683307
	37.919416	20.682053
4	37.918057	20.680913
	37.917200	20.680052
	37.917262	20.678454
5	37.915507	20.677604
	37.916350	20.676925
	37.916125	20.675903
	37.916591	20.676305
6	37.915360	20.673419
	37.915729	20.673786
	37.916529	20.675025
	37.915980	20.673274

	Northing	Easting
7	37.918310	20.675921
	37.914310	20.672848
8	37.913586	20.670868
	37.912775	20.668669
	37.911866	20.670841
	37.910818	20.672797
9	37.911375	20.675040
10	37.911981	20.675431
	37.912874	20.677184
	37.912679	20.679713
	37.912226	20.683244
	37.913398	20.686981
11	37.910215	20.688124
12	37.915198	20.699555
	37.915917	20.702801
13	37.914608	20.704682
	37.914503	20.707735
	37.915904	20.708169
	37.917818	20.708195
	37.920169	20.706376
	37.922300	20.704856
	37.923656	20.703128
14	37.923463	20.701570

Walk 22: Pigadákia hills

Wp	Northing	Easting
1	37.818703	20.762156
	37.819080	20.761912
	37.820143	20.761049
2	37.820730	20.760587
	37.820344	20.760132
	37.820016	20.759991
	37.820520	20.759780
	37.820965	20.759300
	37.821295	20.758563
3	37.821143	20.758259
	37.821319	20.757690
4	37.820481	20.757632
	37.820579	20.757333
	37.821398	20.756243
	37.821678	20.755186
	37.822066	20.754740
	37.822618	20.754318
	37.822615	20.753801
	37.822590	20.753236
5	37.822755	20.752693
4	37.820481	20.757632
	37.817506	20.758272
6	37.815117	20.760247
	37.814746	20.760815
	37.814246	20.761168

	Northing	Easting
	37.814044	20.761663
	37.813747	20.762457
	37.814232	20.762615
	37.815204	20.763185
	37.815399	20.763853
	37.815320	20.764370
	37.815275	20.764605
7	37.815218	20.765122
A	37.821974	20.752706
D	37.819501	20.755050
B	37.814321	20.757193
C	37.814359	20.757816

Note: E-F was severely burnt in 2005 and too overgrown to be walked at time of writing. Contact Spíros Vertzágias (page 172, 'Alternative routes') to guide you.

● Index

Only geographical entries are included here; for other entries, see Contents on page 3.
To save space, beaches and churches/monasteries have been grouped together.

Photographs of flora and fauna